CIMA Exam Practice Kit

F3 – Financial Strategy

CIMA Exam Practice Kit

CIMA PUBLISHING

F3 – Financial Strategy

John Ogilvie

ELSEVIER

Amsterdam • Boston • Heidelberg • London • New York • Oxford
Paris • San Diego • San Francisco • Singapore • Sydney • Tokyo

CIMA Publishing is an imprint of Elsevier
The Boulevard, Langford Lane, Kidlington, Oxford, OX5 1GB
30 Corporate Drive, Suite 400, Burlington, MA 01803, USA

First edition 2009
Reprinted 2010 (twice)

British Library Cataloguing in Publication Data
A catalogue record for this book is available from the British Library

Library of Congress Cataloging-in-Publication Data
A catalog record for this book is available from the Library of Congress

ISBN: 978-1-8561-7789-4

For information on all CIMA publications
visit our website at www.elsevierdirect.com

Printed and bound in Great Britain

10 11 12 13 14 8 7 6 5 4 3

Contents

Syllabus Guidance, Learning Objectives and Verbs

A The Syllabus

The syllabus for the CIMA Professional Chartered Management Accounting qualification 2010 comprises three learning pillars:

- Enterprise pillar
- Financial pillar
- Operational pillar

Subjects within each learning pillar of the qualification are set at three levels, Operational level, Managerial level and Strategic level. The pass mark is 50%.

For further syllabus information please see CIMA's website www.cimaglobal.com.

B Aims of the Syllabus

The aims of the syllabus for the CIMA Professional Chartered Management Accounting qualification 2010 are:

- To provide for the Institute, an adequate basis for assuring society that those admitted to membership are competent to act as management accountants for entities, whether in manufacturing, commercial or service organisations, in the public or private sectors of the economy.
- To enable the Institute to examine whether prospective members have an adequate knowledge, understanding and mastery of the stated body of knowledge and skills.
- To enable the Institute to assess whether prospective members have completed initial professional development and acquired the necessary work-based practical experience and skills.

C Study Weightings

Within a syllabus subject, a percentage weighting is shown against each section topic and is intended as a guide to the proportion of study time each topic requires.

It is essential that all topics in the syllabus are studied, since any single examination question may examine more than one topic, or carry a higher proportion of marks than the percentage study time suggested.

The weightings *do not* specify the number of marks that will be allocated to topics in the examination.

D Learning Outcomes

Each subject within the three learning pillars of the syllabus is divided into a number of broad syllabus topics. The topics contain one or more lead learning outcomes, related component learning outcomes and indicative knowledge content.

A learning outcome has two main purposes:

(a) to define the skill or ability that a well-prepared candidate should be able to exhibit in the examination;
(b) to demonstrate the approach likely to be taken by examiners in examination questions.

The learning outcomes are part of a hierarchy of learning objectives. The verbs used at the beginning of each learning outcome relate to a specific learning objective e.g.

Evaluate performance using fixed and flexible budget reports

The verb ***'evaluate'*** indicates a high, level 5, learning objective. Because learning objectives are hierarchical, it is expected that at this level, students will have knowledge of fixed and flexible budget techniques, to be able to apply them and assess performance using relevant reports.

The following table lists the learning objectives and the verbs that appear in the syllabus learning outcomes and examination questions:

Learning Objective		**Verbs Used**	**Definition**
1	Knowledge *What you are expected to know*	List State Define	Make a list of Express, fully or clearly, the details/facts of Give the exact meaning of
2	Comprehension *What you are expected to understand*	Describe Distinguish Explain Identify Illustrate	Communicate the key features of Highlight the differences between Make clear or intelligible/state the meaning or purpose of Recognise, establish or select after consideration Use an example to describe or explain something
3	Application *How you are expected to apply your knowledge*	Apply Calculate Demonstrate Prepare Reconcile Solve Tabulate	Put to practical use Ascertain or reckon mathematically Prove with certainty or exhibit by practical means Make or get ready for use Make or prove consistent/compatible Find an answer to Arrange in a table

4	Analysis *How you are expected to analyse the detail of what you have learned*	Analyse Categorise Compare and contrast Construct Discuss Interpret Prioritise Produce	Examine in detail the structure of Place into a defined class or division Show the similarities and/or differences between Build up or compile Examine in detail by argument Translate into intelligible or familiar terms Place in order of priority or sequence for action Create or bring into existence
5	Evaluation *How you are expected to use your learning to evaluate, make decisions or recommendations*	Advise Evaluate Recommend	Counsel, inform or notify Appraise or assess the value of Pro pose a course of action

E Study Weightings

Within a syllabus subject, a percentage weighting is shown against each section topic and is intended as a guide to the proportion of study time each topic requires.

It is essential that all topics in the syllabus are studied, since any single examination question may examine more than one topic, or carry a higher proportion of marks than the percentage study time suggested.

The weightings *do not* specify the number of marks that will be allocated to topics in the examination.

Key to Icons

 Exam focus

 Key points

 Questions

 Answers

Paper F3 – Financial Strategy

Syllabus Overview

Paper F3 deals with the key elements in designing and managing the organisation's financial strategy, in the context of contributing to achieving the organisation's objectives and within its external constraints, such as the general regulatory and investment environment. The features and implications of the full range of major financing instruments are covered. A broad range of types of investment decision is also covered and it is recognised throughout that such decisions need to take account of broader strategic issues as well the financial analysis.

Syllabus Structure

The syllabus comprises the following topics and study weightings:

A	Formulation of Financial Strategy	25%
B	Financing Decisions	30%
C	Investment Decisions and Project Control	45%

Assessment Strategy

There will be a written examination paper of 3 hours, plus 20 minutes of pre-examination question paper reading time. The examination paper will have the following sections:

Section A – 50 marks

A maximum of four compulsory questions, totalling 50 marks, all relating to a pre-seen case study and further new un-seen case material provided within the examination. (Note: The pre-seen case study is common to all three of the Strategic level papers at each examination sitting i.e. paper E3, P3 and F3.)

Section B – 50 marks

Two questions, from a choice of three, each worth 25 marks. Short scenarios will be given, to which some or all questions relate.

Learning Outcomes and Indicative Syllabus Content

F3 – A. Formulation of Financial Strategy (25%)

Learning Outcomes On completion of their studies students should be able to:		Indicative Syllabus Content
Lead	**Component**	
1. Identify and discuss potential strategic financial objectives, and the relationships among and constraints on the elements of financial strategy. (4)	(a) discuss the potential strategic financial objectives that of an organisation; may have; (b) discuss the interrelationships between decisions concerning investment, financing and dividends; (c) identify, analyse and discuss the impact of internal and external constraints on financial strategy, including the impact of regulation on business combinations.	• The financial and non-financial objectives of different organisations (e.g. value for money, maximising shareholder wealth, providing a surplus). (A) • The three key decisions of financial management (investment, financing and dividend) and their links. (B) • Benefits of matching characteristics of investment and financing in the longer term (e.g. in cross-border investment) and in short-term hedging strategies. (B) • Considerations in the formulation of dividend policy and dividend decisions, including meeting the cash needs of the business. (B, C) • External constraints on financial strategy (e.g. funding, regulatory bodies, investor relations, strategy and economic factors). (C) • Developing financial strategy in the context of regulatory requirements (e.g. price and service controls exercised by industry regulators) and international operations. (C) • The implications of regulation for business combinations. (Note: Detailed knowledge of the City Code and EU competition rules will not be tested.) (C)

2. Recommend strategic financial objectives for an organisation, and evaluate the extent of their attainment; evaluate the strategic financial strategies and objectives of an organisation and the extent of their attainment. (5)	(a) identify an organisation's objectives in financial terms; (b) evaluate the attainment of an organisation's financial objectives; (a) evaluate current and forecast performance taking account of potential variations in economic and business factors; (b) recommend and evaluate alternative financial strategies for an organisation taking account of external assessment of the organisation by financiers and other stakeholders, including likely changes to such assessment in the light of developments in reporting.	• Identifying the financial objectives of an organisation and the economic forces affecting its financial plans (e.g. interest, inflation and exchange rates). (A) • Assessing attainment of financial objectives. (A) • Use of financial analysis in the external assessment of the company (e.g. in assessing creditworthiness and compliance with financing covenants). (B) • Modelling and forecasting cash flows and financial statements based on expected values for economic variables (e.g. interest rates) and business variables (e.g. volume and margins) over a number of years. (B) • Analysis of sensitivity to changes in expected values in the above models and forecasts. (B) • Assessing the implications for shareholder value of alternative financial strategies, including dividend policy. (Note: Modigliani and Miller's theory of dividend irrelevancy will be tested in broad terms. The mathematical proof of the model will not be required, but some understanding of the graphical method is expected.) (C) • The lender's assessment of creditworthiness. (C) • Current and emerging issues in financial reporting (e.g. proposals to amend or introduce new accounting standards) and in other forms of external reporting (e.g. environmental accounting). (C)

F3 – B. Financing Decisions (30%)

Learning Outcomes On completion of their studies students should be able to:		Indicative Syllabus Content
Lead	**Component**	
1. Analyse the financing requirements of an organisation and recommend a strategy for their satisfaction (5); evaluate the financing requirements of an organisation and recommend a strategy for meeting those requirements. (5)	(a) analyse the short- and long-term financing requirements of an organisation; (b) evaluate and compare alternative methods of meeting financing requirements, taking account of the implications for the organisation's financial statements, its tax position and financial stakeholders; (c) calculate and evaluate the weighted average cost of capital of an organisation; and discuss its meaning and application; (d) recommend methods of funding specific investments, taking account of basic tax considerations and risk exposures (to interest and currency exchange rate fluctuations); (e) recommend optimal strategies for the management of working capital and satisfaction of longer-term financing requirements.	• Identifying financing requirements (both in respect of domestic and international operations) and the impacts of different types of finance on models and forecasts of performance and position. (A) • Working capital management strategies. (Note: No detailed testing of cash and stock management models will be set since these are covered at a lower level within the syllabus.) at the Managerial level (A, B, E) • Types and features of domestic and international long-term finance: share capital (ordinary and preference shares, warrants), long-term debt (bank borrowing and forms of securitised debt, e.g. convertibles) and finance leases, and methods of issuing securities. (B, E) • The operation of stock exchanges (e.g. how share prices are determined, what causes share prices to rise or fall, and the efficient market hypothesis). (Note: No detailed knowledge of any specific country's stock exchange will be tested.) (B) • The impact of changing capital structure on the market value of a company. (Note: An understanding of Modigliani and Miller's theory of gearing, with and without taxes, will be expected, but proof of their theory will not be examined.) (B, E)

		• The capital asset pricing model (CAPM): calculation of the cost of equity using the dividend growth model (knowledge of methods of calculating and estimating dividend growth will be expected), the ability to gear and un-gear betas and comparison to the arbitrage pricing model. (B) • The ideas of diversifiable risk (unsystematic risk) and systematic risk. (Note: use of the two-asset portfolio formula will not be tested.) (B) • The cost of redeemable and irredeemable debt, including the tax shield on debt. (C, E) • The weighted average cost of capital (WACC): calculation, interpretation and uses. (C, E) • The lease or buy decision (with both operating and finance leases). (D, E) • Criteria for selecting sources of finance, including finance for international investments. (E) • The effect of financing decisions on balance sheet structure and on ratios of interest to investors and other financiers (gearing, earnings per share, price-earnings ratio, dividend yield, dividend cover gearing, interest cover). (E)
2. Discuss the role and management of the treasury function. (4)	(a) discuss the role and management of the treasury function.	• The role of the treasury function in terms of setting corporate objectives, liquidity management, funding management and currency management. • The advantages and disadvantages of establishing treasury departments as profit centres or cost centres, and their control.

Examination Techniques

Essay questions

Your essay should have a clear structure, i.e. an introduction, a middle and an end. Marks will depend on the depth of discussion ranging from a brief bullet point to a well described point.

Numerical questions

It is essential to show workings in your answer. If you come up with the wrong answer and no workings, the examiner cannot award any marks. However, if you get the wrong answer but apply the correct technique then you will be given some marks.

Reports and memorandum

Where you are asked to produce an answer in a report type format you will be given easy marks for style and presentation.

- A *report* is a document from an individual or group in one organisation sent to an individual or group in another.
- A *memorandum* is an informal report going from one individual or group to another individual or group in the same organisation.

You should start a report as follows:

To: J. SMITH, CEO, ABC plc

From: M ACCOUNTANT

Date: 31st December 200X

Terms of Reference: Financial Strategy of ABC plc

All questions

The integrative nature of the syllabus should not be overlooked and you should be able to relate topics to each other. A good example of this is the integration of the investment and financing decision. These are often considered separately but may need to be considered together in, for example, a takeover bid.

It should be emphasised that few examination questions are limited to one syllabus topic and candidates are expected to be able to use a particular technique in a variety of different circumstances. The case study questions in Chapter 10 of this kit provide good examples of combining various aspects of financial strategy in one question. The whole syllabus is examinable, and questions will be asked on every topic over three or four diets.

For all sections of the syllabus you should be aware that extra examination marks can be gained by an ability to refer to, and demonstrate some understanding of, recent relevant discussions on a topic, either by reference to the financial press or academic journals.

Part 1

Formulation of Financial Strategy

1

Formulation of Financial Strategy

Formulation of Financial Strategy

1

Financial and non-financial objectives

Questions on this section will typically be asked in conjunction with aspects of one of the other main syllabus areas. For example, the objectives of not-for-profit entities combined with an investment appraisal. For profit making entities the main strategic objective is to maximise the wealth of the proprietors. This means investing in projects that expect to generate a positive NPV at a specific risk adjusted rate that on average provides a return commensurate with investors' expectations and risk profile. In practice this may be interpreted as achieving maximum profits for shareholders, measured by the return generated from ownership. This might be considered too narrow a view and the achievement of this single objective is subject to various constraints, both internal and external, and conflicting demands on management by self-interest groups.

The concept of shareholder wealth is absent in not-for-profit entities. The objectives of the entity will be determined by the purpose for which it was established. This might be set out in a charter or trustee arrangement. However, many of the general principles of financial strategy are still available for these entities to help them manage their finances to meet their objectives and maintain their duty of care to their key stakeholders. The differences between financial management in the private and public sectors are diminishing as governments seek to make the public sector more commercially aware.

The three key decisions of financial management

The practical application of financial strategy can be grouped into three main areas of decision that reflect the responsibilities of acquiring financial resources and managing those resources:

- Investment decisions are those which determine how scarce resources are committed to projects; e.g. acquisition of new plant, takeovers and mergers, divestment from unsuccessful projects.
- Financing decisions relate to acquiring the optimum finance to meet financial objectives and seeing that non-current assets and working capital are effectively managed.
- Dividend decisions relate to the determination of how much and how frequently cash can be paid out of the profits of an entity as income for its proprietors.

Dividend policy and dividend decisions

In theory, and within a narrow range of assumptions, the value of an entity is unaffected by dividend decisions. In reality, dividend policy, and in particular the signalling effect of dividend announcements is considered to be extremely important. This section of the syllabus requires a thorough knowledge of the various policies available to an entity and the implications of each for investors.

Modigliani and Miller expressed the view that dividends are irrelevant to the value of the entity. Their argument is that the entity has a duty to maximise the value of that entity, and that involves investing in all positive NPV projects. If shareholders need cash they can sell some of their shares. However, this assumes:

- No taxes or transaction costs
- Fixed investment and borrowing programmes
- Additional needed funds come from retained earnings and extra cash is paid as dividends
- Capital markets are efficient.

External constraints on financial strategy

External constraints imposed on managers by governments and society include: legislation, e.g. laws to protect the environment or employees; accounting concepts and conventions; economic factors, and the effect of regulatory controls. Detailed knowledge of any specific legislation, accounting or reporting standard, or regulatory control is not required. What is required is an understanding of how the broad concepts and conventions affect business operations and strategic decisions.

Use of financial analysis

An ability to calculate ratios and performance measures based on accounting numbers is taken for granted at this level. What is more important is an ability to select appropriate information and evaluate it as part of an entity's strategy.

It is important to realise that a ratio on its own tells you very little and no absolute targets can be set without reference to the circumstances of a particular organisation. To make informed comments we need to make comparisons. These can be with:

- the previous year
- the budget
- an investor's expectations
- a competitor
- the industry average.

Profitability ratios

(a) Return on capital employed (ROCE) $= \dfrac{\text{Profit before interest + tax (PBIT)}}{\text{Long-term debt + equity}}$

(b) Operating profit margin $= \dfrac{\text{PBIT}}{\text{Sales revenue}}$

(c) Asset turnover $= \dfrac{\text{Sales revenue}}{\text{Capital employed}}$

(d) Return on equity $= \dfrac{\text{Profit after interest and tax}}{\text{Shareholders' funds}}$

(e) Expense ratio $= \dfrac{\text{Expense}}{\text{Sales revenue}}$

Modelling and forecasting cash flows and financial statements

Questions on this area of the syllabus usually require the construction of forecast income statements, balance sheets, and cash flow statements from base year data. The construction of these statements may require you to make a number of assumptions. Discussion or analysis of the financial performance and position may constitute a significant proportion of the marks available.

Sensitivity analysis

Sensitivity analysis will almost always be examined in conjunction with modelling and forecasting cash flows and financial statements. An ability to describe and discuss the steps required to undertake sensitivity analysis, its usefulness, and the problems that might be encountered is required.

Questions

Question 1 – Objectives

This question concerns two entities, one in the private sector and one in the public sector.

Entity 1
This is a listed entity in the electronics industry. Its stated financial objectives are:

- to increase earnings per share year on year by 10% per annum; and
- to achieve a 25% per annum return on capital employed.

This entity has an equity market capitalisation of £600 m. It also has a variety of debt instruments trading at a total value of £150 m.

Entity 2
This entity is a newly established purchaser and provider of healthcare services in the public sector. The entitie's legal status is a trust. Its total income for the current year will be almost £100 m. It is considering funding the building of a new healthcare centre via the Private Finance Initiative (PFI). The total debt will be £15 m. Capital and interest will be repaid over 15 years at a variable rate of interest, currently 9% each year. The trust's sole financial objective states simply 'to achieve financial balance during the year'. Its other objectives are concerned with qualitative factors such as 'providing high quality healthcare'.

Requirements

(a) Discuss

(i) the reasons for the differences in the financial objectives of the two types of entity given above; and

(ii) the main differences in the business risks involved in the achievement of their financial objectives and how these risks might be managed.

Use the scenario details given above to assist your answer wherever possible.

(18 marks)

(b) Explain how the financial risks introduced into the public sector organisation by the use of PFI might affect the achievement of its objectives and comment on how these risks might be managed.

(7 marks)

Note: Candidates from outside the UK may use examples of private financing of public sector schemes in their own country in answering part (b) of this question if they wish.

(Total = 25 marks)

Question 2 – Educational

(a) You are a newly appointed Finance Manager of an Educational Institution that is mainly government funded, having moved from a similar post in a service company in the private sector. The objective, or mission statement, of this Institution is shown in its publicity material as:

> To achieve recognised standards of excellence in the provision of teaching and research.

The only financial performance measure evaluated by the government is that the Institution has to remain within cash limits. The cash allocation each year is determined by a range of non-financial measures such as the number of research publications the Institution's staff have achieved and official ratings for teaching quality.

However, almost 20% of total cash generated by the Institution is now from the provision of courses and seminars to private sector companies, using either its own or its customers' facilities. These customers are largely unconcerned about research ratings and teaching quality as they relate more to academic awards such as degrees.

The Head of the Institution aims to increase the percentage of income coming from the private sector to 50% over the next five years. She has asked you to advise on how the management team can evaluate progress towards achieving this aim as well as meeting the objective set by government for the activities it funds.

Requirement

Discuss the main issues that an institution such as this has to consider when setting objectives.

Advise on

- whether a financial objective, or objectives, could or should be determined; and
- whether such objective(s) should be made public.

(9 marks)

(b) The following is a list of financial and non-financial performance measures that were in use in your previous company:

Financial	*Non-financial*
Value added	Customer satisfaction
Profitability	Competitive position
Return on investment	Market share

Requirement

Choose two of each type of measure, explain their purpose and advise on how they could be used by the Educational Institution over the next five years to assess how it is meeting the Head of the Institution's aims.

(16 marks)

Note: A report format is NOT required in answering this question.

(Total = 25 marks)

Question 3 – Police

A regional police force has the following corporate objectives:

- to reduce crime and disorder
- to promote community safety
- to contribute to delivering justice and maintaining public confidence in the law.

The force aims to achieve these objectives by continuously improving its resources management to meet the needs of its stakeholders. It has no stated financial objective other than to stay within its funding limits.

The force is mainly public-funded but, like other regional forces, it has some commercial operations, for example policing football matches when the football clubs pay a fee to the police force for its officers working overtime. The police force uses this money to supplement the funding it receives from the government. The national government is proposing to privatise (i.e. sell off) these commercial operations and has already been in preliminary discussions with an international security company. This company's stated financial objectives are:

- to increase earnings per share year on year by 5% per annum; and
- to achieve a 20% per annum return on capital employed.

Arguments put forward by government in favour of privatisation focus on the conflict of objectives between mainstream operations and commercial activities, and savings to the taxpayer. However, the proposals have met with strong opposition from most of the force's stakeholders.

Requirements

(a) Discuss the reasons for the differences in the objectives of the two types of organisation given above. Use the scenario details given above to assist your answer wherever possible.

(12 marks)

(b) Discuss the influence the commercial operations might currently have on the police force's ability to meet its stated objectives. Include in your discussion an evaluation of the possible effects on mainstream services and the various stakeholder groups if the commercial operations were to be privatised.

(13 marks)
(Total = 25 marks)

Question 4 – Healthcare

Two senior executives have recently met on a course where they were being taught about setting financial objectives and the three key policy decisions listed below:

1 the investment decision
2 the financing decision
3 the dividend decision.

One of the executives works for a large healthcare company listed on the stock exchange, the other works in the public sector health service where all services are provided free of charge to users at the point of delivery. The public sector health service is financed through an annual cash budget funded entirely by taxes and government borrowing and has no treasury department.

The following extracts are from their conversation after the course:

Healthcare company executive

Life must be so much easier for you. We have to raise finance from various sources to fund any new investment. We also have to ensure that we pay a dividend that keeps our shareholders happy.

Public sector health service executive

I don't think you would find a cash-constrained life, as we experience it, very easy. I would like to be able to raise money on the stock market to fund our business requirements. I would also much prefer to have my own treasury department to go to at any time rather than having to wait and see what we have been allocated in our annual budget.

Requirements:

(a) Identify in which of the three key policy decisions listed above the public sector health service would have **least** involvement, and explain why. Additionally, identify in which of the three key policy decisions listed above a treasury department would have **most** involvement, and explain why.

(8 marks)

(b) Describe each of the three key policy decisions listed and discuss the importance of each of them to the shareholders in the healthcare company.

(9 marks)

(c) Describe the main methods of raising new equity finance and recommend the most appropriate method for the healthcare company to raise equity finance on the stock market.

(8 marks)
(Total = 25 marks)

Question 5 – RJ

RJ plc is a supplier of surgical instruments and medical supplies (excluding drugs). Its shares are listed on the UK's Alternative Investment Market and are currently quoted at 458 pence per £1 share. The majority of its customers are public sector organisations in the UK. RJ plc is doing well and now needs additional capital to expand operations.

The forecast financial statements are given below.

Extracts from the Income Statement for the year ended 31 December 2005

	£'000
Revenue	30,120
Costs and expenses	22,500
Operating profit	7,620
Finance costs	2,650
Profit before tax	4,970
Tax	1,491

Note: Dividends declared for 2005 are £1,392,000 *Balance Sheet as at 31 December 2005*

	£'000	£'000
TOTAL ASSETS		
Non-current assets		14,425
Current assets		
Inventories	4,510	
Trade receivables	3,700	
Cash	198	
		8,408
		22,833

	£'000	£'000
EQUITY AND LIABILITIES		
Equity		
Share capital	8,350	
Retained earnings	4,750	
		13,100
Non-current liabilities		
(Secured bonds, 6% 2008)		4,000
Current liabilities		
Trade payables	2,850	
Other payables (tax and dividends)	2,883	
		5,733
		22,833

You have obtained the following additional information:

1 Revenue is expected to increase by 10% per annum in each of the financial years ending 31 December 2006 and 2007. Costs and expenses, excluding depreciation, are expected to increase by an average of 5% per annum. Finance costs are expected to remain unchanged.
2 RJ plc expects to continue to be liable for tax at the marginal rate of 30%. Assume tax is paid or refunded the year following that in which the liability or repayment arises.
3 The ratios of *trade receivables to revenue* and *trade payables to costs and expenses* will remain the same for the next two years. The value of inventories is likely to remain at 2005 levels.
4 The non-current assets are land and buildings, which are not depreciated in RJ plc's books. Capital (tax) allowances on the buildings may be ignored. All other assets used by the entity (machinery, cars and so on) are either rented or leased on operating leases.
5 Dividends will be increased by 5% each year.
6 RJ plc intends to purchase for cash new machinery to the value of £6,000,000 during 2006, although an investment appraisal exercise has not been carried out. It will be depreciated straight line over 10 years. RJ plc intends to charge a full year's depreciation in the first year of purchase of its assets. Capital (tax) allowances are available at 25% reducing balance on this expenditure.

RJ plc's main financial objectives for the years 2006-2007 are to earn a pre-tax return on the closing book value of equity of 35% per annum and a year-on-year increase in earnings of 10%.

Requirements

Assume you are a consultant working for RJ plc. Evaluate the implications of the financial information you have obtained. You should:

(i) Provide forecast income statements, dividends and retentions for the two years ending 31 December 2006 and 2007.

(6 marks)

(ii) Provide cash flow forecasts for the years 2006 and 2007. Comment briefly on how RJ plc might finance any cash deficit.

(8 marks)

Note: This is **not** an investment appraisal exercise; you may ignore the timing of cash flows **within** each year and you should not discount the cash flows. You should also ignore interest payable on any cash deficit.

(iii) Discuss the key aspects and implications of the financial information you have obtained in your answer to (i) and (ii) of the question, in particular whether RJ plc is likely to meet its stated objectives. Provide whatever calculations you think are appropriate to support your discussion. Up to 4 marks are available for calculations in this section of the question.

(11 marks)
(Total = 25 marks)

Answers

Question 1 – Objectives

(a) (i) **Differences in financial objectives**

Objectives in the private and public sectors have come closer together in recent years, as private companies appreciate the needs of other stakeholders apart from shareholder, and the public sector concentrates more on value for money and the best use of the financial resources.

However, the financial objectives remain the key areas for the private sector, whose primary responsibility is to their shareholders, and the public sector's primary objectives are the provision of a quality service.

In addition, the private sector will generally set their objectives, by reference to the needs of their stakeholders, while the public sector organisation will have many of its objectives imposed by the government.

EPS
Earnings per share are used by shareholders to judge the growth achieved. While it can be misleading, it gives an idea of the profits generated in the year. The public sector generally does not have such a financial measure but concentrates more on the service provided.

ROCE
The private sector company has to give a sufficient return to its investors for the risk they perceive in the investment. This can be approximated by tracking the return on capital employed.

In the public sector, to convince the 'investors', usually the government, to release funds and not to withdraw resources, the organisation needs to persuade them that the activities represent value for money. This is often politically driven rather than being based on long-term financial analysis.

Cash limits
The public sector has a major objective to achieve financial balance during the year, as it is unable to raise more during the year. The private sector charges customers and can raise more revenue by selling more.

(ii) **Business risks and management**

A major difference between the two is how risk in the organisation is built into the objective. A private sector company has the risk that it may fail to attract any customers and hence any revenue. Hence the objectives are focused around the revenues and profits generated.

In the trust, the 'customers' have little choice in the healthcare in the area, so there is little risk to the trust in terms of the quantity of service required dropping. However, there is a major risk in terms of the quality of service delivered, so the main objectives relate to this. This is bound to be more difficult to measure, so a number of targets have been developed by government to assess progress in these areas.

Generally, we could say the main risk to a private sector organisation is that demand for the product falls, while for a public sector one, demand for the service increases beyond what can be managed within its resources.

The private sector company could manage its major commercial risk by:

- maintaining and monitoring its quality
- analysing customers and competitors
- ensuring against risks where possible.

The public sector trust has to manage the risk that it fails to give a service of sufficient quality within its financial constraints, by:

- monitoring value for money of the services provided, both internally and externally
- ensuring that services bought are the most effective
- using private finance where possible to ease financial constraints.

(b) **Financial risks**

The original aim of PFI was to allow services to be expanded and quality enhanced without increasing the public funds provided. This was done by private sector providing assets such as the new centre for relatively low financial rates; this is possible because there is much less risk of default on payments and the private sector company is therefore happy with a lower return than normal.

The main risks to the trust's financial objective from this PFI debt are:

- interest rates might rise and not be matched by government finance
- income falls but interest and capital still have to be paid.

However, annual payments will be £15m/8.06 = £1.86m which is less than 2% of annual income, so it is unlikely that this will be a problem for the trust. If it does materialise, the trust may be able to negotiate longer terms (15 years is shorter than the usual PFI).

Question 2 – Educational

(a) **Setting objectives**

The main issues to consider in setting objectives are:

- deciding who the main stakeholders are
- assessing and estimating the level of financial resources which are likely
- whether one objective can meet all the needs of the various stakeholders
- can the objective be measured
- should the objectives and performance be made public.

A financial objective is fairly easy to measure against progress, and performance can also be compared to other similar educational institutions. However, one objective is probably not sufficient, given the different nature of the two markets.

However, other educational institutions may not have the same political influences. In addition, the results of the two areas will be affected by the apportionment of costs between them. Lastly, the institution may not be in full control of its policies in areas such as fees and selection, so that it may be misleading to draw conclusions from its performance, particularly in comparison with others.

(b) **Performance measures**

Financial measures were traditionally those used by management, but there has been an increasing focus on non-financial areas as well in order to judge success in terms of meeting objectives. These will tend to pick up objectives relating to the needs of different stakeholders.

Financial measures

(i) Value added

This measure looks at the performance of an organisation by trying to identify the value added to the service by the organisation's own efforts. It is more common in the private sector, but has been introduced in some areas of the public sector to allow better comparisons to be made. A school with an intake from a wealthy intelligent background would be expected to produce better results than one with a poor deprived intake, but the second school might have added more value in terms of improving the level which the children attained between entering and leaving the school.

The institution could try to look at the background of students and assess the improvement made, compared with competitors or against expected performance based on their prior attainment. This would be complicated to undertake and an approximation might look at the student body for each year as a whole, comparing the average intake background and attainment to the average results on leaving. An even cruder measure would be to look at the average degree class or the percentage of firsts and 2.1s.

This measure is included under financial measures as the private sector often use (Sales value – Cost of purchases and services) to measure it. The public sector is less likely to use financial terms to measure it, as seen above.

(ii) Profitability

This measure looks at the profits generated per unit of input (such as per staff member), but does not look at the *quality* of those profits. It can therefore lead to short-term focus, as the risk to longer-term profits is not considered. In the context of the institution, this might mean putting a very large number of students in one lecture room in order to decrease cost per student or increase revenue per lecturer.

However, in the long term, results and hence the reputation and recruitment might suffer, leading to lower profits.

Used in conjunction with other measures, it can give useful information on how the institute compares to others.

This measure does not connect directly to the stated mission statement of the institute, so it may need to rethink its objectives as discussed in part (a) before introducing this measure.

(i) Customer satisfaction

This is an important measure because if customers are not satisfied, they could go elsewhere and other potential customers could be discouraged. In the context of the institution, the two sets of 'customers' are government-funded students and companies. Although the first group have limited ability to seek redress if not satisfied, poor performance in exams could reduce government funding, as could a high percentage of student drop-out, and reduce applications for courses. The second group could show their disappointment much more quickly by not booking further courses or seminars and having an immediate impact on income.

Measuring customer satisfaction can be difficult, but course assessments at the end of every course, quality audits by regulatory bodies, company discussions and peer reviews could help.

(ii) Competitive position

In a competitive marketplace, an organisation needs to be aware of its position in that market. The institution needs to be aware of how it is doing compared with its competitors. Government funding now partly relies on the level and quality of research, and as this is externally assessed it will make comparisons in this area easier. The amount of revenue generated by company work for competitors will be less easy to ascertain. Student courses can be easily compared against competitors as the number on particular courses are publicly available, and absolute numbers and trends can be compared for all the courses offered.

Question 3 – Police

(a) **Differences in objectives**

Objectives in the public and private sectors have been coming closer together, as the public sector has become more aware of the need to give value for money, and the private sector has started to recognise other stakeholders apart from shareholders.

Despite this, the private company's primary responsibility is to their shareholders within the constraints imposed by society and government. Public bodies generally have their objectives imposed by government rather than setting their own.

EPS
Earnings per share are used by shareholders to judge performance by looking at the growth achieved. While it can be misleading, it gives an idea of the profits generated in the year. The public sector generally does not have such a financial measure but concentrates more on the service provided. Indeed, some public sector organisations would consider it a failure to have not spent all the revenue received (i.e. to have achieved a 'nil profit' position).

ROCE
The private sector company has to give a sufficient return to its investors for the risk they perceive in the investment. This can be approximated by tracking the return on capital employed.

In the public sector, to convince the 'investors', usually the government, to release funds and not to withdraw resources, the organisation needs to persuade them that the activities represent value for money. This is often politically driven rather than being based on long-term financial analysis.

Cash limits
The public sector has a major objective to stay within its cash resources, as it is unable to raise more during the year. The private sector charges customers and can raise more revenue by selling more.

Risk
A major difference between the two is how risk in the organisation is built into the objectives. A private sector company has the risk that it may fail to attract any customers and hence any revenue. Hence the objectives are focused around the revenues and profits generated.

In the police force, the 'customers' have little choice in the police services in the area, so there is little risk to the police operations in terms of the quantity of the service required falling. However, there is a major risk in terms of the quality of service delivered, so the main objectives relate to this. This is bound to be more difficult to measure, so a number of targets have been developed by government to assess progress in these areas.

Generally, we could say the main risk to a private sector organisation is that demand for the service falls, while for a public sector one its demand for the service increases beyond what can be managed within its resources.

(b) **Influence of commercial operations**

The government has argued that there is a conflict of objectives, as they feel that senior police officers may divert resources to activities such as football matches, which will have a negative impact on the resources available for other mainstream operations, in order to ease financial constraints.

However, it could be argued that a visible police presence at football matches will help to maintain public confidence in the law and reduce crime and disorder on the streets.

Additional finance raised could also help the force to meet its other objectives by providing more resources.

The impact on the various stakeholder groups is likely to be:

- Senior police officers will probably fear a reduction in the financial resources and hence a reduction in mainstream activities, unless the government make up the shortfall.
- Police officers will lose a major opportunity to earn overtime and is likely to be an unpopular move.
- Football clubs and other organisations that have the police force may be concerned that the quality of service will deteriorate. The police have wide experience of managing crowds at matches and have wider powers than a private company if there are problems in surrounding streets.
- The local community is likely to be concerned in a similar way that trouble in the area on football match days will not be dealt with effectively.
- The government will receive cash for selling the service.

Question 4 – Healthcare

(a) **Key policy decisions**

The public sector health service will have little involvement in a dividend decision. This determines how much of the surplus cash is returned to shareholders. As the public sector health service does not have shareholders, this is not relevant; surplus cash is used to provide additional services.

A treasury department in a private sector company is likely to have most involvement in the financing decision. Although the department may be involved in the dividend decision and, to some extent, assessing investment opportunities, this is to the extent that they impinge on their primary role. This is to ensure that funds are available when needed and that surplus funds are put to good use.

(b) **Importance to shareholders**

The investment decision considers the benefits of investing cash, either in projects or in working capital, or even in high yield deposit accounts. This is important to shareholders, as it will determine the cash flows which are generated by the company and will ultimately affect the dividends paid and the share price. Assessing projects in the healthcare industry can be difficult as large investments are often required which promise the possibility of returns over many years, making the cash flows hard to estimate. Shareholders will also be concerned to compare the risk as well as the return between profits, as a higher risk investment should carry a higher return to compensate.

The financing decision considers the source of the finance required for the business operations. This will be a mixture of equity and long-term debt finance; companies need to balance the benefits to their shareholders – debt is a cheaper form of finance as the returns required are lower (due to lower risk) and the debt interest is tax allowable, but excessive gearing can increase the risk to the company, and hence the shareholders, dramatically.

The dividend decision looks at how much of the surplus cash generated should be paid out to the shareholders, and how much retained for future investments. Companies often make two payments a year, and shareholders generally prefer a predictable, steadily rising, dividend rather than one, which follows the fluctuations of the profits. A dividend policy is often declared for a number of years to give this predictability. A company which then delivers what it promised will generally be regarded as less risky, and hence more valuable, by shareholders.

(c) **Raising equity finance**

Equity can be raised via a placing, an offer for sale or a public offer.

A placing is when shares are offered to a small number of investors, usually institutions. The costs are likely to be lower but will concentrate ownership.

An offer for sale allots shares to an issuing house which then offers them to the public. Issuing costs are higher, but it will create a wider share base.

In a public offer, the company itself offers them to the public. This will involve high issue costs to cover publicity and underwriting.

The healthcare company is already listed on the stock exchange; it is likely that a rights issue, in which existing shareholders are given the right to subscribe for more shares, will be the method used. The shareholders buy them at a price below the market price, but can sell these rights if they cannot afford to subscribe. Theoretically, although the proportional shareholdings may change, an investor should be no worse off or better off whether they take up or sell the rights.

Question 5 – RJ

(i) *Extracts from the Income Statements for the years ended 31 December*

	2005	*2006*	*2007*
	£'000	£'000	£'000
Revenue	30,120	33,132	36,445
Costs and expenses (including depreciation)	(22,500)	(24,225)	(25,406)
Operating profit	7,620	8,907	11,039
Less: Finance costs	(2,650)	(2,650)	(2,650)
Profit before tax	4,970	6,257	8,389
Tax*	(1,491)	(1,607)	(2,359)
Profit after tax (earnings)	3,479	4,650	6,030
Dividends declared	(1,392)	(1,462)	(1,535)
Retained earnings for year	2,087	3,188	4,495

Examiner's Note

The question did not require candidates to show the figures for 2005; they are shown here in italics for convenience.

Capital allowances calculation:

Cost of machinery	6,000
2006WDA@25%	1,500
WDV	4,500
2007WDA@25%	1,125
WDV	3,375

* Tax is calculated on profit plus depreciation less capital allowances

2006 (6,257 + 600 − 1,500) X 30% = 1,607

2007 (8,389 + 600 − 1,125) X 30% = 2,359

Examiner's Note

It was not intended that candidates should consider the impact of deferred taxation in their answer here. Credit was available for those who did so.

(ii) *Cash flow forecasts for 2006 and 2007*

Calculations of cash receivable and cash payable:

	2006	*2007*
Revenue	33,132	36,445
O/B trade receivables	3,700	4,075
C/B trade receivables at 12.3% (2005 - 3,700/30,120 X 100%)	(4,075)	(4,483)

	2006		*2007*	
Cash receivable	32,757		36,037	
Costs and expenses	23,625		24,806	
O/B trade payables	2,850		2,993	
C/B trade payables at 12.67%	(2,993)		(3,143)	
(2005 - 2,850/22,500 X 100%)				
Cash payable	23,482		24,656	
Cash flow forecasts				
Cash received from sales	32,757		36,037	
Costs and expenses	23,482		24,656	
Machinery	6,000			
Tax	1,491		1,607	
Dividends	1,392		1,462	
Finance costs	2,650		2,650	
Total outflows		35,015		30,375
Net cash flow		(2,258)		5,662
Opening balance		198		(2,060)
Closing balance		(2,060)		3,602

An alternative, equally acceptable, approach to presenting the cash flow forecasts is as follows. Note that IAS 7 allows for some discretion in the presentation format of cash flow statements. The question here required a forecast rather than a published statement and any sensible format gained credit. There is also the potential for different figures depending on rounding assumptions on accounts receivable and accounts payable.

	2006 £'000	*2007* £'000
Operations		
Operating profit	8,907	11,039
Add back depreciation	600	600
Change in receivables	(375)	(407)
Change in payables	143	149
Sub-total	9,275	11,381
Interest paid	(2,650)	(2,650)
Taxation	(1,491)	(1,607)
Net cash flow from operations	7,519	7,124
Investments		
New Machinery	(6,000)	
Financing		
Dividends paid	(1,392)	(1,462)
Total net cash flows	(2,258)	5,662
Opening cash balance	198	(1,060)
Closing cash balance	(2,060)	(3,602)

Examiner's Note

The question stated dividends of £1,392,000 were declared in 2005. It would be usual, but not inevitable that these would be paid in 2006. Candidates who assumed payment would be made in 2005 were not penalised.

There is need to finance a cash shortfall of just over £2m by the end of 2006. Of course, if the machinery was bought early in 2006, there may well be a requirement to finance a much greater cash shortfall earlier in the year. There is insufficient information in the question to comment further on this. However, this would be a very short-term requirement as by the end of 2007 there is a healthy cash surplus of £3.6m. As the shortfall is caused by the purchase of new machinery, there should be no problem in raising finance. Suitable methods include bank overdraft, supplier credit or short-term leasing. However, as this is a long-term asset, it could be argued it should be funded by long-term finance and the cash surplus used for additional investments or, alternatively, repaid to shareholders.

(iii) *Key aspects and implications Preliminary calculations:*

	2005	*2006*	*2007*
Total equity			
Share capital	8,350	8,350	8,350
Retained earnings	4,750	7,938	12,433
Total equity	13,100	16,288	20,783
Return on equity %	37.9	38.4	40.4
	(4,970/13,100) × 100	(6,257/16,288) × 100	(8,389/20,783) × 100
EPS - pence	41.6	55.7	72.2
% increase		33.9	29.6
Market value of company if P/E — 11 (Share price of 458/EPS)	38,269	51,160*	66,316*
Dividend payout percentage	40%	31.4%	25.5%
DPS - pence	16.7	17.5	18.4

Examiner's Note

The figures would be 51,150 and 66,330, respectively if calculations were total earnings X 11.

Return on equity
The entity easily meets its objectives of return on equity in all three years, even though a target of 35% is quite high for an entity such as this.

Investment and financing
No investment appraisal has been carried out for the purchase of the new machinery. This should be done before the investment is made, even though the entity appears more than capable of funding the purchase out of cash flow.

Increase in earnings and dividends
Earnings increase almost 34% in 2006 over 2005 and 30% in 2007 over 2006. Figures are not available for years before 2005, but an increase in two consecutive years of over 30% suggests either 2004 was an unusually poor year or there has been a substantial improvement in prospects.

Effect of government/policy changes
The entity's main customer is the government which means RJ may be vulnerable to changes in government, government policy or regulation - or all three.

Effect on market value/rating
If the P/E ratio stays at 11, then the company can expect a significant increase in its market value in 2006, from £38 m to £51 m. However, the comment above about apparent lack of investment opportunities could have an adverse effect on its growth rating and the P/E ratio could actually fall despite the forecast increase in profits over the next two years.

Part 2

Financial Management

2

Financial Management

Financial Management

2

Investor ratios

(a) Earnings per share (EPS) $= \dfrac{\text{Distributable profit for the year}}{\text{Number of shares in issue}}$

(b) P/E ratio $= \dfrac{\text{MPS}}{\text{EPS}}$

(c) Dividend yield $= \dfrac{\text{Dividend}}{\text{Share price}}$

(d) Payout ratio $= \dfrac{\text{Dividend}}{\text{Distributable profit for the year}}$

(e) Dividend cover $= \dfrac{\text{Distributable profit for the year}}{\text{Dividend}}$

Operating cycle

(a) Receivables collection period $= \dfrac{\text{Average trade receivables}}{\text{Annual credit sales}} \times 365 \text{ days}$

(b) Payables payment period $= \dfrac{\text{Average trade payables}}{\text{Annual purchases}} \times 365 \text{ days}$

(c) Inventory holding period $= \dfrac{\text{Average inventory}}{\text{Annual cost of sales}} \times 365 \text{ days}$

(d) Current ratio (liquidity ratio) $= \dfrac{\text{Current assets}}{\text{Current liabilities}}$

(e) Quick ratio (Acid test) $= \dfrac{\text{Current assets excluding inventory}}{\text{Current liabilities}}$

Working capital management strategies

Two aspects of working capital policy that require managerial decisions are the level of current assets and the manner in which they are financed. In conditions of uncertainty entities must hold some minimum level of cash and inventories based on expected revenues, plus additional safety stocks. With an aggressive working capital policy, an entity would hold minimal safety stock. Such a policy would minimise costs, but it could lower revenues because the entity could not respond rapidly to increases in demand. Generally the expected return is higher under an aggressive investment policy than a conservative policy, but the risks are higher.

Working capital financing decisions involve the determination of the mix of long-term and short-term debt. When the yield curve is upward sloping, short-term debt is cheaper than long-term debt. With an aggressive financing policy, the entity finances part of its permanent asset base with short-term debt. This policy generally provides the highest expected return because short-term debt costs are typically less than long-term costs, but it is very risky. Under a conservative financing policy, the entity would have permanent financing that exceeds its permanent asset base of assets. The conservative policy is the least risky but it also results in the lowest expected return.

Operation of the securities markets

Detailed procedural knowledge is not required for this exam. However, an understanding of the relationships between entities, the securities markets and the macro-economic environment is required. Merchant banks and other financial institutions provide a range of advice and support services to entities, for example during a takeover bid, a reconstruction, or when issuing capital.

Efficient market hypothesis

Financial strategy theory depends on the assumption that the capital markets are informationally efficient. There are three forms of the efficient market hypothesis (weak, semi-strong and strong).

The role of the treasury function

In a large entity the finance function may be split between treasury and financial control. A treasurer is usually responsible for obtaining finance and managing relations with the bank, and capital markets, and generally managing the entity's funds. The financial controller is usually more concerned with the allocation and effective use of resources and has responsibility for the investment decisions, budgeting, planning and accounting. In small entities these various functions may be combined.

Treasury can be treated as a cost centre or a profit centre. A profit centre might mean charging business units a market rate for services and encouraging an effective service, but may tempt the treasury department to speculate as well as involve additional administration time and costs.

? Questions

Question 1 – ZX Inc.

ZX is a relatively small US-based company in the agricultural industry. It is highly mechanised and uses modern techniques and equipment. In the past, it has operated a very conservative policy in respect of the management of its working capital. Assume that you are a newly recruited management accountant. The Finance Director, who is responsible for both financial control and treasury functions, has asked you to review this policy. You assemble the following information about the company's forecast end-of-year financial outcomes. The company's year-end is in six months' time.

	US$'000
Receivables	2,500
Inventory	2,000
Cash at bank	500
Current assets	5,000
Fixed assets	1,250
Current liabilities	1,850
Forecast sales for the full year	8,000
Forecast operating profit (18% of sales)	1,440

You wish to evaluate the likely effect on the company if it introduced one of two alternative approaches to working capital management. The Finance Director suggests you adjust the figures in accordance with the following parameters:

	'Moderate' policy	*'Aggressive' policy*
Receivables and inventory	−20%	−30%
Cash	Reduce to $250,000	Reduce to $100,000
Fixed assets	No change	No change
Current liabilities	+10%	+20%
Forecast sales	+2%	+4%
Forecast profit	No change in percentage profit/sales	

Requirements

Write a report to the Finance Director that includes the following:

(a) A discussion of the main aspects to consider when determining policy in respect of the investment in, and financing of, working capital, in general and in the circumstances of ZX.

(10 marks)

(b) Calculations of the return on net assets and the current ratio under each of three scenarios shown below:

- the company continues with its present policy
- the company adopts the 'moderate' policy
- the company adopts the 'aggressive' policy.

(8 marks)

(c) A recommendation to the company of a proposed course of action. Your recommendation should be based on your evaluation as discussed above and on your opinion of what further action is necessary before a final decision can be taken.

(7 marks)
(Total = 25 marks)

Question 2 – UR

UR is a privately owned machine tool manufacturing company based in the Republic of Ireland. For the past five years, it has operated an aggressive policy in respect of the management of its working capital. The following information concerns the company's forecast end-of-year financial outcomes if it continues with this type of policy.

	Euro'000
Receivables	5,200
Inventory	2,150
Cash at bank	350
Total current assets	7,700
Fixed assets	14,500
Trade payables	4,500
Sales	17,500
Operating costs	14,000
Operating profit	3,500
Earnings	2,625

There are 2.5 m shares in issue.

The company has been experiencing a series of problems because of the type of working capital management policy it has been following and is considering an alternative approach to working capital management.

The percentage figures shown below are changes to the above forecast. These changes are anticipated to occur if a more conservative policy is adopted.

Receivables	−40%
Inventory	+20%
Cash (figures in Euro'000) Increase to Euro	1,000
Fixed assets	No change
Current liabilities	−30%
Forecast sales	−5%
Operating profit and earnings	+5%

Requirement

Evaluate the two working capital management policies described above and recommend a proposed course of action. Include in your evaluation a discussion of the problems that might have arisen as a result of operating aggressive working capital management policies and the key elements to consider and actions to take before making a decision to change. You should calculate appropriate and relevant ratios or performance measures to support your arguments.

[The calculations will earn up to 8 marks]
(25 marks)

Question 3 – Hotel (Practice Question)

A family run hotel has 60 rooms and a dining room and is located in Edinburgh. Suggest four ways in which they could attempt to measure customer satisfaction.

Question 4 – ML

ML plc is a large company that is listed on a major international stock exchange. Its shares are held mainly by large financial institutions which have, in general, favoured a generous dividend payout policy.

ML plc manufactures consumer electrical goods. This is a rapidly changing industry that requires significant new investment in developing new products every few years. Failure to make such investment is likely to result in reduced competitiveness. The following data are relevant to the company for each of the years ended 30 September:

	2000	*2001*	*2002*	*2003*
£1 ordinary shares (million)	300	300	300	450
Dividend (£ million)	50	55	55	70
Retained profit for year (£ million)	200	250	100	300
Total debt (£ million)	1,000	1,100	1,350	850
Share price at 30 September (£)	4		6	
New investment in fixed assets (£ million)	190	260	100	290

The company made a rights issue on 1 October 2002 of 1 for 2 at an issue price of £4 per share. All debt carries interest at 10% per annum and any new debt is taken on at the end of each year. Prior to the year 2000, debt had stood at £ 1,000m for some years.

The company has not made any takeovers and there has been no significant divestment of fixed assets.

Requirements

(a) Suggest possible explanations as to why the share price has:

- risen in the year to 30 September 2002 despite a loss being made;
- fallen in the year to 30 September 2003 despite a profit being made.

(4 marks)

(b) Using the information available in the table, calculate the following ratios for ML plc for both the year to 30 September 2000 and the year to 30 September 2003:

- Earnings per share
- Price earnings ratio (using the share price at 30 September)
- Dividend cover.

Briefly explain each of the three types of ratio, commenting on any changes in the ratios you have calculated for ML plc.

(11 marks)

(c) Analyse the investment, financing and dividend decisions of ML plc and discuss how they interrelate. Refer to the table provided and use supporting calculations where appropriate.

(10 marks)

Ignore taxation.

(Total = 25 marks)

Question 5 – XYZ training

XYZ is *a* financial publishing and training company that helps to prepare students for professional exams. Its activities are concentrated in North America and Europe and include classroom tuition and book publishing. It has recently expanded its publishing activities into e-learning (mainly CD ROMs). Customers include professional firms, self-paying students, college lecturers and bookshops throughout America and Europe, with growing export sales to the Far East. XYZ is carefully reviewing all aspects of its business and is currently focusing on working capital management in its publishing division. Recent data shows the following:

	XYZ Publishing	*XYZ Publishing*	*Industry average of publishing companies*	*Industry average of publishing companies*
Year	2002	2003	2002	2003
	$m	$m		
Sales	30	31	10% growth in 2002	8% growth in 2003
Cost of sales	20*	22*	70% of sales	70% of sales
Average inventory	18**	19**	75 days based on cost of sales	70 days based on cost of sales
Average receivables	10	11	62 days	61 days
Average payables	3	3	70 days	73 days
Bad debts	1	1.5	0.5% of sales	0.5% of sales
Inventory write-off	3	4	13% of sales	13% of sales

* 50% of the cost of sales relates to print costs and cost of sales excludes any inventory write-off cost or bad debt cost. ** If on-demand printing were introduced, physical inventories would be expected to fall by 80% from their current level.

(On-demand printing is where books are only printed when orders are received. The current method is to print for the estimated demand over the following 12 months.) The cost of capital is 5%.

At a recent Board Meeting the following comments were made on how to maximise the use of working capital:

Director of Publishing:
Inventory control has been a big problem. We have been particularly badly hit in 2003 by a large number of changes in syllabi for the various professional bodies. This has made it difficult to predict demand when setting print quantities. Changing syllabi has also resulted in a large number of books needing to be re-printed at higher per unit costs while other books were substantially overprinted, requiring large quantities of books to be thrown away. On-demand printing, while costing 20% more to print compared with current printing, may be worth considering. To manage the information needs of on-demand printing an upgraded computer system would be needed costing $0.5 m per annum.

Sales Director:
I think our receivables position needs some attention. I would recommend extra staffing in credit control to reduce receivable days and the use of aggressive legal action in an attempt to reduce our bad debt levels. The extra staffing we would need to reduce

the receivable days would cost $250,000 per annum. By putting this resource in place, I estimate that our receivable days would fall to the 2003 industry average. Estimating the cost of taking legal action is more difficult, but current estimates show that an investment of about $200,000 per annum would reduce bad debts to 0.4% of sales.

The Finance Director has asked you to produce a draft response to the following memorandum received from the Chief Executive.

MEMORANDUM

To: Finance Director From: Chief Executive Date: 25 May 2004 Subject: Working capital	Approximate number of marks available for the points raised by the Chief Executive
I need your guidance on how to manage our working capital. I would like a report on the following:	
(a) Compare the inventory control, receivable control and gross margin record for our Publishing Division with the industry average and interpret your results.	**(9 marks)** [5 marks of which are for calculations]
(b) Advise on whether we would have been better off in 2003 to have printed using on-demand printing.	**(9 marks)** [6 marks of which are for calculations]
(c) Evaluate the recommendations of the Sales Director. (Use 2003 data and assume that all sales are on credit.)	**(7 marks)** [4 marks of which are for calculations]

Requirement

Prepare a draft response to the Chief Executive's memorandum.

(Total = 25 marks)

Question 6

CBA Limited is a manufacturing entity in the furniture trade. Its sales have risen sharply over the past 6 months as a result of an improvement in the economy and a strong housing market. The entity is now showing signs of 'overtrading' and the financial manager, Ms Smith, is concerned about its liquidity. The entity is 1 month from its year end. Estimated figures for the full 12 months of the current year and forecasts for next year, on present cash management policies, are shown below.

	Next year £'000	*Current year* £'000
Income account		
Revenue	5,200	4,200
Less :		
Cost of sales[1]	3,224	2,520
Operating expenses	650	500
profit from operations	1,326	1,180
Interest paid	54	48
Profit before tax	1,272	1,132
Tax payable	305	283
Profit after tax	967	849
Dividends declared	387	339
Current assets and liabilities as at the end of the year		
Inventory/work in progress	625	350
Receivables	750	520
Cash	0	25
Trade payables	464	320
Other payables (tax and dividends)	692	622
Overdraft	11	0
Net current assets/(liabilities)	208	(47)
Note:		
1. Cost of sales includes depreciation of	225	175

Ms Smith is considering methods of improving the cash position. A number of actions are being discussed:

Receivables

Offer a 2% discount to customers who pay within 10 days of despatch of invoices. It is estimated that 50% of customers will take advantage of the new discount scheme. The other 50% will continue to take the current average credit period.

Trade payables and inventory

Reduce the number of suppliers currently being used and negotiate better terms with those that remain by introducing a 'just-in-time' policy. The aim will be to reduce the end-ofyear forecast cost of sales (excluding depreciation) by 5% and inventory/WIP levels by 10%. However, the number of days ' credit taken by the entity will have to fall to 30 days to help persuade suppliers to improve their prices.

Other information

- All trade is on credit. Official terms of sale at present require payment within 30 days. Interest is not charged on late payments.
- All purchases are made on credit.
- Operating expenses will be £ 650,000 under either the existing or proposed policies.
- Interest payments would be £ 45,000 if the new policies are implemented.
- Capital expenditure of £ 550,000 is planned for next year.

Requirements

(a) Provide a cash-fl ow forecast for next year, assuming:
  (i) the entity does not change its policies;
  (ii) the entity's proposals for managing receivables, payables and inventories are implemented.

  In both cases, assume a full 12-month period, that is the changes will be effective from day 1 of next year.

(14 marks)

(b) As assistant to Ms Smith, write a short report to her evaluating the proposed actions. Include comments on the factors, financial and non-financial, that the entity should take into account before implementing the new policies.

(6 marks)
(Total marks 20)

Answers

Question 1 – ZX Inc.

REPORT

To: Finance Director
From: Management Accountant
Date: x of xx 2001

Working capital management

This report discusses the main aspects of working capital management, calculates the return on assets and current ratio under the different proposals and recommends a course of action.

(a) *Main aspects of working capital management*

Working capital consists of the investment in inventory, receivables and cash; these are partly financed by trade payables and sometimes an overdraft. The amount held in each of these assets and the extent to which the current liabilities cover the current assets give an idea of a company's approach to working capital. A conservative policy would have high inventory levels to ensure that demand can always be met instantly, and high cash levels in order to meet any unforeseen liabilities. A conservative policy would normally mean playing safe and not offering extended credit, while an aggressive policy would try to boost sales by tactics such as giving better credit terms. ZX has included a reduction in credit terms offered, or at least an improvement in collection, as an aggressive policy; this might be described as an aggressive cash management policy as it will collect cash more quickly.

The financing of working capital can also be described as conservative or aggressive. Using only trade payables, by increasing the credit period taken, can be viewed as an aggressive approach, while reducing payables and using long-term finance would be safer and more conservative. Short-term finance is often less expensive (in the case of trade payables almost costless if there is no impact on the trading relationship but is more risky for ZX as the facility can be withdrawn at short notice).

In considering the appropriate policy for ZX, we need to consider the nature of the business and the industry:

- Terms offered by competitors will probably have to be matched by ZX which is a small company. The receivables days are currently 114 and would fall to 89 (moderate) or 77 (aggressive). Whether this will be acceptable to the customers will depend on whether our competitors can supply a comparable product on better terms.
- The type of product will have a major impact on the working capital as a long production process will tie up far more inventory in terms of work-in-progress and may mean that higher finished goods have to be held to meet unexpected demand. ZX has a highly mechanised process and uses modern techniques and equipment which would suggest a shorter production process. If this compares

favourably with its competitors, ZX could reduce its inventory levels below those of the industry average without harming its business relationships with customers.

- The efficiency of operations, particularly in terms of credit control and invoicing immediately, will have a direct impact on our working capital in terms of the receivables and cash, but as long as aggressive collection techniques are not employed, there should be little impact on customer relations.

(b) *Ratios under different policies*

The return on net assets and current ratio under the different policies suggested and the current policy are as follows:

Policy	Current	Moderate	Aggressive
Sales	8,000	8,160	8,320
Profit	1,440	1,469	1,498
Receivables	2,500	2,000	1,750
Inventory	2,000	1,600	1,400
Cash	500	250	100
Current assets	5,000	3,850	3,250
Fixed assets	1,250	1,250	1,250
Current liabilities	1,850	2,035	2,220
Net assets	4,400	3,065	2,280
Return on net assets	32.7	47.9	65.7
Current ratio	2.7	1.9	1.5

(c) *Recommendations*

The above ratios would suggest that the aggressive policy is the most attractive as it has the best return on net assets, at double the current return, but only sees the current ratio drop to 1.5, which should still give the company sufficient cover to meet its ongoing liabilities. However, before applying this policy we need to look at the impact this will have on our relationship with our customers and our suppliers. This will depend to a large extent on the terms offered by our competitors as an attempt to reduce our credit period could adversely affect our sales. To this extent, as a small company ZX has less leeway in adjusting its policies than it might appear as it will probably have to follow the industry practices. In addition, cutting inventory levels and reducing the current account cash could incur costs if demand exceeds the inventory held (lost contribution and reputation) or more funds are required (finance costs or bank charges for transferring between accounts). In the light of this, I recommend that we look closely at the industry norms in this area and go for the more cautious approach of the moderate policy. This will allow an increase in the return on net assets, but give sufficient liquidity to compete on an equal basis with the rest of the industry.

Question 2 – UR

Calculations

	Aggressive	*Conservative*
EPS	2.625/2.5 = E 1.05	2.756/2.5 = E 1.10
ROCE	3,500/17,700 = 19.8%	3,675/18,050 = 20.4%
Current ratio	7,700/4,500 = 1.71	6,700/3,150 = 2.13
Quick ratio	5,500/4,500 = 1.23	4,120/3,150 = 1.31
Inventory days	2,150/14,000 × 365 = 56.1 days	2,580/12,950 × 365 = 72.7 days
Receivables days	5,200/17,500 × 365 = 108.5 days	3,120/16,625 × 365 = 68.5 days
Payable days	4,500/14,000 × 365 = 117.3 days	3,150/12,950 × 365 = 88.8 days
Operating cycle	47.3 days	52.4 days
Op profit margin	3,500/17,500 = 20%	3,675/16,625 = 22.1%

Working capital

Working capital typically consists of inventories, receivables, cash and other short-term assets. Because of uncertainty, companies must hold some inventory and cash based on the forecasts made as well as some surplus. The amount of excess inventory and cash held will be a compromise between the risk of running out, and causing commercial problems, and holding too much, which is a waste of money. An aggressive policy would hold lower safety inventories, a conservative one would hold higher levels. An aggressive policy is therefore more risky.

In a similar way, a conservative policy would not want to take as much risk (of customers not paying) and so is likely to extend less generous payment terms than under an aggressive policy, which would be prepared to take the risk of non-payment in order to increase sales.

Whilst trade payables are not an investment, by taking credit a company can reduce the overall net investment required. An aggressive policy would take as long as possible to pay as long as it did not undermine the commercial relationship with the supplier. This effectively means funding much of the current assets through short-term finance which is inherently more risky than using long-term finance.

Problems of an aggressive policy

UR might have encountered a number of commercial problems in operating its aggressive policies. These might include:

- losing sales or having to stop production because the company ran out of inventory
- overdraft charges due to unexpected cash payments taking the account into overdraft
- legal action from suppliers because of late payment
- increased prices from suppliers or low priority for work
- bad debts and more expensive credit control and debt chasing due to liberal credit policies offered.

Key elements to consider in change

UR needs to look closely at the impact on its relations with customers and sales, and to review carefully the projections made if the change is implemented.

Assuming that the forecasts are reliable, UR should consider the following:

- What are the equivalent credit terms offered by competitors in the industry. Unless UR has a product which is so different that no customer would dream of going to a competitor, any terms which are much worse than the industry average could lead to lost sales.
- The receivable days would fall from 109 to 69 days; this will be beneficial for the company on the face of it but we need to compare it with the terms offered by competitors.
- The operating cycle would reduce slightly from 47 to 52 days which will not make a significant difference to profits. The profit margin also increases slightly from 20 to 22%.
- The current ratio seems relatively high under both policies and actually rises under the proposal. This would suggest that current assets are under-utilised.
- This is particularly true of cash as leaving it in a bank account is not an effective use. Detailed cash-flow projections should be prepared and excess funds invested elsewhere.

Conclusion

Although the proposed change has a beneficial effect on profits, EPS and ROCE, the impact is small. It might be more sensible to review management procedures for each component of working capital. A more rapid invoicing of customers, a tighter and more efficient credit control department or a better inventory control system may do more than this suggested change in policy. External changes in policy will have an impact on the commercial relationships with customers and suppliers, leading to loss of business, while tightening up internal processes will have less impact.

Question 3 – Hotel

Ways in which customer satisfaction could be measured include:

- feedback forms with scoring on a scale 1–5
- percentage of guests who return
- percentage of hotel rooms occupied
- number of bookings for next 6 months
- percentage of guests eating in the hotel.

Question 4 – ML

(a) **Share price movements**

The stock market seems in practice to be closest to the semi-strong form of efficiency which states that the share price reflects all publicly available information.

2002 price rise

Although the company made a loss in the year to 30 September 2002, the share price reflects public information which impacts on expectations for the future. Thus it appears to feel profits will recover (as they did). Additionally, the market may have already built in the expectation of a loss, and a smaller loss than expected had a favourable impact on the price.

2003 price drop

As there has been a rights issue, there are more shares representing the overall market value. We would expect a price ex-rights of:

$$\frac{[(2 \times 6) + (1 \times 4)]}{3} = £5.33$$

The current price of £5 is slightly lower, possibly reflecting a lower profit than had been expected, which affected the market's view of future prospects.

(b) **Ratios**

	2000	*2003*
EPS	250/300 = 83.3 pence	370/400 = 82.2 pence
P/E ratio	400/83.3 = 4.8	500/82.2 = 6.1
Dividend cover	250/50 = 5	370/70 = 5.3

EPS looks at the profits available for distribution generated per share. The results are only comparable if the number of shares is constant; in this case the rights issue means that a holder of 2 shares in 2000 would now hold 3 shares in 2003.

The P/E ratio gives the multiple linking the share price to the earnings per share. This gives an indication of future expectations, and incorporates growth estimates and an allowance for risk. A higher ratio suggests higher expectations compared with current performance. This may mean the market expects higher growth or lower risk than envisaged in 2000, but may also mean that current earnings are not as good as the long-term trend expected.

Dividend cover indicates the ease with which dividends can be covered by profits generated in the year. This will tend to fluctuate, as profits are more volatile than the steady dividend policies usually followed, and therefore needs to be analysed as a long-term trend. A cover of 5 is fairly safe, but does not mean that the company will always have the cash available to maintain the dividend.

(c) **Investment, financing and dividend decisions**

Investment in positive NPV projects will increase the present value of cash for the company, which will lead ultimately to an increase in the present value of the cash paid to shareholders. This in turn, assuming a relatively efficient market, will increase the share price and hence shareholders' wealth.

In order to finance these investments, cash will be needed and this can be from raising new finance or by using cash the company already has. The former is more expensive in that it will incur issue costs, while the latter reduces the cash available for dividends. In most markets, information is less than perfect and a reduction in dividends may cause the market to reduce its future expectations, and hence the share price, unless it understands the future benefits to be obtained by withholding the cash. There is therefore a compromise to be reached between the dividend policy and the financing decision.

In ML, there appears to have been investments and funding as follows:

In£m	*2000*	*2001*	*2002*	*2003*
Investment	190	260	100	290
Funding				
Cash retained	NA	160	–	190
New equity	NA	–	–	600
New debt	NA	100	250	(500)
Dividends	50	55	55	70

It would therefore appear that the dividends are kept in place and steady growth allowed, while issuing new debt annually when needed to make up the cash required for investment. This accesses outside finance in the cheapest way, but ML reduces the risk to shareholders engendered in a high gearing level by periodically raising more equity to lower the debt level. This has higher issue costs and is unlikely to be popular with shareholders on an annual basis, so is kept to a larger issue every few years.

Question 5 – XYZ training

DRAFT REPORT

To: Chief Executive
From: Finance Director
Date: 25 May 2004

Management of working capital

This report will consider the performance of the Publishing Division, advise on whether we would have been better using on-demand printing and evaluate the recommendations of the Sales Director.

1 *Publishing division performance*

	Division		*Industry*	
Year	2002	2003	2002	2003
Inventory days	328 days	315 days	75 days	70 days
Inventory write-offs	10%	12.9%	13%	13%
Receivables days	122 days	130 days	62 days	61 days
Bad debts	3.3%	4.8%	0.5%	0.5%
Gross margin	33%	29%	30%	30%

Inventory write-offs have increased to industry levels, probably due to the change in syllabuses. The division holds a much higher level of inventory than the industry average, probably because they print to meet the whole year's estimated demand. This may well lead to further write-offs if demand turns out to be lower than expected. It is also possible that growing overseas sales have led to inventories being held overseas as well.

Receivables days are twice the industry average and rising. In addition bad debts are now nearly ten times the industry level and have risen from last year. The receivables collection and bad debts need urgent attention. It is possible these are linked to the expansion overseas, but care needs to be taken before offering credit. It is possible that the results have been distorted by a major customer going into liquidation.

The gross margin has fallen from its position above the industry average to below it. This has been caused in part by the printing costs associated with the change in syllabuses.

2 *On-demand printing*

Based on 2003, the current system compared with on-demand printing shows the following:

	Current *$m*	*On-demand* *$m*
Print costs	11.00	13.20
Inventory write-offs	4.00	0.00
Computer	0.00	0.50
Finance cost of stock		
5% × $19 m	0.95	
5% × $19 m × 1.20 × 0.20		0.23
	15.95	13.93

The financial analysis shows an annual cost saving of $2.02m in moving to on-demand printing. In addition, the lower inventories may mean a saving in storage costs, which have not been quantified. However, it will need careful management to ensure that large orders can be met on time and that peak demand periods can be managed. Despite these concerns, the financial case for moving to on-demand printing is compelling.

3 *Sales Director's recommendations*

Based on 2003 data, the current position compared with the Sales Director's suggestions shows the following:

	Current *$m*	*Suggested* *$m*
Extra staffing		
Current receivables	11	
New receivables = $31 m × 31/365		5.18
Finance cost at 5%	0.55	0.26
Salaries		0.25
	$0.55 m	$0.51 m
Legal action		
Bad debts	1.50	0.12
Legal action		0.20
	$1.50 m	$0.32 m

These show that based on the financial estimates, we would save $40,000 from introducing extra staffing in credit control and $1.16 m by taking more aggressive legal action. While this suggests we should implement both, it is important to consider other alternatives such as factoring our debts, undertaking stricter credit checks before granting credit and reviewing our terms of trade. It is also important to consider the impact on our relationship with customers if we tighten our credit periods or pursue aggressive legal action.

It is likely that this analysis would benefit from looking at each type of receivable, by nature of business and location, separately so that the key areas of concern can be highlighted and appropriate action taken.

Question 6

(a) *All figures in £'000s*

	No change in policy	*Changes implemented*
Profit from operations	1,326	1,424
Add depreciation	225	225
+/− change in receivables	−230	+72
+/− change in payables	+144	−86
Cash flow from operations	1,465	1,635
Interest paid	−54	−45
Tax paid	−283	−283
Dividends paid	−339	−339
Investing activities		
Non-current assets	−550	−550
Inventory	−275	−212
Net cash flow	−36	206
Opening balance	25	25
Closing balance	−11	231

Changes implemented

1. Profit from operations:

Revenue	=	5,200
Less discounts	=	−52
CoS (3,224 − 225) × 95% + 225	=	−3,074
Operating expenses (unchanged)	=	−650
	=	1,424

2. Decrease in receivables:

£ 520 − [(£2,600/365 × 53) + (£2,600/365 × 10)]	=	72
Decrease in trade payables:		
[£320 − (£2,849/365 × 30)]	=	86

3. Inventory:

[£350 − (625 × 90%)]	=	212

(b) **Report**

To : Ms Smith

From : Assistant

Subject : Proposed working capital policy changes

> ! The solution provided here is the published solution for this examination question. While covering the key points required by the question, it should not be considered an ideal solution, either in terms of its presentation or content.

To include:

- Comment that cash flow is improved by almost a quarter of a million pounds if the proposed changes are made.
- Problems appear to have arisen because credit and stock control have not been adequate for increased levels of turnover.
- Liquidity: current ratio was 0.95:1 (all current assets to trade and other creditors), will be around 1.2:1 under both options. Perversely, ratio looks to improve even if company takes no action and causes an overdraft. This is because of high debtors and stock levels. Moral: high current assets do not mean high cash. Cash ratio is perhaps a better measure.
- Customers' days last year was 45, forecast to rise to 53 on current policies despite 'official' terms being 30. Company could perhaps look to improve its credit control before offering discounts.
- Suppliers' days were 46, forecast to rise to 52. Are discounts being ignored? Are relationships with suppliers being threatened?*
- Dramatic increase in inventory levels forecast: 50 days last year, 71 days forecast this year. If change implemented, inventory will still be 67 days.*
- Operating profit percentage forecast to fall to 25.5% from 281.1% if no changes made. Percentage will fall to 27.4% if changes implemented; a fall probably acceptable if cash flow improved and overdraft interest saved.
- Non-financial factors include relationships with customers and suppliers.
- Other financial factors, is increase in turnover sustainable?

*Using cost of sales figures including depreciation.

3

Sources of Long-term Finance

Sources of Long-term Finance 3

Types of long-term finance

Sources of finance are frequently discussed under two broad headings: equity and debt. Equity is the risk, and permanent, capital of an entity. In balance sheet terms it is represented by ordinary share capital and reserves. The difference between book values, market values, and nominal values of equity needs to be fully understood. Bank borrowing has historically been the most popular form of debt to be raised. Preference shares are a hybrid between debt and equity and account for a small proportion of corporate finance.

The ability to match sources of finance to an entity's requirements and circumstances is required for this examination. Sources of capital also need to be discussed in relation to the use to which that finance will be put and the duration of the investment. Matching the maturity of the investment to the maturity of the finance is often considered to be the preferred approach.

Criteria for selecting a source of finance

- Duration
- Amount
- Accessibility of the finance
- Administration costs
- Servicing costs – for example interest or dividends
- Gearing
- Dividend policy (if choosing between retained profits and equity issues)
- Pricing issues
- Security
- Tax implications.

Issue of shares to new shareholders

(a) Offer for sale by prospectus: shares are offered at a *fixed price* to the public and are presented in a prospectus.

(b) Offer for sale by tender: potential shareholders are asked the number of shares and the amount they are prepared to pay. The issuing house then ranks the bids to determine which applicants are at the top of the list, and who therefore become shareholders.

(c) A placing: shares are placed with a broker who sells the shares to its clients. This tends to be the cheapest way to issue new shares.
(d) Introduction: shares have already been issued, for example on an overseas stock exchange or already have a wide distribution, and are introduced to the marketplace.

Rights issues

This is an issue of shares to existing shareholders in proportion to their current holding.

Considerations when issuing debt

Security – fixed and floating charge
Gearing and interest cover
Impact on EPS
Interest rates
Duration of the loan
Risk
Size of the loan
Yield curve

A financial manager must consider the likely movement in interest rates when choosing the type of finance, for example whether to borrow short or long term. It shows the market expectation of interest rates and should be reviewed before making large borrowing decisions.

Lease or buy decision

There are two main types of lease: finance leases and operating leases. In both cases the lessor is the legal owner. In a finance lease the terms will allow for full recovery of the cost to the lessor. In an operating lease the costs may not be recovered as the lease may be cancellable before full recovery is assured. The risk of a lease is therefore with the lessee in a finance lease and with the lessor in an operating lease.

The discount rate to use in a lease or buy decision is usually assumed to be the rate for secured bank borrowing, as finance leases are usually considered to be equivalent to secured bank borrowing.

Funding of SMEs

SMEs (Small and Medium Enterprises) often find themselves with a funding gap. They are too small for a full stock market quotation but need to raise significant finance which proves very expensive/impossible through basic loans or increasing the overdraft.

Venture Capital entities, such as 3i, and some banks provide equity finance to SMEs. Venture Capitalists retain an interest in an entity for a number of years, before looking for an exit route.

Venture Capitalists invest after assessing the viability of an entity, credibility of its management, realistic forecasts of growth, retention and distribution of profits, prospects of a successful future listing and the proportion of shareholding on offer. However, as they are accepting a high level of risk, they will require a very high return. This is usually in the form of a capital gain over 5–7 years.

Business Angels are often business people who provide relatively small capital amounts for an equity stake (sometimes called the informal venture capital market). They may also offer their management expertise.

Questions

Question 1 –

Praktika plc has a capital structure consisting of 50p ordinary shares with a paid-up value of £45m, and 14% debentures to the face value of £40 m. The shares are currently trading at 400p, and the market price of the loan stock is £120 per £100 nominal.

The entity is concerned about the relatively high coupon rate it is committed to pay on the debentures, which still have several years to maturity. It is therefore proposed to make a 1- to-6 rights issue at a discount of 30% to the current market price, and use the proceeds for part repayment of the debentures.

Praktika's annual after-tax earnings have regularly been in the region of £ 36m for the last few years, and its P/E ratio is not expected to be materially affected by the change in gearing. The company pays corporate tax at the rate of 30%.

Requirements

(a) Using the information provided, numerically assess whether the rights issue would create value for Praktika's shareholders, in the form of a share price that is higher than the theoretical ex-rights price. Comment upon your results. **(8 marks)**

(b) Distinguish between a rights issue and a vendor consideration placing; to what extent does the latter encroach on shareholders' pre-emptive rights? **(5 marks)**

(c) Briefl y describe the primary documentation necessary for a rights issue, and the nature of information that is required to be contained in it. **(4 marks)**

(d) Briefl y discuss the role of underwriting in rights issues. **(3 marks)**

(Total marks=20)

Question 2 –

XYZ plc is a large entity whose shares are listed on a major international stock exchange. It manufactures a variety of concrete and clay building materials. It has decided to replace 100 of its grinding machines with 100 of a new type of machine that has just been launched. The entity is unable to issue any further equity and is therefore considering alternative methods of financing the new machines.

The entity's accounting year end is 31 December.

Option 1 — Issue debt to purchase the machines
The machines are expected to cost $720,000 each on 31 December 2001 and on average are expected to have a useful economic life of 10 years. After this time, the entity expects to scrap the machines, but it has no idea what proceeds would be generated from the sale.

If XYZ plc issues debt, it would do so on 31 December 2001 for the full purchase price in order to finance the investment. The debt would be issued at a discount of 10% on par value (that is, at $90 per $100 nominal) being redeemable at par on 31 December 2011 and carrying a coupon annual interest rate of 6%. Debt interest is tax allowable and the corporate tax rate can be assumed to be 30% (ignore any tax on the redemption).

The debt would be secured by fixed and floating charges.

Option 2 — Long-term lease
The machines can be leased with equal annual rentals payable in arrears. The lease term would be 8 years, but this can be extended indefinitely at the option of the entity at a nominal rent. The lease cannot be cancelled within the minimum lease term of 8 years. The entity would need to pay its own maintenance costs.

Option 3 — Short-term leases
The machines can be leased using a series of separate annual contracts. Maintenance costs would be paid by the lessor under these contracts but, even so, the average lease rentals would be much higher than under Option 2. There is no obligation on either party to sign a new annual contract on the termination of the previous lease contract.

Requirements

(a) Calculate the after tax cost of debt at 31 December 2001 to be used in *Option 1*.
(8 marks)

(b) Explain whether the after tax cost of debt would be an appropriate discount rate for evaluating XYZ plc's investment in grinding machines. **(4 marks)**

Calculations are not required.

(c) Write a memorandum to the directors of XYZ plc which discusses the factors that should be considered when deciding which of the three methods of financing the grinding machines is the most appropriate. **(8 marks)**
(Total = 20 marks)

Question 3 – PJH

Assume you are the Management Accountant in PJH Limited. The company manufactures soft furnishings (such as curtains and drapes) for theatres, exhibitions and concert halls in the United Kingdom. It has been trading for 20 years. 55% of the shares are owned between 10 members of the founding family. There are also 25 other shareholders with holdings of various sizes.

Two years ago, the company received an offer of £25 m for its entire equity, which the Board of Directors rejected without conducting any serious evaluation. The company is forecasting pre-tax earnings of £4.5 m on turnover of £32 m for the current year. These sales and earnings levels are expected to continue unless new investment is undertaken. The Managing Director, Mrs Henry, who is also a major shareholder, is planning a major expansion programme that will require raising £5 m of new finance for capital investment. This investment yields a positive net present value (NPV) of £1.2 m when evaluated at the company's post-tax cost of capital of 9%.

The Board is considering two alternative methods of financing this expansion:

1 A rights issue to vexisting shareholders plus a new issue of shares to employees and trading partners.
2 Medium-term (5 years) debt, interest rate fixed at 7%, secured on the company's fixed assets, mainly land and buildings. The company at present has no long-term debt. It has an overdraft facility that is used for short-term financing needs.

The company pays tax at 30%. Mrs Henry is aware that the method of financing chosen might have an impact on the valuation of the company and also on the company's long-term objectives.

Requirements

Write a report to Mrs Henry that advises on:

(a) the factors that need to be considered by the Board when deciding to raise new equity.
(8 marks)

(b) the effect of each suggested method of financing on the valuation of the company. You only need provide some simple calculations here to support your arguments. You do not have enough information to do a detailed valuation.
(10 marks)

(c) appropriate long-term financial objectives for a company such as PJH Limited.
(7 marks)
(Total = 25 marks)

Question 4 – VID

VID Inc. is a US-based company, which was established 15 years ago. It makes and distributes videos, both for the general market and to customer specifications. Its common stock (shares) have been listed on a US stock exchange for the past 8 years. However, there are relatively few stockholders and the stock is not traded in large volumes. The founders of the company no longer participate in its management but own around 10% of the stock in issue.

VID Inc. borrowed US$65m to purchase new premises three years ago, which have recently been valued at US$85m. The company is now considering diversifying into mainstream film production which will require raising US$50m for additional fixed and working capital. This new business will involve joint ventures with UK partners and much of the filming will be done in the UK or Spain. The new investment is not expected to have a significant effect on profits for at least 18 months.

The three methods being considered for raising capital are:

(i) New equity in the UK, subject to US stockholders' approval;
(ii) Long-term fixed rate US$ debt;
(iii) Floating rate sterling-denominated Eurobonds.

Summary financial statistics for the last financial year for VID Inc. are as below.

	US$m
Turnover	175.00
Operating profit	45.00
Post-tax profits	31.36
Non-current assets (book value)	95.00
Net current assets	58.00
Long-term loans	
8% redeemable 2030	65.00
Common stock (in units of US$1)	25.00
Retained earnings	63.00

Share price (US$)	
High for year	28.56
Low for year	18.50
As at today (25 May 2004)	22.58

Current annual fixed interest rates for secured long-term borrowing are as follows:

US$6%   UK£7%   European common currency area Euro 5%

Floating rate sterling Eurobond notes are available at the bank base rate +0.5%. Tax will continue to be payable at 20% per annum.

Requirement

Assume you are a financial adviser to VID Inc. Evaluate the three methods of finance being considered at the present time and advise the directors of VID Inc. Support your advice with any calculations you consider appropriate. Assume, for the purposes of this evaluation, that the P/E ratio of the company will rise to 20 if equity finance is used, or 19 if fixed or floating rate debt is issued. Make only other simplifying assumptions you think necessary and appropriate.

(Total=25 marks)

Note: Up to 10 marks are available for calculations. A report structure is not required for this question.

Question 5 – Rump

Rump plc is an all-equity financed, listed company which operates in the food processing industry. The Rump family owns 40% of the ordinary shares; the remainder are held by large financial institutions. There are 10 m £1 ordinary shares currently in issue.

The company has just finalised a long-term contract to supply a large chain of restaurants with a variety of food products. The contract requires investment in new machinery costing £24 m. This machinery would become operational on 1 January 2002, and payment would be made on the same date. Sales would commence immediately thereafter.

Company policy is to pay out all profits as dividends and, if Rump plc continues to be all-equity financed, there will be an annual dividend of £9 m in perpetuity commencing 31 December 2002.

There are two alternatives being considered to finance the required investment of £24 m:

1 A 2-for-5 rights issue, in which case the annual dividend would be £9 m. The cum rights price per share would be £6.60.
2 Issuing 7.5% irredeemable debentures at par with interest payable annually in arrears. For this alternative, interest would be paid out of the £9 m otherwise available to pay dividends.

For either alternative, the directors expect the cost of equity to remain at its present annual level of 10%.

Requirements

(a) Calculate the issue and ex-rights share prices of Rump plc assuming a 2-for-5 rights issue is used to finance the new project at 1 January 2002. Ignore taxation.

(6 marks)

(b) Calculate the value per ordinary share in Rump plc at 1 January 2002 if 7.5% irredeemable debentures are issued to finance the new project. Assume that the cost of equity remains at 10% each year. Ignore taxation.

(4 marks)

(c) Write a report to the directors of Rump plc which:
  (i) compares and contrasts the rights issue and the debenture issue methods of raising finance – you may refer to the calculations in your answer to requirements (a) and (b) and to any assumptions made; and
  (ii) explains and evaluates the appropriateness of the following alternative methods of issuing equity finance in the specific circumstances of Rump plc:
  - a placing
  - an offer for sale
  - a public offer for subscription.

(15 marks)
(Total = 25 marks)

Question 6 – RZ

RZ is a privately owned textile manufacturer based in the UK with sales revenue in the last financial year of £68 m and earnings of £4.5 m. The directors of the company have been evaluating a cost saving project, which will require purchasing new machinery from the USA at a capital cost of $1.5 m. The directors expect the new machinery to have a life of at least 5 years and to provide cost savings (including capital allowances) of £240,000 after tax each year. Cash flows beyond 5 years are ignored by RZ in all its investment decisions. The discount rate that the company applies to investment decisions of this nature is its post-tax real cost of capital of 9% per annum.

RZ at present has no debt in its capital structure. The directors, who are the major shareholders, would be prepared to finance the purchase of the new machinery via a rights issue but believe an all-equity capital structure fails to take advantage of the tax benefits of debt. They therefore propose to finance with one of the following methods:

(i) Undated debt, raised in the UK and secured on the company's assets. The current pre-tax rate of interest required by the market on corporate debt of this risk is 7% per annum. Interest payments would be made at the end of each year.

(ii) A finance lease raised in the USA repayable over 5 years. The terms would be 5 annual payments of US$325,000 payable at the *beginning* of each year. The machinery could be bought by RZ from the finance company at the end of the five year lease contract for a nominal amount of $ 1. Assume the whole amount of each annual payment is tax deductible.

(iii) An operating lease. No cost details are available at present.

Other information

- The company's marginal tax rate is 30%. Tax is payable in the year in which the liability arises.
- Capitval allowances are available at 25% reducing balance.

- If bought outright, the machinery is estimated to have a residual value in real cash flow terms, at the end of five years, of 10% of the original purchase price.
- The spot rate US$ to the £ is 1.58.
- Interest rates in the USA and UK are currently 2.5 and 3.5%, respectively.

Requirements

(a) Discuss the advisability of the investment and the advantages and disadvantages of financing with either (i) undated debt, (ii) a finance lease or (iii) an operating lease compared with new equity raised via a rights issue and comment on whether the choice of method of finance should affect the investment decision. Provide appropriate and relevant calculations and assumptions to support your discussion.

(18 marks)

(b) Discuss the benefits and potential problems of financing assets in the same currency as their purchase.

(7 marks)
(Total=25 marks)

Question 7 – EFG

EFG is a South American entity specialising in providing information systems solutions to large corporates. It is going through a period of rapid expansion and requires additional funds to finance the long-term working capital needs of the business.

EFG has issued one million $1 ordinary shares, which are listed on the local stock market at a current market price of $15, with typical increases of 10% per annum expected in the next five-year period. Dividend payout is kept constant at a level of 10% of post-tax profits. EFG also has $10 m of bank borrowings.

It is estimated that a further $3 m is required to satisfy the funding requirements of the business for the next five-year period beginning 1 July 2006. Two major institutional shareholders have indicated that they are not prepared to invest further in EFG at the present time and so a rights issue is unlikely to succeed. The directors are, therefore, considering various forms of debt finance. Three alternative structures are under discussion as shown below:

- Five-year unsecured bank loan at a fixed interest rate of 7% per annum;
- Five-year unsecured bond with a coupon of 5% per annum, redeemable at par and issued at a 6% discount to par;
- A convertible bond, issued at par, with an annual coupon of 4.5% and a conversion option in five years' time of five shares for each $100 nominal of debt.

There have been lengthy boardroom discussions on the relative merits of each instrument and you, as Finance Director, have been asked to address the following queries:

Sr. A: 'The bank loan would seem to be more expensive than the unsecured bond. Is this actually the case?'
Sr. B: 'Surely the convertible bond would be the cheapest form of borrowing with such a low interest rate?'
Sr. C: 'If we want to increase our equity base, why use a convertible bond, rather than a straight equity issue?'

Requirements

(a) Write a response to Sr. A, Sr. B and Sr. C, directors of EFG, discussing the issues raised and advising on the most appropriate financing instrument for EFG. In your answer, include calculations of:

- expected conversion value of the convertible bond in five years' time;
- yield to maturity (redemption yield) of the five-year unsecured bond. Ignore tax.

(18 marks)
(including up to 8 marks for calculations)

(b) Advise a prospective investor in the five-year unsecured bond issued by EFG on what information he should expect to be provided with and what further analysis he should undertake in order to assess the creditworthiness of the proposed investment.

(7 marks)
(Total = 25 marks)

A report format is **not** required for this question.

Question 8 – TFC

The Translavian Ferry Company (TFC) operates four ferries. It wishes to acquire a further new ferry due to high demand for its services from passengers.

At a Board meeting, proposals were put forward for three different methods of financing the new ferry. It was made clear at the meeting that the company is unable to raise any further equity finance.

The ferry being acquired is identical under all three methods of financing. The price of the ferry will be $10m at 1 January 2004 and it will have a 10-year life. After this time, the terms of the operating licence given by the Translavian government require that the ferry should be scrapped for health and safety reasons. The net proceeds are expected to be zero. The company's accounting year end is 31 December. The entity uses an annual net of tax discount rate of 7% to evaluate financing projects.

Method 1 – Long-term lease

The ferry can be leased with equal annual rentals of $2.8m payable in arrears. The lease term would be 5 years, but this can be extended indefinitely, at the option of the entity, at a nominal rent. The lease cannot be cancelled within the minimum lease term of 5 years. TFC would incur all the maintenance costs of $200,000 per year, payable at the end of each year of the life of the asset.

Method 2 – Short-term lease

The ferry can be leased using a series of separate annual contracts. The annual expected lease rental would be $1.7m payable annually in advance, with the first payment being on 1 January 2004. Maintenance costs would be paid in full by the lessor. There is no obligation on either party to sign a new annual contract on the termination of the previous lease contract.

Method 3 – Loan

TFC's bank is willing to make a 4-year loan of $10m so that the ferry can be purchased. Annual repayments would be $3.154m including both capital and interest. These payments are to be made at the end of each of the four years. The loan would be secured by fixed and floating charges over the company's assets.

Taxation

Taxation payments are made one year after the relevant transaction occurs. The tax rate is 30%. All lease payments, interest payments and maintenance charges are allowable in full for tax. Similarly, the purchase price of the ferry is allowable in full as a tax deduction in the year in which the expenditure is incurred. The company has sufficient profits from the existing ferries to ensure that tax allowances can be offset immediately.

The Marketing Director's view

After the meeting, the Marketing Director expressed concerns about the Board's decision to consider only the three funding methods proposed. He argued that: 'All three methods involve financing charges. Yet we can obtain just about enough cash to fund the new ferry from our own resources, even though we may need to sell some of our short-term investments. Why should we pay interest and other finance charges to outsiders when we can fund the new ferry for free ourselves?'

Requirements

(a) Calculate the pre-tax rate of interest implicit in the 4-year loan under financing Method 3 above.

(4 marks)

(b) Calculate the present values at 1 January 2004 of Method 1 and of Method 2 for financing the new ferry. Use the specified annual net of tax discount rate of 7%.

(9 marks)

(c) As a consultant, write a memorandum to the Board of TFC which:

(i) discusses the non-quantitative factors that should be considered when deciding which of the three methods of financing the new ferry is the most appropriate; and

(ii) evaluates the concerns of the Marketing Director.

(12 marks)

(Total = 25 marks)

Answers

Question 1 –

(a)

Current number of shares	=	45 m/0.50	=	90 m
Market capitalization	=	90 m × 4	=	£360 m
Current EPS	=	£36 m/90 m	=	40p
Current P/E ratio	=	400/40	=	10
Rights issue price	=	400 × 0.7	=	280p
Number of rights shares at 1:6	=	15 m		
Amount of rights issue	=	15 m × £2.80	=	£42 m
Number of shares ex-rights	=	90 + 15	=	105 m
Theoretical ex-rights price	=	(360 + 42)/105	=	**383p**
Debentures redeemed	=	£42 m/1.20	=	£35 m
Interest saved	=	35 m × 0.14	=	£4.9 m
Tax saving forfeited	=	4.9 – 0.30	=	£1.47 m
Net saving	=	4.9 – 1.47	=	£3.43 m
New earnings fi gure	=	36 + 3.43	=	£39.43 m
New EPS	=	39.43/105	=	37.5
New share price	=	37.5 × 10	=	**375p**

As this is less than the theoretical ex-rights price, the proposal would have a negative impact on shareholder value. However, the expectation that the P/E ratio would be unaffected by the reduction in gearing does not seem realistic. If, as is more likely, the reduced gearing results in increasing the P/E ratio, the impact may be favourable.

(b) A rights issue is an offering of new shares for subscription by existing shareholders in proportion to their existing shareholdings, in accordance with the principle of pre-emptive rights. Any new issue of shares in excess of 5% of a company's issued share capital (or 7.5% maximum in a rolling 3-year period) would be subject to pre-emptive rights. Shareholders who do not wish to take up the rights can sell them on a nil-paid basis. A rights issue can be made at any time.

A VCP, on the other hand, is made specifically in connection with acquisitions. It occurs when an acquiring company issues new equity in exchange for an acquired company's assets, and places them with institutions for cash that is received by the owners of the acquired company. Thus, although the acquisition is effected by exchange of equity shares, the vendors still receive payment in cash. Pre-emption rights do not, therefore, apply. However, if the VCP relates to over 10% of the issuing company's share capital, or if the shares are offered at a discount to the market price greater than 5%, existing shareholders are entitled to a 100% clawback – that is, they are entitled to purchase shares at the placing price on a basis pro rata to their existing shareholding, to maintain their percentage holding and benefit from the discount offered (but these rights cannot be sold on a nil-paid basis, as in a conventional rights issue).

(c) *Listing particulars.* Provide information about company, and state the purpose for which new funds are required. If for acquisition, information regarding the company to be acquired is to be furnished. Disclosure of material contracts entered into in the preceding year, and any legal or arbitration proceedings, etc., are required. Detailed regulations on what is to be contained in listing particulars are furnished in the Stock Exchange Yellow Book. Full listing particulars are not required for issues of less than 10% of existing issued equity.

Provisional allotment letter. For rights issues, a provisional allotment letter (not a subscription form) is required. Each letter is to be addressed to an individual shareholder, specifying the exact number of shares that have been provisionally allotted.

(d) In return for a fee, underwriters agree to subscribe for all shares not sold. The company effectively purchases a put option which guarantees take-up of all the issue, particularly if the equity market falls significantly between the time of setting the issue price and the closure of the offer. Underwriting is essential when the uncertainty costs of an undersubscribed issue are considerably greater than the costs of underwriting. It is possible to dispense with underwriting in respect of deeply discounted rights issues, which are unlikely to fail. However, it is relatively rare for underwriting to be dispensed with, as the presence of underwriters is a favourable signal to the market.

Question 2 –

(a)

Year	*Cash flow*	*DF 5%*	*PV 5%*	*DF 6%*	*PV 6%*
0	(90.00)	1.000	(90.00)	1.000	(90.000)
1–10	4.20	7.722	32.43	7.360	30.912
10	100.00	0.614	61.40	0.558	55.800
			3.83		(3.288)

By interpolation

$$K_{\mathrm{d}} = 5 + \left(\frac{3.83}{3.83 + 3.288}\right) = 5.538\%$$

(b)

The use of the cost of debt is likely to be inappropriate, no matter which form of financing is used.

If the project merely earned a sufficient return to cover the interest payments, it would fail to recognise the overall impact on existing providers of finance, and that they would be likely to demand a higher return in response to additional financial risk.

This is because the borrowing of additional funds to finance the grinding machines will increase the gearing of the business, possibly significantly. In so doing, the equity shareholders, as the residual claimants on the company's returns, are exposed to greater risk as the returns become more volatile. Also, in the event of corporate failure, they would rank behind a higher level of debt in a distribution from the receiver.

Given that most investors are risk averse, then shareholders are likely to demand a higher return in response to this additional risk.

The exception to this would be if the new project were lease financed, and there was no penalty arising from termination of the contract, other than the return of the asset. In this case, there is no additional exposure to existing shareholders. The lessor would, however, be taking most of the risk and would thus require a significant risk premium.

The grinding machines project, financed by debt, may also change the operating risk of the business, thereby changing the required return on all existing forms of finance.

As an alternative to the cost of debt, the WACC may be an appropriate discount rate. It would first be necessary, however, to calculate the cost of equity.

(c)

Memorandum

To: The Directors	*From:* Management Accountant
Subject: Financing New Grinding Machines	*Date:* 20 November 2001

Introduction
The three methods of fi nancing are likely to give similar conclusions in a competitive-market, otherwise there would be little or no demand for such financing. It would be necessary, however, to carry out detailed calculations of the present values of the cash fl ows for each of the three options before a final decision was taken.

Notwithstanding this, some of the broader issues that would need to be considered are as follows.

Cash flow
Given that the long-term lease is payable in arrears, a short-term cash fl ow advantage is given. The long-term lease is, however, payable equally over 8 years. In contrast, only the interest on the loan is payable over the next 10 years and the capital is not repayable until the end of this period. This gives a significant cash flow advantage to debt financing which may be relevant if capital is constrained.

Risk
The risk of the underlying operations is identical in each case, as the physical assets are the same. This can thus be ignored as a common factor.

A purchase option, however, carries some residual risk in the net realisable value at the end of the machine's life. Given this is some way into the future, it may be regarded as extremely uncertain, particularly if there is a thin market for this type of asset.

Other aspects of risk include breakdown of the machine, which is covered in the short-term lease, but not in the other forms of financing.

Also, the payment terms of the purchase and long-term finance arrangements are fixed, but those of the short lease may vary. Lease rentals may rise with infl ation or a change in market conditions. Alternatively, they may fall if the rate of technological change is greater than expected.

In the extreme, it is possible that the lessor company may collapse and there may be other claims over the asset from creditors arising from this. The fi nancial risk implications have already been discussed in requirement (b) above.

Security
Should the company be unable to repay the debt, then the debt holders' claim would fall not just on the asset (which may have a low net realisable value) but also on other assets in the form of the floating charge. Depending on the terms of the lease contract, the lessor may only have the right to reclaim the asset, perhaps with a penalty. At best, the balance would be an unsecured creditor against XYZ. This relatively higher risk position of the lessor is likely to be reflected in the return demanded in the form of higher lease rentals.

Maintenance
The maintenance contract is included in the short-term lease, but not the other options, although the cost is clearly built into the short-term lease rentals. As already noted, this

gives greater certainty, although perhaps less control, over the type and extent of maintenance than would be the case if it were subject to a separate contract.

Financial reporting considerations
For financial reporting purposes, the long-term lease is probably a finance lease, while the short-term lease is probably an operating lease. From a finance perspective, these definitions are not of themselves signifi cant. Indirectly, however, the operating lease could probably be kept off the balance sheet, while purchase and finance lease options are on balance sheet. This should not make any difference from an information perspective, as stock markets are reasonably efficient and are not normally deceived by changes in disclosed accounting procedures. However, there may be debt covenants (e.g. gearing ratios) or othe accounting-based contracts which may be affected by putting significant assets and matching finance on balance sheet.

Other forms offinance
There may be other forms of finance which may be preferable to those specified. One example may be hire purchase, but also other forms of lease or debt contract may be available.

Signed: Management Accountant.

Therefore, it is cheaper to lease the asset at a cost of £996k, than buy at a cost of £1,000,000. The decision is very marginal.

The NPV will increase from £205,000 to £209,000 if the asset is leased.

Question 3 – PJH

REPORT

To: Mrs Henry
From: Management Accountant
Date: xx of x 2002

Expansion finance, valuations and objectives

This report will consider the factors to be considered when raising new equity, the impact of the method of financing on the valuation of the business and appropriate long-term financial objectives.

1 *Factors to consider*

If the shares are issued to the existing shareholders, the family will have to find 55% of £5 m, which is £2.75 m; this is an average of £275,000 each. The other shareholders only number 25, which mean they would have to contribute an average of £90,000 each. This may be beyond the existing shareholders' means.

However, issuing shares to others will dilute the control of the family, and may mean that decisions are made which are not in their best interests. Ultimately, if the family ends up with a minority stake the company could be sold.

One possibility is to calculate the number of shares the family would have to buy to maintain control.

Suppose the company is worth £35 m (see 'Effect on company value'); this gives a value per share of £35. A rights issue is likely to be at less than current value, say £30.

If the existing shareholders contribute £3 m, this will be 100,000 shares (a 10% rights issue), with the family contributing £1.65 m (an average £165,000 each) and the others £1.35 m (£54,000 each on average). The other £2 m might be raised from new investors at a price of £34.50 (see 'Working'); this would mean issuing a further 57,970 shares.

The family would therefore own (55,000 × 1.10)/(1,100,000 + 57,970) = 52% which still gives them day-to-day control of the company. However, the sums required from existing shareholders may be too much, particularly as the above calculations look at averages - in reality some of the family members will have to find more if they have greater shareholdings than the average.

2 *Effect on company value*

We would start with the bid of £25 m from two years ago and add on the NPV of the project, giving £26.2 m. However, this bid was not evaluated and may not have been a realistic value and it takes no account of what has happened over the last two years.

A better approximation might be the present value of future cash flows, assuming earnings approximate to cash and no growth:

$$\text{Value before project} = \frac{(£4.50\text{ m} \times 0.70)}{0.09} = £35\text{ m}$$

If financed through equity, equity value = 35 m + 5 m + 1.2 m – £41.2 m

If financed through debt, equity value= 35 m + 1.2 m + NPV of tax relief on debt interest and tax relief = £5 m × 7% × 30% = £105,000 pa

PV at 7% = 105,000 × 4.100 = £430,500

Therefore equity value = 35 m + 1.2 m + 430,500 = £36,630,500

Although the equity is worth more under equity financing, bear in mind that £5 m of this is because we have issued more shares!

The second calculation assumes a very efficient market and that debt is effectively risk-free, while both assume that there is no change in the operating risk of the company.

3 *Appropriate long-term financial objectives*

In theory, a company should maximise shareholders' wealth through a combination of dividends and capital value increase. However, other stakeholders set constraints on this objective which will need to be observed if the company is going to thrive in the long term. These include commitments to staff, customers and suppliers. Combining these interests with those of shareholders might give the following objectives:

- dividend payout ratio
- market share and growth in sales
- sales per employee
- amount of repeat business
- employee remuneration as a percentage of costs
- percentage of creditors paid on time.

In addition, the intentions of the family members in the medium term might influence the objectives decided upon.

Working

Existing	1,000,000 shares at £35	£35,000,000
Rights	1,000,000 shares at £30	£3,000,000
	X shares at y	£2,000,000
		£40,000,000

But to ensure no instant gain to the new shareholders, y should be the theoretical price after the issues = £40 m/(1.1 m + X)

$$= X \times 40/(1{,}100{,}000 + X) = 2$$

$$40\,X = 2{,}200{,}000 + 2\,X$$

$$X = 57{,}895 \text{ shares}$$

Question 4 – VID

Calculations	*Existing*	*+ Equity*	*± Debt*
Operating profit ($m)	45	45	45
Finance costs ($m)	5.2	5.2	8.2
	39.8 m	39.8 m	36.8 m
Tax ($m)	8	8	7.4
Post-tax profits ($m)	31.8	31.8	29.4
Number of shares (m)	25	27.5	25
EPS ($)	1.27	1.16	1.18
P/E ratio	17.75	20	19
Mkt value equity ($m)	564.5	636	558.6
ROCE(bk values) (%)	29.4	22.2	22.2
ROE (bk value) (%)	36.1	23.0	33.4
Interest cover	8.7	8.7	5.5
Profit margin (%)	18	18	17
Debt/Debt & Equity (book values) (%)	42.5	32.0	56.7%
Debt/Debt & Equity (market values) (%)	13.3	12	19.7

Assumptions

New equity is issued at US$20 or its sterling equivalent.

The current loan is valued as (65 × 0.08)/0.06 = $86.7 m, which approximates it as an irredeemable debt.

Generally, the company does not appear to be particularly highly geared (based on market values), although it would be useful to know the average for the industry. The interest cover is also reasonable even if new debt is issued.

The market appears to like the prospects for the investment, given that the P/E ratio is expected to increase. If equity is raised, the total market capitalisation is expected to increase by $72 m, representing the $50 m investment and an additional $22 m for the expected NPV of the project.

The return on capital employed and return on equity both look healthy, but again we need industry averages to be able to comment more. The project will not produce profits for 18 months; the market needs to be aware of this or the disappointment will depress the share price in the short term.

Considering the three financing methods mentioned:

1 *Equity*

- existing shareholders will need to waive their pre-emptive rights
- an equity issue will be more expensive than a debt issue
- equity will have a higher cost than debt, although annual payments do not have to be made unlike debt interest
- the price may have to be lower than $20 to attract investors and this will affect the calculations of the ratios
- gearing will decrease if equity is issued
- EPS will be diluted in the short term to $1.16.

2 *Fixed interest debt*

- easier and cheaper to raise
- gearing increases to roughly 20% by market values
- EPS would still dilute to $1.18 but not as much as with equity.

3 *Floating rate debt*

- interest payments would be affected by market conditions. It is therefore important to take account of the director's expectations of future market rates, given the loan will be in sterling, there will also be a currency exchange rate risk.

Question 5 – Rump

(a) **Rights issue**

$$\text{Offer price} = \frac{\text{Finance needed}}{\text{Number of shares issued}}$$

$$= \frac{£24\,\text{m}}{4\,\text{m}} = £6 \text{ per share}$$

$$\text{Ex-rights price} = \frac{[(5 \times £6.60) + (2 \times £6)]}{7}$$

$$= £6.43$$

(b) **Irredeemable debentures**

Dividends per annum $= £9\,\text{m} - (7.5\% \times £24\,\text{m}) = £7.2\,\text{m}$

Dividend per share $= £0.72\,\text{pa}$

Share price = PV of dividends $= \frac{0.72}{0.1} = £7.20$

(c)

REPORT

To: Directors of Rump plc
From: Accountant
Date: xx of 20xx

Raising new finance

The project represents a sizeable increase in the company's operations and the financing of it will have a material impact on the capital structure and the shareholders' wealth.

(i) *Debenture issue or rights issue*

The debentures would introduce significant gearing, and may include restrictive covenants which dictate the repayment timings. In addition there may be restrictions on the operations of the business in order to maintain certain gearing ratios or interest cover. They will probably require security over assets, or compensate for the additional risk of less than full security by applying a higher interest charge.

However, the issue costs associated with the debentures are likely to be lower than those incurred on a rights issue. In addition, the fixed income and asset security will lead to a cheaper cost than the equity which is enhanced by the tax relief available on debt interest.

The calculations in (b) have assumed the cost of equity (and hence the total market value) would stay the same under a debenture issue. However, the risk to the shareholders would increase (as the financial risk of the interest being paid out of profits increases the fluctuation in returns) and so the return required would increase. It therefore may not be as beneficial to shareholders as it appears, as the share value may drop from the price calculated.

Finally, it is possible that not all shareholders will want to take up their rights, which will involve the company selling the rights to other shareholders or the general public if possible. The family would see its shareholding reduced if it could not finance its share of the rights issue.

(ii) *Alternative methods of issuing equity*

A wider issue of equity than a rights issue would have more chance of success but would reduce the holding of current shareholders such as the family, and is likely to have higher issue costs.

A placing is where an issuing house places shares with clients, and is likely to have relatively low costs as it avoids underwriting and much of the advertising. It is likely, however, to concentrate shareholdings which will threaten the family's control. An offer for sale is when an issuing house buys the shares and then offers them to the public, at a fixed price or via a tender, by circulating a prospectus. The costs are likely to be higher as the fees effectively incorporate underwriting of the issue.

A public offer for subscription means that Rump plc itself would issue the prospectus and invite subscription at a fixed price. Costs are likely to be high, as they will have to cover underwriting, publicity and specialist advice.

Question 6 – RZ

(a) **Assessment of investment**

Using equity:

PV of cost savings for 5 years	= £240,000 × 3.890	= £933,600
Capital expenditure	= \$1.5m/1.58	= (949,367)
		(15,767)

While the net present value is negative, it is fairly marginal and the tax benefits which come with other forms of financing may be enough to make it positive.

(i) *Undated debt*

Assume we raise £950,000.

Additional benefit = PV of the tax relief on interest payments
950,000 × 0.07 × 0.30 = £19,950 per annum
Over 5 years this gives 19,950 × 4.100 = £81,795
As a perpetuity it gives 19,950/0.07 = £285,000

Strictly, a risk-free rate should be used to calculate the present value, but the yield on the debt has been used as an approximation.

Advantages

- The benefits of the tax relief on the interest will make the net present value positive (81,795 − 15,767 = £66,000 approximately).
- The financing will not dilute share ownership and is likely to be cheaper and easier to administer than equity.

Disadvantages

- As the debt is undated (in practice this is unusual), the interest will have to be covered indefinitely, even after the benefits from the investment have ceased.

(ii) *Finance Lease*

The easiest way to assess this financing source is to compare the present value of the difference in cashflows from debt finance. This is normally discounted at the post-tax cost of borrowing:

Benefits of leasing over borrow and purchase (in £'000)

	t_0	t_1	t_2	t_3	t_4	t_5
Lease payments	(325)	(325)	(325)	(325)	(325)	
X/R	1.58	1.56	1.55	1.53	1.52	
In £'000	(206)	(208)	(210)	(212)	(214)	
Tax saved		62	62	63	64	64
Purchase saved	949					(95)
Tax benefits lost		(71)	(53)	(40)	(30)	(62)
	743	(217)	(201)	(189)	(180)	(93)
	1	0.952	0.907	0.864	0.823	0.784
	743	(207)	(182)	(163)	(148)	(73)

As the net present value is negative (£30,000), it means that leasing appears to be less beneficial than borrowing using straight debt.

Advantages

- The leasing has a definite five-year life compared with the uncertainty of the undated debt or equity.
- There are quite often lower arrangement costs for leasing than for debt or equity.

- Although our calculation suggests it is more expensive, this is greatly influenced by the resale value estimate and the timing of the cashflows. Further analysis may alter the result.

Disadvantages

- A finance lease will still involve placing an asset and a long-term liability on the balance sheet, and hence will have a similar impact on any ratios as raising finance through debt. This may not be a problem for a (currently) all-equity private company.
- As it entails another four years of payments in US$, it will introduce currency risk.

(iii) *Operating Lease*

With an operating lease, the risks and rewards of ownership remain with the lessor, so that the lessee does not have to include assets, and associated liabilities, on the balance sheet.

Advantages

- There are not likely to be any other costs, such as maintenance or insurance, payable.
- There are likely to be points in the lease at which it can be abandoned.
- There will be no balance sheet impact (although, as above, this may not be an issue for RZ).

Disadvantages

- It may be more expensive as the lessor has to cover all the other costs.
- Operating leases will not be available on all types of machinery.

(b) **Same currency financing**

In this question, RZ could have raised finance in US$ to finance the purchase.

Advantages

- The changes in balance sheet values of the asset and liability would be in the same currency and will offset each other to a large extent.
- There might be cheaper finance available in the US to encourage export sales.

Disadvantages

- The tax implications will be more complex.
- If cashflows are generated in sterling, this will produce currency risk as the interest and capital payments will be made in US$.
- In some cases, exchange controls might be introduced which would cause problems in making the payments.

Question 7 – EFG

(a) **Response to Board members**

Response to Sr. A:

- the redemption yield (YTM) allows the cost of the loan and bond to be compared on the same basis;

- the redemption yield is effectively the IRR of the cash flows under the debt instrument and so takes into account the time value of money;
- the bond is slightly cheaper than the loan, with a redemption yield of 6.45% instead of 7%;
- this result would be expected, since the bond is marketed to a wider investor base and so finer rates can be obtained;
- issue costs must also be taken into account; no information is provided in the question, but costs can be expected to be significantly higher for the bond because of the publicity and underwriting required.

Response to Sr.B:

- looking at coupon rates in isolation, the convertible bond appears to cost less than the bond; certainly the interest cost would be lower over the five-year period;
- however, if the share price rises by 10% a year as predicted, each convertible bond worth $100 on redemption will convert to 5 shares worth $120.80. This capital gain is equivalent to a compound yield of 3.85% per annum. This is in addition to the 4.5% coupon on the convertible, making it overall significantly more expensive than the unsecured bond (*Workings* $3.85\% = (120.80/100)^{1/5} - 1$);
- in addition, from year 6 onwards, the entity will need to pay dividends on the shares created on conversion which is likely to increase the cost of capital since the cost of equity is generally higher than the cost of debt.

Response to Sr.C:

- investors may have concerns about the future growth of the entity and be reluctant to subscribe to shares at the present time, as indicated by the two major institutional shareholders;
- the convertible bond gives investors the opportunity to acquire new shares, but they have the assurance that they do not need to convert the bond into shares unless the entity performs well in the next five-year period;
- in the meantime, the entity benefits from lower financing costs for five years.

Recommendation

For a rapidly expanding entity such as EFG, the convertible bond may be the most appropriate. The convertible bond provides low cost finance for five years and may result in the desired equity base at the end of the five year period.

Appendix: Calculations and workings

Calculation of the expected conversion value of the convertible on 1 July 2011:

Share price now:	$15
Share price in five years' time:	$24.16 ($= 15 \times (1 + 10\%)^5$)
So conversion value is:	$120.80 per $100 nominal ($= 5 \times \$24.16$)
Capital gain is:	

Yield to maturity (YTM) calculations:

Loan: The YTM for the bank loan is equal to the annual coupon of 7%.

Bond:

Based on $100 nominal for simplicity:

Using a 6% discount rate:

Year	*Cash flow*	*Discount factor*	*PV (= cash flow × discount factor)*
	$		$
0	94	1.000	94.00
1–5	(5)	4.212	(21.06)
5	(100)	0.747	(74.70)
TOTAL NPV			(1.76)

Using a 7% discount rate:

Year	*Cash flow*	*Discount factor*	*PV(= cash flow × discount factor)*
	$		$
0	94	1.000	94.00
1–5	(5)	4.100	(20.50)
5	(100)	0.713	(71.30)
TOTAL NPV			2.20

So, by interpolation, the YTM of the bond is approximately:

$$6\% + 1\% \times \frac{1.76}{(1.76 + 2.20)} = 64.4\ \%$$

Alternative approach based on actual cashflows:

Using a 6% discount rate:

Year	*Cash flow*	*Discount factor*	*PV (= cash flow × discount factor)*
$m	$m		$m
0	3.00	1.000	3.000
1–5	(0.16)	4.212	(0.674)
5	(3.19)	0.747	(2.383)
TOTAL NPV			(0.057)

Using a 7% discount rate:

Year	Cash flow	*Discount factor*	PV (= *cash flow × discount factor)*
	$m		$m
0	3.00	1.000	3.000
1–5	(0.16)	4.100	(0.656)
5	(3.19)	0.713	(2.274)
TOTAL NPV			0.070

So, by interpolation, the YTM of the bond is approximately:

$$6\% + 1\% \times \frac{0.057}{(0.057 + 0.070)} = 6.45\%$$

Workings:

- Borrowings needed of \$3 m;
- The bond is issued at a 6% discount, so issue nominal of \$3 m/0.94 = \$3.19 m in order to raise \$3 m;
- Annual interest at 5% on a nominal value of \$3.19 m is \$3.19 m × 5% = \$0.16 m.

(b) In assessing creditworthiness, a prospective investor should be provided with the following information:

- financial statements for the last three years;
- cash flow forecasts;
- long- and short-term ratings from rating agencies of this and similar entities' bonds;
- business prospects;
- prospects for the market sector.

and undertake the following analyses:

- calculate ratios (gearing, interest cover, dividend cover, working capital ratios);
- analyse free cash flow;
- carry out a risk assessment of the business and the market sector.

Question 8 – TFC

(a) **Pre-tax implicit interest rate**

Rate given by 10 m = 3.154 m × 4 year Annuity Factor
4 year AF = 3.171
From the tables, this gives the implicit rate as approximately 10% per annum.

(b) **Present values**

Method 1 (long-term lease)

PV of rentals	= 2.8 m × 4.1	= (11.48 m)
PV of maintenance	= 0.2 m × 7.024	= (1.405 m)
PV tax relief of rentals	= (11.48 × 0.30)/1.07	= 3.219 m
PV tax relief of maintenance	= (1.405 × 0.30)/1.07	= 0.394 m
		(9.272 m)

Method 2 (short-term lease)

PV of rentals	= 1.7 m × (6.515 + 1)	= (12.776 m)
PV of tax relief	= (12.776 × 0.30)/1.07	= 3.582 m
		(9.194 m)

(c)

MEMORANDUM

To: Board of TFC
From: Consultant
Date: xx of xx 2003

Financing considerations

The three methods of financing considered are likely to have similar financial results in a competitive market, but other, non-financial, considerations may be important.

1 *Risk*

The short-term lease covers the potential breakdown of the ferry, whereas the others do not. The short-term lease is also renewed annually, which means we cannot guarantee that the terms will remain the same, unlike the other two proposals.

On the other hand, the short-term lease allows TFC to terminate the operation earlier than planned if circumstances change.

2 *Security on assets*

The bank loan is likely to be secured on other assets of the company in the form of fixed or floating charges. The lease arrangements will only give the lessor the right to reclaim the ferry if the lease payments are not kept up, even if the value of the ferry is exceeded by the amounts owed.

3 *Cash flow*

The loan is payable over 4 years, while the long-term lease is payable over 5 years and the short-term over the full 10 years. This gives the short-term lease a significant cash-flow advantage. This is despite having to pay annually in advance (the other two are in arrears).

4 *Gearing ratios*

The long-term lease is probably classified as a finance lease and would therefore be included as an asset and long-term debt, like the bank loan. The short-term lease is probably an operating lease, which would not affect the balance sheet. There could therefore be a difference in the gearing ratios calculated, which can be specified as covenants for debt finance.

5 *Marketing Director's View*

The Marketing Director feels that internal resources should be used to finance the new ferry. This is sensible if the company has sufficient cash resources as it will involve no arrangement fees and the lost investment income is likely to be lower than the interest rate charged by an outside provider of finance.

However, internal cash is not costless as it belongs to the company, which in turn belongs to the shareholders; they require a return on the funds used which matches the risk they perceive in the investment.

6 *Conclusion*

It might be sensible to use some of the company's own resources, leaving some for other opportunities that might present themselves, and some externally. This might suggest the straight loan, rather than leasing, which can be reduced to the amount required. However, this will depend on the confidence of the company in being able to meet the cash-flow commitments and the importance of maintaining a certain gearing ratio.

4

Capital Structure and Cost of Capital

Capital Structure and Cost of Capital

4

Cost of equity

Dividend valuation model:

$$k_e = \frac{d_1}{P_0} + g$$

where,
d_1 = dividend in one year's time
P_0 = Today's ex div share price
g = constant annual dividend growth

Remember:

(a) It assumes constant dividend growth
(b) P_0 is ex div
(c) d_1 probably has to be estimated as $d_0 (1 + g)$, where d_0 = today's dividend.

Estimating g

From past dividends:

$$20(1 + g)^5 = 28$$
$$1 + g = 1.4^{0.2}$$
$$1 + g = 1.0696$$
$$\text{so } g = 6.96\%$$

where the dividend paid in 2001 was 20 and the dividend paid in 2006 was 28.

Using Gordon's growth model:

$$g = b \times r$$

where,
b = proportion of profits retained (i.e. not paid out as dividends)
r = return achieved on funds invested

You are less likely to make mistakes if you input both b and r as decimals.

Capital asset pricing model (CAPM)

$$k_e = R_f + [R_m - R_f]\beta$$

where the expected return depends on:
R_f = return required if there was no risk (the 'risk-free rate')
R_m = expected average return on the stock market
β = the risk of investing in the company compared with the whole stock market.

Remember that:

(a) $[R_m - R_f]$ is called the market premium for risk
(b) β is unlikely to be outside the range 0.5 – 2.0
(c) It assumes that investors in the stock market hold diversified portfolios of shares
(d) It assumes a perfect capital market is in operation.

Cost of debt

Corporate debt is normally traded in the UK in £100 nominal value. However, the market price could be very different and is expressed in different ways:

£120 or 120% or a 20% premium (to par) = a price of £120

The yield to an investor $= \dfrac{\text{Interest paid}}{\text{Market price}}$

The cost of debt to the company, k_d $= \dfrac{\text{Interest paid}}{\text{Market price}} \times (1 - t)$

When we have redeemable debt, the interest payments will cease so we do not have a perpetuity of interest and we have to estimate the discount rate used to equate the future interest payments and redemption received by the investor to the current market price.

Weighted average cost of capital (WACC)

The company's cost of capital will be the weighted average of all the costs of long-term finance. Total market values are used to weight the costs together.

$$k_e = \frac{V_E}{V_E + V_D} + k_d(1 - t)\frac{V_D}{V_E + V_D}$$

where
V_E and V_D = total market value of equity and debt respectively and
k_d = pre-tax cost of debt

Assumptions and use of WACC

All of the above rely on the market price of any traded investment in the entity's equity or debt reflecting the expected risks and returns of holding that investment. This implies a rational, reasonably perfect (or efficient) capital market.

In addition, the cost of capital derived will only be appropriate if the risk in the project is the same as that currently perceived by the investor in the entity.

In effect, this means:

- The project must be in the same line of business as the rest of the entity (business risk stays the same)
- There must be no change in the gearing level (financial risk stays the same).

Financial risk and the cost of capital

Traditional view
The Traditional view was based on observations of the impact of gearing on the market value of an enetity and its cost of capital. It observed that shareholders viewed some debt as beneficial, as it was cheaper finance and had the effect of magnifying returns to equity.

As a result the weighted average cost of capital, with more cheap debt and no or little increase in the cost of equity, drops before rising as shareholders start to adjust the return required at higher levels of gearing.

However, this was not much good for predicting exactly what would happen to the cost of capital when the gearing changed, as it depended on shareholders' views in a particular company on the appropriate level of debt.

M&M with corporation tax
M&M showed that in a perfect capital market the value of a geared entity was higher than that of an identical ungeared entity and that the difference was the present value of the tax relief on the debt interest.

i.e. $$V_g = V_u + TB$$

where:
V_g = total market value of the geared company = $E + D$
V_u = market value of the equity in an identical all-equity entity
TB = PV of the tax relief on debt interest.

If the debt is irredeemable and the discount rate used on the tax relief is the pre-tax cost of debt, TB is simply the market value of the debt multiplied by the tax rate. If the value is increasing as gearing increases, the WACC must be decreasing.

$$k = k_{eu}(1 - TL)$$

where:

$$L = \frac{V_D}{V_E + V_D} \text{ for the finance used}$$

M&M with corporate taxes implies that the value of the entity can be increased by becoming very highly geared. In practice this is unlikely and the theory becomes less useful at higher level of gearing as it did not take account of:

- the entity not having any taxable profits left to obtain tax relief on the extra interest (tax exhaustion);
- debt becoming more risky to hold at high gearing levels, thus increasing the cost of debt;
- the additional costs of doing business when supplies and customers see you as at risk of bankruptcy;
- personal tax positions.

In addition, there are practical considerations, such as the assets the entity can offer for security, which limit the level of debt which can be issued.

Adjusted present values (APV)

Instead of calculating a new cost of capital for assessing a project, an adjusted present value approach can be used, which separates the investment decision from the financing decision.

This uses the formula:

$$V_g = V_u + PV \text{ of tax relief on debt interest}$$

It evaluates the NPV from the perspective of an ungeared entity (giving the increase in V_u) before looking at the benefit to the entity of increasing the debt for its funding.

Business risk and the cost of capital

Business risk

Business risk (or operating risk) includes all the risks in an entity, apart from financial risk. In other words, it includes the character of the directors, the cost structure of the entity and the type of business in which the entity operates, as well as other factors.

However, the only one which might be different in a project being considered by an entity from that known by investors is the type of business in which it operates. Investors in a brewer of beer, for example, would not have allowed for the risk of book publishing even though the brewer might be considering such a project. The cost of capital derived would, therefore, be inappropriate for the project.

Capital asset pricing model (CAPM)

CAPM states that expected return on an investment is

$$R_f + [R_m - Rf]\beta$$

For a quoted entity we would assume the average investor is well diversified. In other words, β only reflects the systematic risk of the investment which cannot be avoided if the portfolio is held in the stock market. The unsystematic risk is diversified away in the portfolio.

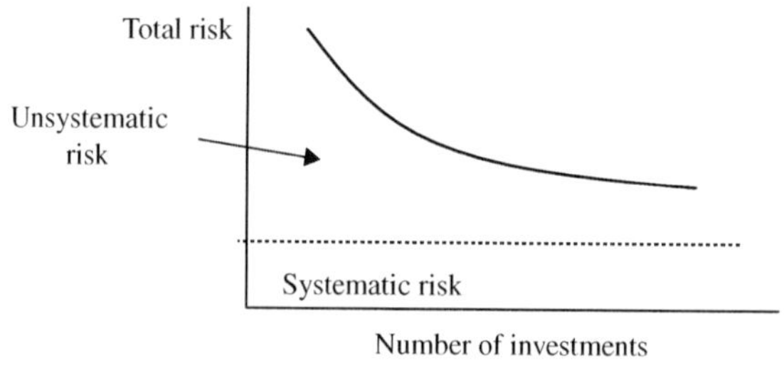

Changing business risk

A brewer, thinking about a project in book publishing, would find the average beta for book publishing by looking at companies already involved in that sector. The cost of equity derived would then be built into the WACC along with the various costs of debt. In practice the brewer should probably make some adjustment to the cost of equity derived, as it reflects the return required by investors from an experienced publisher.

Beta and gearing

One major difference between the brewer and the publishing entity, from which it derives the beta, may be in the level of gearing. This will clearly affect the risk to the investor and hence the beta.

We need to strip out the publishing entity's gearing and replace it with the brewer's gearing, using:

$$\beta_U = \beta_G \frac{V_E}{V_E + V_D(1 - t)} + \beta_D \frac{V_D(1 - t)}{V_E + V_D(1 - t)}$$

Although this seems complex, B is the debt beta and measures the risk of the debt. As debt carries much less risk than equity, its beta is relatively small; many questions do not mention a debt beta, in which case we would assume that it is approximately zero (i.e. the debt is risk-free) and the final term in the above equation disappears.

Combining betas

An entity may comprise several divisions with different risk characteristics. The entity's beta will be a weighted average (by total value) of the divisions' betas. In the same way, the beta of a portfolio of shares will be the weighted average, by market value, of the betas of the individual investments.

Arbitrage pricing theory

APT suggests that various independent factors affect the return required, rather than just the systematic risk used by CAPM. However, it is difficult to predict these factors in practice.

Questions

Question 1 – LS

LS is a mature consumer goods company with limited scope for turnover growth in its stable market. The following information is known about the company and its main competitors:

	LS	*Competitor A*	*Competitor B*
Equity beta	0.5	0.9	Not available
Actual return on equity per annum (%)	8	9	11 (estimate)
Risk-free return per annum (%)	5	5	5
Market return per annum (%)	10	10	10
Current share price ($)	$2	$3	Not available
Historic turnover growth per annum (%)	3	5	Not available

A recent press announcement from competitor A stated: 'We believe in delivering a return above the norm in our sector of the market and are pleased that we have delivered returns of 1% more than our main competitor. Investors wanting a high return in exciting markets need look no further.'

It is also known that competitor B is looking for financial backing to commence trading and is predicting average annual returns of 11% to equity investors. The company will also be funded with high levels of debt. After five years, the intention is to float the company on the main stock exchange.

The Chief Executive of LS is concerned about these developments and is expecting some shareholders of LS ask some difficult questions. The Chief Executive has made the following three comments to the management team in response to the current situation:

> I have heard that the capital asset pricing model has some limitations, for example it only looks at one part of risk, the risk related to the market. Don't you think we should consider total risk?
> Shouldn't we be comparing actual returns on equity with the weighted average cost of capital rather than with the required return calculated by using the capital asset pricing model?
> I've heard that our stock market is semi-strong. Is that why our share price is low? If our stock market were strong, would our share price be higher? Can we do anything about our share price if we think it is undervalued?

Requirements

You are a member of the management team. To assist the Chief Executive, set out answers to the following:

(a) Calculate the required return on equity for both LS and competitor A based on CAPM and comment on the results. Compare the actual return with the required return in each case and advise whether LS or competitor A is providing the best performance.

(8 marks)

(b) Assuming the estimated return of 11% accurately reflects the level of systematic risk of competitor B, calculate its beta factor. Discuss the potential risks for a shareholder of investing in competitor B.

(7 marks)

(c) Discuss each of the Chief Executive's three comments.

(10 marks)
(Total = 25 marks)

Question 2 – CAP

CAP plc is a listed company that owns and operates a large number of farms throughout the world. A variety of crops are grown.

Financing structure
The following is an extract from the balance sheet of CAP plc at 30 September 2002.

	£m
Ordinary shares of £1 each	200
Reserves	100
9% irredeemable £1 preference shares	50
8% loan stock 2003	250
	600

The ordinary shares were quoted at £3 per share ex div on 30 September 2002. The beta of CAP plc's equity shares is 0.8, the annual yield on treasury bills is 5%, and financial markets expect an average annual return of 15% on the market index.

The market price per preference share was £0.90 ex div on 30 September 2002.

Loan stock interest is paid annually in arrears and is allowable for tax at a corporation tax rate of 30%. The loan stock was priced at £100.57 ex interest per £100 nominal on 30 September 2002. Loan stock is redeemable on 30 September 2003.

Assume that taxation is payable at the end of the year in which taxable profits arise.

A new project
Difficult trading conditions in European farming have caused CAP plc to decide to convert a number of its farms in Southern Europe into camping sites with effect from the 2003 holiday season. Providing the necessary facilities for campers will require major investment, and this will be financed by a new issue of loan stock. The returns on the new campsite business are likely to have a very low correlation with those of the existing farming business.

Requirements

(a) Using the capital asset pricing model, calculate the required rate of return on equity of CAP plc at 30 September 2002. Ignore any impact from the new campsite project.

Briefly explain the implications of a beta of less than 1, such as that for CAP plc.

(6 marks)

(b) Calculate the weighted average cost of capital of CAP plc at 30 September 2002 (use your calculation in answer to requirement (a) above for the cost of equity). Ignore any impact from the new campsite project.

(12 marks)

(c) Without further calculations, identify and explain the factors that may change CAP plc's equity beta during the year ending 30 September 2003.

(7 marks)
(Total = 25 marks)

Question 3 – WEB

WEB plc operates a low-cost airline and is a listed company. By comparison to its major competitors it is relatively small, but it has expanded significantly in recent years. The shares are held mainly by large financial institutions.

The following are extracts from WEB plc's budgeted balance sheet at 31 May 2002:

	$m
Ordinary shares of $1	100
Reserves	50
9% debentures 2005 (at nominal value)	200
	350

Dividends have grown in the past at 3% a year, resulting in an expected dividend of $1 per share to be declared on 31 May 2002 (Assume for simplicity that the dividend will also be paid on this date.) Due to expansion, dividends are expected to grow at 4% a year from 1 June 2002 for the foreseeable future. The price per share is currently $10.40 ex div and this is not expected to change before 31 May 2002.

The existing debentures are due to be redeemed at par on 31 May 2005. The market value of these debentures at 1 June 2002 is expected to be $100.84 (ex interest) per $100 nominal. Interest is payable annually in arrears on 31 May and is allowable for tax purposes. The corporation tax rate for the foreseeable future is 30%. Assume taxation is payable at the end of the year in which the taxable profits arise.

New finance

The company has now decided to purchase three additional aircraft at a cost of $10 m each. The Board has decided that the new aircraft will be financed in full by an 8% bank loan on 1 June 2002.

Requirements

(a) Calculate the expected weighted average cost of capital of WEB plc at 31 May 2002.

(10 marks)

(b) Without further calculations, explain the impact of the new bank loan on WEB plc's
  (i) cost of equity
  (ii) cost of debt
  (iii) weighted average cost of capital (using the traditional model).

(10 marks)

(c) Explain and distinguish
   (i) debentures
   (ii) a bank loan.

   In so doing, explain why, in the circumstances of WEB plc, the cost of debt may be different for the two types of security.

(5 marks)
(Total = 25 marks)

Question 4 – REM

REM is a family-owned business. The family owns 80% of the shares. The remaining 20% is owned by four non-family shareholders. The Board of Directors is considering the purchase of two second-hand (i.e. previously used) freight planes to deliver its goods within its key markets in the USA. The Managing Director, an ex-pilot and one of the non-family shareholders, commissioned an evaluation from the company's accountants and was advised that the company would save money and be more efficient if it performed these delivery operations itself instead of 'outsourcing' them to established courier and postal services. The accountants built into their evaluation an assumption that the company would be able to sell spare capacity on the planes to other companies in the locality.

The Managing Director has decided that the accountants' recommendation will be conducted as a 'trial' for 5 years when its success or otherwise will be evaluated. The net, post-tax operating cash flows of this investment are estimated as:

Year(s)	$m
0	−12.50 (the initial capital investment)
1–4	3.15 each year
5	5.85

Year 5 includes an estimate of the residual value of the planes.

The company normally uses an estimated post-tax weighted average cost of capital of 12% to evaluate investments. However, this investment is different from its usual business operations and the Finance Director suggests using the capital asset pricing model (CAPM) to determine a discount rate. REM, being unlisted, does not have a published beta so the Finance Director has obtained a beta of 1.3 for a courier company that is listed. This company has a debt ratio (debt to equity) of 1:2, compared with REM whose debt ratio is 1:5.

Other information:

- The expected annual post-tax return on the market is 9% and the risk-free rate is 5%.
- Assume both companies' debt is virtually risk-free.
- Both companies pay tax at 30%.

Requirements

(a) Using the CAPM, calculate:

   (i) an asset beta for REM
   (ii) an equity beta for REM

(iii) an appropriate discount rate to be used in the evaluation of this project
(iv) the NPV of the project using the discount rate calculated in (iii); and comment briefly on your choice of discount rate in part (iii).

(11 marks)

(b) Evaluate the benefits and limitations of using a proxy company's beta to determine the rate to be used by REM in the circumstances here, and recommend alternative methods of adjusting for risk in the evaluation that could be considered by the company.

(9 marks)

(c) Advise the Managing Director on the benefits of a post-completion audit. A report format is not required in answering this question.

(5 marks)
(Total = 25 marks)

Question 5 – DEB

DEB plc is a listed company that sells fashion clothes over the Internet. Financial markets have criticised the company recently because of the high levels of debt that it has maintained in its balance sheet.

The company's debt consists of $150m of 8% debentures that are due for repayment by 31 March 2005. Financial markets indicate it would not be possible to issue a new loan under the same conditions. The market value of the debentures is $90 per $100 nominal.

DEB plc's draft balance sheet at 31 March 2002 was as follows:

	$m
Ordinary shares of $1	100
Reserves	20
	120
8% debentures (at nominal value)	150
	270
Fixed assets	200
Net current assets	70
	270

Fixed assets consist of $150m of capitalised development costs and $50m of land and buildings. The company's share price has fallen consistently over the past two years as follows:

Price per share

31 March 2000	$20
31 March 2001	$8
31 March 2002	$4

The company intends to make a 1-for-2 rights issue at an issue price of $2.50 on 30 June 2002. It is assuming that the cum rights price at the issue date will be $4. Immediately thereafter, all the proceeds will be used to redeem debt at its nominal value and thereby reduce its gearing.

Requirements

(a) Calculate the gearing (i.e. debt/equity) of DEB plc at 31 March 2002 using both
  (i) book values
  (ii) market values.

(3 marks)

(b) Evaluate the weaknesses and benefits of the two methods used to calculate gearing in requirement (a) above.

(6 marks)

(c) Calculate the gearing of DEB plc in market value terms, immediately after the rights issue and redemption of debt.

(8 marks)

(d) Briefly explain the advantages and disadvantages for DEB plc of redeeming part of its debt using an issue of equity shares.

(8 marks)
(Total = 25 marks)

Question 6 – Imlico

Imlico plc is an all-equity financed listed company. It develops customised software for clients which are mainly large civil engineering companies. Nearly all its shares are held by financial institutions.

Imlico plc's chairman has been dissatisfied with the company's performance for some time. Some directors were also concerned about the way in which the company is perceived by financial markets. In response, the company recently appointed a new Finance Director who advocated using the capital asset pricing model as a means of evaluating risk and interpreting the stock market's reaction to the company.

The following initial information was put forward by the Finance Director for two rival companies operating in the same industry:

Company	*Beta*
Aztaz plc	0.7
Borran plc	1.4

The Finance Director suggests that the betas of the two companies are used by the stock market to calculate their required rates of return. He also notes, however, that the risk-free rate is 5% each year and the expected return on the market portfolio is 15% each year.

The chairman set out his concerns at a meeting of the Board of Directors: 'I fail to understand these calculations. Aztaz plc operates largely in overseas markets with all the risk which that involves, yet you seem to be arguing that it is a lower risk company than Borran plc, whose income is mainly derived from long-term contracts in our domestic UK building industry. I am very concerned that we can take too much notice of the stock market. Take last year for instance, we had to announce a loss and the share price went up.'

Requirements

(a) Calculate, using the capital asset pricing model, the required rate of return on equity of:

(i) Aztaz plc
(ii) Borran plc.

(6 marks)

(b) Calculate the beta of Imlico plc assuming its required annual rate of return on equity is 17% and the stock market uses the capital asset pricing model to calculate this return.

(3 marks)

(c) As the new Finance Director, write a memorandum to the chairman which explains, in language understandable to a non-financial manager, the following:

(i) the assumptions and limitations of the capital asset pricing model; and (ii) an explanation of why Imlico plc's share price could rise following the announcement of a loss.

In so doing, comment upon the observations and concerns expressed by the chairman. You may refer, where appropriate, to your calculations in (a) and (b) above.

(16 marks)
(Total = 25 marks)

Question 7

WEB plc operates a low-cost airline and is a listed entity. By comparison to its major competitors it is relatively small, but it has expanded significantly in recent years. The shares are held mainly by large fi nancial institutions.

The following are extracts from WEB plc's budgeted balance sheet at 31 May 2002:

	$ million
Ordinary shares of $1	100
Reserves	50
9% debentures 2005 (at nominal value)	200
	350

Dividends have grown in the past at 3% a year, resulting in an expected dividend of $1 per share to be declared on 31 May 2002. (Assume for simplicity that the dividend will also be paid on this date.) Due to expansion, dividends are expected to grow at 4% a year from 1 June 2002 for the foreseeable future. The price per share is currently $10.40 ex div. and this is not expected to change before 31 May 2002.

The existing debentures are due to be redeemed at par on 31 May 2005. The market value of these debentures at 1 June 2002 is expected to be $100.84 (ex interest) per $100 nominal. Interest is payable annually in arrears on 31 May and is allowable for tax purposes. The corporate tax rate for the foreseeable future is 30%. Assume taxation is payable at the end of the year in which the taxable profi ts arise.

New finance

The entity has now decided to purchase three additional aircraft at a cost of $10 m each. The board has decided that the new aircraft will be financed in full by an 8% bank loan on 1 June 2002.

Requirements

(a) Calculate the expected WACC of WEB plc at 31 May 2002.

(8 marks)

(b) *Without further calculations*, explain the impact of the new bank loan on WEB plc's

(i) cost of equity;
(ii) cost of debt;
(iii) WACC (using the traditional model).

(8 marks)

(c) Explain and distinguish

(i) debentures; and
(ii) a bank loan.

In so doing, explain why, in the circumstances of WEB plc, the cost of debt may be different for the two types of security.

(4 marks)
(Total marks 20)

Question 8

DDD plc runs a chain of twenty-six garden centres which sell plants, gardening implements and a range of other gardening products. It is listed on an international stock exchange and it has an accounting year end of 30 June.

The entity plans to open three new garden SuperCentres in 2004. Unlike existing stores, they will also sell garden furniture.

Answers

Question 1 – LS

(a) **Required return on equity**

LS $5 + (10 - 5)\,0.5 = 7.5\%$
A $5 + (10 - 5)\,0.9 = 9.5\%$

Beta measures the responsiveness of the returns to changes in the market, so A, having a higher beta, is more risky to shareholders and will require a greater return to compensate.

Shareholders require a return of 7.5% from LS, but it is managing to exceed this by giving 8%. On the other hand, they require 9.5% from A but it is only giving 9%. Even though it gives a higher return than LS, it is not high enough for the risk perceived by shareholders. A is therefore an 'inefficient' investment and LS, which is exceeding the return required in compensation for its risk, is providing the better performance.

(b) **Competitor B**

$11 = 5 + (10 - 5)\beta$
So $\beta = 1.2$

As B has not yet started trading and has no track record, investors are bound to view it as a more risky investment. In addition, the company intends to raise high levels of debt which will increase the risk to shareholders; this is because interest will be paid before any returns to shareholders and if interest rates rise, could force the company into liquidation. Finally, shareholders will probably only be able to realise their holding in five years' time when the company is floated. All this means that B is a much riskier investment than A (or LS), as reflected in the beta, and hence the return required is higher.

(c) **Chief executive's comments**

(i) *Market risk*

The Capital Asset Pricing Model (CAPM) has a number of assumptions and limitations. Investors are assumed to be fully diversified within the stock market, so that their portfolio reflects the market index. Total risk can be split into market, or systematic risk and specific or unsystematic risk. The unsystematic risk can be diversified away so if our assumption is correct, investors with diversified portfolios will only be interested in the systematic risk. This is measured by beta, which then, via CAPM, gives the return required.

If investors have not diversified their portfolios, there would be some benefit in the company considering total risk and effectively reducing the unsystematic risk by diversifying for these shareholders.

Conversely, investors can diversify outside the stock market (unquoted companies and property, for example) thus reducing their risk further. In this situation, CAPM will overstate the risk and the return required.

(ii) *Weighted average cost of capital* (WACC)

We always need to compare like with like: CAPM gives the required return for equity and should therefore be compared with the actual returns on equity. The

WACC estimates the average return required for all sources of capital, including long-term debt, and so should be compared to the average return generated for equity and debt holders. However, the gearing structure will affect the WACC calculation and make it more difficult to compare with other companies which have different gearing levels.

(iii) *Efficiency*

If a market is efficient, then the share price reflects all information that would be relevant to buyers and sellers; this means the price changes rapidly as new information arises. There are three forms described:

1 The weak form states that share prices always reflect past share price movements and trends.
2 The semi-strong form states that share prices always reflect all publicly available information (such as annual reports and media).
3 The strong form states that share prices always reflect all public and private information (including inside information).

Therefore, a semi-strong market does not indicate a share price will be low or high, simply that the share price takes into account all information in the public domain. If the share price is undervalued, it must be that the market is not fully aware of some information about the company and its prospects. This information needs to be identified and released to the public so that it is understood and reflected in the share price.

Question 2 – CAP

(a) Required return on equity = 5 + (15 − 5) 0.8
= 13%

Beta measures the extent to which CAP's share price has moved with changes in the average market returns. A beta less than 1 means that the share price does not fluctuate as much as the market average (on average it only moves 80% of the change in the market average).

As the fluctuations are lower, it is less volatile, or risky, than the average and will therefore require a lower return than the market average (25%) in compensation.

(b)

Cost of preference shares	9/90	10%
Cost of debt	(105.6/100.57) − 1	5%
WACC =	[(13% × 600) + (10% × 45) + (5% × 251.43)]/896.43	10.6%

(c) **Equity Beta**

Beta is a measure of the risk to a well-diversified stock market investor; changes to both the business risk and the financial risk of CAP will therefore affect beta in the company year.

The new business venture will diversify the company's operations but this will affect the unsystematic risk, not the systematic risk which is measured by beta. The impact on beta will depend on the new business's correlation with the market, not with the current operations. The new beta will then be (ignoring any change in financing) a weighted average of the two betas for the two different operations.

The new debt finance for the camping sites will increase the risk to shareholders, as the interest paid out will make their returns more volatile. This will therefore increase the equity beta.

It is unclear if the current loan stock is to be re-financed next year, or whether this has been allowed for in the new issue. A reduction in the debt finance will reduce the risk to shareholders and hence the beta.

In addition to the above influences, beta changes over time as investors build in expectations of the farming industry. Beta is calculated by looking at historical returns and therefore it can change gradually as new information about the industry and the company emerges; however, this is unpredictable by its very nature.

Question 3 – WEB

(a) **Weighted average cost of capital**

$$K_e = \frac{1 \times 1.04}{10.40} + 0.04 = 14\%$$

K_d given by:

t_0		(100.84)
$t_1 - t_3$	9×0.70	6.30
t_3		100

At 6%, NPV $= (6.30 \times 2.673) + (100 \times 0.840) - 100.84 = 0$
So, K_d $= 6\%$
WACC $= (14\% \times 1{,}040/1{,}241.68) + (6\% \times 201.68/1{,}241.68)$
$= 12.7\%$

(b) **Impact of new bank loan**

(i) *Cost of equity*

The new bank loan will increase the gearing of the company and therefore make the returns to equity more volatile as interest has to be paid before any payment is made to shareholders. In addition, on liquidation the bank loan will be paid in full before any distribution to shareholders. This means that the risk to shareholders increases and therefore the cost of equity will increase to compensate shareholders for this risk.

(ii) *Cost of debt*

Gearing is currently fairly low (measured by market values) but the bank loan will increase this. However, the bank value of assets less current liabilities would appear to be roughly \$350m. This easily covers the \$232m of debt, even with the new \$30m loan and as long as the book values of the fixed assets do not massively exceed their market values, the increase in debt should not affect the risk perceived by the debt-holders. Therefore, we would not expect the cost of debt to change.

(iii) *Weighted average cost of capital* (WACC)

As more debt is introduced, it will tend to reduce the WACC as it is a cheaper form of finance than equity. However, the cost of equity is likely to rise, as noted above.

As debt is introduced initially, the overall effect, according to the traditional theory, is to decrease until shareholders perceive the risk to be much greater, at which point the cost of equity rises dramatically and pulls the WACC up again. Whether the increase in WEB's debt causes the WACC to increase or decrease depends on whether its current gearing structure is below or above this optional point.

(c) **Debenture or bank loan**

A debenture is a written acknowledgement of a company debt, stating the interest coupon and repayment provisions as well as other conditions. These can be offered to the public if a prospectus is prepared and can be held in trust on behalf of many different investors and traded on a secondary market.

A bank loan is not normally trded and is arranged with a single bank or a syndicate of banks.

The cost of debt may be different between the two for WEB as:

- The current interest rates will affect the terms when issued, so the 9% coupon rate on the debentures will have been influenced by the interest rates ruling at the time.
- The covenants to protect the investor may be different; the one with more protection will be less risky and hence carry a lower cost.
- The debentures are marketable, thus reducing the risk to holders and leading to a lower cost.
- The debentures may have been issued at a premium or a discount and the future cash flows increased or decreased to compensate.
- The cost of debt is not very different between the two. The bank loan is 8% pre tax, whereas the debenture is 6% post tax. Pre tax, the cost of the debenture (or yield) is 8.7%.

Question 4 – REM

(a) (i) *Asset Beta*

given by: $\dfrac{1.3 \times 2}{(2 + 0.7)} = 0.96$

(ii) *Equity Beta*

$$0.96 = \frac{\text{Beta} \times 5}{(5 + 0.7)}$$

Equity Beta = 1.09

(iii) *Discount rate*

$$\begin{aligned} K_e &= \text{rf} + (\text{r}_\text{m} - \text{rf})\ \text{Beta} \\ &= 5 + (9 - 5)\ 0.96 \\ &= 8.84\% \end{aligned}$$

This is the discount rate appropriate to the risk of the business of the delivery proposal. It does not take into account the method in which the investment will be financed.

(iv) *Net present value*

Time	t_0	t_1	t_2	h	h	t_5
Cash flow ($m)	(12.50)	3.15	3.15	3.15	3.15	5.85
Discount factor	1	0.919	0.844	0.776	0.713	0.655
Present value	(12.50)	2.89	2.66	2.44	2.25	3.83

Net present value = $1.57 m

(b) **Using a proxy Beta**

Benefits include:

- It gives an idea of the risk of the project as perceived by stock market investors.
- It looks specifically at the risk of the new project.

Limitations include:

- No two companies are identical in their operations, so it will only be an approximation.
- Beta can vary over time, and the estimate only gives a long run average.
- CAPM is a single period model, deals only with systematic risk and is based on historical data.
- CAPM assumes fully diversified investors who are only concerned about systematic risk, while REM being 80% family owned is unlikely to be in that position.

Financial Strategy Alternative methods might be:

- Using the company's cost of equity. While this assumes the project is a similar risk to the existing business, shareholders may feel that it is simply an extension of the existing operations.
- Using the company's weighted average cost of capital. However, it is not theoretically correct, as there will be a change in the business risk and probably financial risk. It is also unclear how the WACC has been estimated.
- Using certainty equivalents to reduce the cash flows and then using the risk-free rate to discount them. It is, however, difficult to determine appropriate probabilities.

(c) **Post-completion audits**

A post-completion audit (PCA) allows the company to both monitor and control the progress of the investment, and to improve investment appraisal in the future.

The company needs to set out clearly the objectives of the investment and, where possible, state them in measurable terms. It then allows the company to:

- Assess the extent to which objectives are achieved.
- Allow for reconsideration or abandonment where objectives are not forecast to be met.
- Assess the performance of managers in charge of the implementation.
- Improve estimates in future investment appraisals.

Question 5 – DEB

(a) (i) *Book values*

$$\text{Gearing} = \frac{150}{120} = 125\%$$

(ii) *Market values*

$$\text{Gearing} = \frac{135}{400} = 33.75\%$$

(b) **Weaknesses and benefits**

- Measuring gearing using book values has the advantage that it will not fluctuate wildly as the stock market rises and falls, but will be much more closely aligned with the company's historical performance. For this reason, banks and other lenders who have gearing covenants usually base the ratio on book values.
- However, measuring gearing using market values allows the equity to reflect the market expectations of future performance through the share price. This is particularly beneficial when much of the equity value is tied up in intangible assets such as staff and reputation in a service company, which are not reflected in the balance sheet.

(c) $$\text{Ex-rights price} = \frac{[(2 \times 4) + 2.50]}{3} = \$3.50$$

Remaining debt = 150 m − (2.50 × 50 m) = \$25 m nominal value

$$\text{New gearing level} = \frac{(25 \times 0.90)}{(150 \times 3.50)} = 4.29\%$$

This does not take into account the tax relief on the debt interest that the company, and hence the shareholders, would lose. This is interest of \$10 m per annum, so roughly \$3 m tax relief per annum for 3 years. This is worth about \$7 m in present value terms so has little impact on the total market value or the gearing calculation.

(d) **Advantages and disadvantages**

Advantages

- The new equity will reduce the debt levels and so help to address the concerns expressed. This may be important if the company wants to raise more finance, or to refinance the remaining debt, in the future.
- Debt covenants may be based on book values for gearing calculations and repayment of much of the debt will prevent any breach of these.
- The cost of debt may decrease as the \$50 m of land and buildings now covers the remaining debt comfortably and gives the debt-holders some security.

Disadvantages

- In market value terms, the gearing was not particularly high and the new equity will have a higher cost than the debt repaid, despite it being lower than the current cost of equity because of the reduced gearing risk. Under the traditional model, it is difficult to predict if the WACC would increase or decrease. Under the theoretical model, the WACC would increase as the gearing reduced.
- As the market price is below par, this is currently a cheap source of finance, and paying off over 80% appears excessive.

Question 6 – Imlico

(a) **Return on equity**

(i) Aztac $5 + (15 - 5)\,0.7 = 12\%$
(ii) Borran $5 + (15 - 5)\,1.4 = 19\%$

(b) **Beta of Imlico**

$17 = 5 + (15 - 5)\beta$
So $\beta = 1.2$

(c) MEMORANDUM

To: Chairman, Imlico plc
From: Finance Director
Date: xx x 20xx

Returns required and share price

1 *Capital asset pricing model (CAPM)*

CAPM has the following assumptions and limitation:

It assumes that shareholders are diversified and hold a portfolio which mirrors the stock market index. This may be true for the institutional shareholders but is not likely to be so for the directors or employees. It may understate the risk involved for these groups.

Shareholders may be able to diversify more widely than just the market index into such areas as property. It may therefore overstate the risk, and hence return required, for them.

The risk-free rate is approximated by an average treasury bill yield.

Beta is calculated from historical data and assumed to be stable over time. However, beta will change gradually over time, which means there is some risk involved in using a cost of equity derived from past information to make a decision regarding the future.

Aztac operates largely in overseas markets and may well have a higher total risk than Borran. However, its operations are likely to have a lower correlation with the UK stock market than Borran's, and hence its systematic risk, as measured by beta, will be lower.

2 *Share price movements*

The semi-strong form of the Efficient Market Hypothesis states that all publicly available information is reflected in the share price. This means that:

The share price responds immediately and fully to new information as it is released. Analysing information which is already public, including past share price trends, will not benefit an investor.

The Stock market tries to predict future events so that it can profit when the information is confirmed publicly.

In Imlico's case, the stock market had probably already built into the share price an expectation of losses. When the information relating to the actual loss was publicly announced, the share price rose which must mean that it was not as bad as the market had already predicted.

Question 7

(a)
Cost of debt

Year	*Cash flow* *$ million*	*DF 6%*	*DCF 6%* *$ million*
2002	201.68	1.000	(201.68)
2003–2005	18(1 – 0.3)	2.673	33.68
2005	200.00	0.840	168.00
			nil

Thus, cost of debt equals approximately 6%.

Cost of equity

$$K_e = \frac{d_1}{P_0} + g$$

$$K_e = \frac{1(1.04)}{0.40} + 0.04$$

$$= 14\%$$

Weighted average cost of capital

$$\text{WACC} = \frac{(6\% \times \$200\text{m} \times 1.0084) + (14\% \times 100\text{m} \times \$10.40)}{(\$200\text{m} \times 1.0084) + (100\text{m} \times \$10.40)}$$

$$= \left[\frac{(12.1008 + 145.6)}{1,241.68}\right]$$

$$\text{WACC} = 12.7\%$$

(b)

(i) *Cost of equity*

The new bank loan will increase the level of gearing of the company; this will, inturn, increase the required return on equity as it becomes more risky. Investors, being risk-averse, thus demand a higher rate of return.

The primary reason for the increased risk on equity is that interest costs must be paid before dividends. As the residual claimants, the returns to equity become more volatile and thus more risky.

Additionally, debt also ranks in front of equity on liquidation. As a result, the possibilityof equity holders gaining a share of the funds from liquidated assets is reduced as debt increases. Also, as interest must be paid, the probability of liquidation (and thus bankruptcy costs) increases as debt increases.

(ii) *Cost of debt*

The level of gearing is initially low in market value terms, but the issue of new debt will increase it. One concern, however, is that if the company is liquidated, then there may be insuffi cient assets to repay the debt. In the draft balance sheet, capital and reserves are \$150 m. As a result, book net assets are also \$150 m. This is lower than the initial nominal value of debt of \$200 m, and signifi cantly below the new nominal value of debt of \$230 m. It may be that the balance sheet reflects the historic cost of assets, and their revalued amount may be greater. This is possible with land and buildings, but unlikely with aircraft. Moreover, the sale of assets under distress conditions of liquidation may yield proceeds below their historic cost. Thus, the new debt is likely to cause the overall cost of debt to rise as:

- he possibility of full payment on liquidation is reduced.
- the probability of liquidation is increased given the greater interest payments.

(iii) *Weighted averaged cost of capital (WACC)*

There are two factors with opposite effects on WACC as the amount of debt increases.

(1) Both the cost of equity and the cost of debt increase because of increased risk for the reasons noted above.
(2) Debt is lower risk and, therefore, cheaper than equity. Increasing debt increases the proportion of this lower cost source of capital in the financing structure.
It is uncertain as to which effect is greater, and thus whether WACC increases or decreases. The traditional theory argues that as debt increases from a zero level of gearing WACC will initially fall, as the perceived risk to equity is small. It continues to fall until it reaches its optimum point, then begins to increase as the perception of risk increases. The impact on WEB plc's WACC will, therefore, depend on whether the existing level of gearing is below or above the optimal point.

(c)

(i) A debenture is a written acknowledgement of a debt by a company, usually given under seal and normally containing provisions as to repayment of interest and principal together with some conditions.

Debentures can be offered to the public only if the offer is accompanied by a prospectus. In these circumstances, it may differ from a bank loan in that:

- the debenture may be held in trust on behalf of many different investors;
- it may be marketable and thus traded in a secondary market.

(ii) In contrast, a bank loan is usually with a single bank and is not normally traded. However, large corporate loans can be made by a syndicate of banks or other institutions.

Cost of debt differences

The cost of debt may differ on the two types of debt as:

- They cover different periods, thus market interest rates may have changed as might the perception of the company's risk. Thus, the 9% nominal rate on the existing debt may have been prevailing rate some time ago.
- The existing debt may also have been issued at a premium or a discount.
- The terms of the debt may differ. Thus, if one security has more covenants to protect the lender and reduce risk, then a lower rate of interest may be acceptable.
- The debentures are marketable, while the bank loan is unlikely to be. A lower rate of interest may, therefore, be available on debentures to compensate for lower liquidity risk.
- The yield, calculated in *requirement (a)*, of 6% is after tax, while the nominal rate on the bank loan of 8% is before tax.

Question 8

(a)

Alternative 1 – Cost of debt

The cost of debt is calculated after tax, which would mean it would be lower than the nominal cost of 7%. The bonds are however issued at a discount, which would mean the cost of debt would be higher than the nominal cost of 7%. As the discount is small, relative to the tax effect, try 6% for the cost of debt.

Examiner's Note

Linear interpolation is an acceptable alternative to trial and error.

Year 30 June	*Cash flow £ million*	*DF6%*	*DCF6% £ million*
2003	(28.5)	1.0	(28.50)
2004–2008	2.1 (1 – 0.3)	4.212	6.19
2008	30	0.747	22.41
			0.10

Thus cost of debt equals approximately 6%.

Alternative 2 – Cost of debt

The average nominal before tax cost of debt is 7.5%, but this is subject to 30% tax relief, so try 5% as the later cash flows are discounted more heavily than the earlier flows.

Examiner's Note

Linear interpolation is an acceptable alternative to trial and error.

Year *30 June*	*Cash flow* *£ million*	*DF5%*	*DCF5%* *£ million*
2003	(28.5)	1.0	(28.5)
2004–2006	1.425 (1 – 0.3)	2.723	2.716
2007–2009	2.85 (1 – 0.3)	2.723 × 0.864	4.694
2009	28.5	0.746	21.261
			0.171

Thus, the cost of debt is approximately 5%.

Other factors

Other factors that may be considered in choosing between the two types of security are:

- *The amount of funds raised:* In this instance, both methods raise the same amount of £28.5 m after the discount on issue of the bonds is considered.
- *Cash flow:* If DDD plc is facing difficulty in raising funds generally (that is it is capital constrained), then cash flow considerations may be important for liquidity. The bank loan has two cash flow advantages: (i) the interest rate is lower in the first 3 years than the bond issue; (ii) the repayment of capital is 1 year later.
- *Issue costs:* The bond issue is likely to have much higher issue costs than the bank loan. This could be built into the cost of debt, but given that these costs are not currently known, it represents an incremental cost on top of the cost of debt calculated above.
- *Covenants:* Typically, a bank loan will have more restrictive covenants than publicly issued debt and this may reduce financial flexibility.

Thus, while the bank loan is a whole percentage point cheaper than the publicly issued debt, a range of other factors will need to be considered before a final choice is made.

(b)

Memorandum

To: The Board of DDD plc
From: Treasury Department Accountant
Date: 20 May 2003
Subject: Financing the expansion programme

Introduction

The expansion programme is of significant size compared to the existing operations of the company. Existing land and buildings and stocks amount to £42 m, whereas the new venture amounts to £28.5 m (i.e. it is 68% of the existing level).

The estimate of new finance includes the funding of land and building and stock amounting to £28.5m, but no estimate is made of other additional financing need, such as other fixed assets. There may thus be further finance needs, although it may be that these could be financed by:

- Creditors exceeding debtors, as is usual in a retail business, where customers pay in cash or by credit card while suppliers tend to extend credit.
- Operating cash flows.
- Existing cash of £1 m.

Given, this problem is common to all the finance methods being suggested, it will thus be assumed that £28.5 m is the total financing need in each case.

Chief executive (new equity)

The chief executive is suggesting that new equity is issued. If new equity is issued then gearing (debt/equity) will fall as follows:

	Book values	*Market values*
Previous**	24/30 = 80%	24/60 = 40%
Revised**	24/58.5 = 41%	24/88.5* = 27%

* Assumes no increase in share price arises from the announcement of the new projects.

** Assumes market value of debt equals its book value.

Thus, there will be lower financial risk arising from the use of new equity to finance the expansion. This may be appropriate as there is likely to be increased business risk in the new venture, which involves both a different retailing format in SuperCentres but also a new product market in garden furniture.

Also, at 40%, market value gearing (80% in book terms, although this is less valid) may be regarded as relatively high. This is particularly the case as the value of existing land and buildings (£26m) is only just sufficient to provide security for loans (£24). The increase in assets financed by equity will thus give greater assurance to existing debt holders and added debt capacity for further expansion in future. While the suggestion of the chief executive to issue equity is credible, the reasoning for the decision is more questionable.

I believe that we should take advantage of this high share price and issue shares now in case the share price falls again.

If share prices have risen, the semi-strong efficient markets hypothesis (EMH) would suggest that this is because the market is acting rationally and is valuing the company on the basis of publicly available information, including historic share price movement. As a result, even though the share price has risen substantially over the past year, it is no more likely to fall than it would be if the share price had been constant, or had fallen, over the past year.

As such, there is no reason to 'take advantage' of of the previous share price rise unless, on the basis of inside information, the chief executive believes that share prices will fall in future. This view is consistent with the strong form of the efficient markets hypothesis.

Our dividend yield is only 3% – this is cheap finance at low risk.

The dividend yield of 3% does not represent the required return on equity and may not be regarded as low risk. This is the case for a number of reasons:

- The dividend yield is only the current dividend, divided by the share price. If the dividend valuation model is used, it would also reflect anticipated future growth in dividends, which would not be included in the current dividend yield.
- An alternative approach is that the shareholder will require a capital gain and a dividend. The total required return on equity will reflect both of these elements, rather than just the dividend yield which thus understates the required return on equity.
- Market based models such as CAPM may best be used to determine the level of market risk associated with this security but, typically, equity shares will have more significant risk than debt finance. Any new equity finance will however reflect not just the risk of the new project, but also the collective risk of all projects in the company.

Non-executive director (retained profit and divestment)

We should use our retained profits of £20m to finance most of the new land, buildings and stocks.

Unfortunately, the use of retained profits to finance new ventures represents a fundamental misunderstanding of accounting. The retained profits of £20 m in the balance sheet are not represented by cash assets, but by a variety of different assets. Indeed, it can be seen that the company only has cash of £1 m. This is not, therefore, a feasible proposition.

To finance the remaining amount we should sell the least profitable of our existing garden centres. This approach will save all the issue costs and all the uncertainty involved in raising external new finance.

It might be possible to combine a divestment policy with some other form of financing (for example raising only £20 m in debt or equity rather than the full £28.5 m). A number of factors need to be considered:

- Issue costs and uncertainty in raising new finance will be replaced by transaction costs involved in selling existing sites, with the associated uncertainty in these transactions.
- The 'least profitable' of of the existing centres may still be making reasonable profits, thus the opportunity cost of raising funds by closures may represent an additional cost in financing the new venture.
- To the extent of divestment, the existing sites will be replaced by new sites, and thus there is no expansion in the overall asset base. Fewer assets thus exist, for example to secure debt – although less debt would need to be raised.
- Where new sites are in a similar location to old sites, it may be appropriate to divest to avoid duplication.

Finance director (new debt)

The finance director is in favour of issuing new debt to finance the expansion in the form of abond issue or a bank loan. The choice between these two types of debt has already been considered (see (a)). This section thus considers debt as opposed to other types of finance to fund the new expansion. If new debt is raised then gearing (debt/equity) will increase as follows:

	Book values	*Market values*
Previous	24/30 = 80%	24/60 = 40%
Revised**	52.5/30 = 175%	52.5/60* = 88%

*Assumes no change in the share price arises from the announcement of the new projects or their financing.

**Assumes market value of debt equals its book value.

Thus, there will be significantly increased financial risk arising from the use of new debt to finance the expansion. This may be inappropriate, as there is also likely to be increased business risk in the new venture. While there will be additional assets to secure the additional debt, the company remains near its debt capacity for using land and building to secure loans. Thus, the decision to use debt to finance expansion is questionable. Also, however, the reasoning of the finance director is questionable.

The return on these new SuperCentres is bound to be greater than the cost of debt, so a profit is assured and thus the risk is minimal.

Even if the expected return on the new venture, is greater than the cost of debt, this does not make the venture viable. Consider also:

- The operating risk of the new venture which may be significant and thus requires a risk premium.
- The increase in debt that adds financial risk and raises the cost of equity.
- Existing debt holders who may be exposed to greater risk, and thus their required rate of return may increase.
- Overall, the WACC, which may either increase or decrease depending (according to the traditional model) on whether the company is currently below or above the optimal level.

The overall change in the opportunity cost of capital is thus a more appropriate benchmark to judge the returns on the new project than the cost of debt.

Part 3

Investment Decisions and Project Control

5

Valuations

Valuations 5

Asset valuations

The asset values in the balance sheet are historical and are not usually reliable estimates of the current market values. In addition, intangible assets such as inherent goodwill are not recorded.

Where realisable values can be found, it will give the lowest price a vendor will accept, even if he is desperate to sell, as he could break the entity up himself and sell off the assets.

Intellectual capital

Intellectual capital forms a major part of the value of many entities. However, it is difficult to measure separately, and is often viewed as the difference between an income based valuation (or current market value) and the book value of the assets. Alternatively, calculate the present value of the excess returns over the industry average.

Present value of future cash flows

In an ideal world the value of a business should be the present value of the cash flows it generates. However, predicting all of the future cash flows and finding a suitable discount rate is fraught with difficulties and potential buyers will have different estimates both from each other and from the vendor.

The cash flows will also vary with the different plans each has for the business.

The valuation techniques used are all approximations to this, but will often lead to very different results, allowing for a negotiated price.

Price/earnings ratio

Value per share = EPS X P/E ratio.

For a private company this can be a useful technique as the P/E ratio of similar listed entities can be applied to its EPS to arrive at the approximate value it would have if it was quoted. This is often discounted substantially for the lack of liquidity, and hence additional risk, in its shares.

Dividend valuation model

$$P_0 = \frac{d_1}{k_e - g}$$ if we assume constant growth in dividen(

In a private entity, dividends can be more haphazard as owners are also rewarded through salaries. Adjustments may be needed to alter salaries to market rates before using 'potential' dividends. The cost of equity can be estimated from CAPM using the beta of similar listed entities.

Dividend yield

$$\text{Value} = \frac{\text{Dividend}}{\text{Dividend yield}}$$

An average dividend yield for a similar listed sector can be applied to the target entity's dividend.

General comments

(a) The number of potential buyers and the number of potential targets will affect the price.
(b) The asset valuations are likely to be lower than the income-based valuations. For a service business, with few assets, the difference could be very great. In this situation, an asset valuation would be misleading.
(c) Up to 20% premium may be added to a publicly listed share price to gain a controlling interest.
(d) Up to 30% discount may be applied to a private entity compared with an equivalent quoted entity.

Questions

Question 1 – Target (Practice Question)

Target company recently made a profit of £500,000 and had a pay out ratio of 80% (which is higher than the average for this sector). The average P/E ratio for this sector is 9.

The company's balance sheet shows Shareholder's Funds of £2.25 m for 1 m shares, but the buildings are worth £1 m more than their balance sheet value and stocks would be worth £250,000 less in a break-up of the company.

Dividend growth in the sector is expected to be 4% per annum, the risk-free rate is 6%, the market return 11% and the company's beta estimated as 1.2. The average dividend yield for the sector is 6%.

Find valuations of Target using

(a) P/E ratio
(b) Dividend yield
(c) Dividend valuation model
(d) Balance sheet book values
(e) Net realisable value.

Question 2 – CD

CD Limited is a private company in a computer-related industry. It is based in India and has been trading for 6 years. It is managed by its main shareholders, who are the original founders of the company. Most of the employees are also shareholders, having been given shares as bonuses in 1999. None of the shareholders has attempted to sell shares in the company so the problem of placing a value on them has not arisen.

Turnover last year, the 12 months to 31 December 2002, was 356 m Rupees.

The table below shows earnings and dividends for CD Limited since its creation:

	Earnings after tax		*Dividend declared*
Year	*Million Rupees*	*Rupees per share*	*Rupees per share*
1997	25	8.33	0.00
1998	120	40.00	20.00
1999	145	48.33	24.20
2000	185	52.86	26.40
2001	195	55.71	27.80
2002	203	58.00	26.30

Between 1997 and 1999 there were 3 m shares in issue. This was increased to 3.5 m by the issue of bonus shares at the end of 1999. The par value of the shares is 1 Rupee. The company is all-equity financed. The company pays tax at 30%. Dividends declared in one year are paid the following year.

In the current year (2003), earnings are likely to be slightly below 2002 at around 200 m Rupees. The company's directors have decided to pay a maintained dividend for 2003.

They are now evaluating investment opportunities that would require all the company's free cash flow for 2003 plus borrowings of 150 m Rupees of undated debt. If the company does not borrow to invest, growth in earnings and dividends will be zero for the foreseeable future. If the company does borrow and invest, then it expects growth in earnings and dividends of 5% in 2004 (from the 2003 base). The company's expected post-tax cost of equity capital is estimated at 14% per annum, assuming the borrowing takes place. Ignore the effects of inflation.

Requirements

(a) Discuss the relationship between dividend policy, investment policy and financing policy in the context of the scenario and recommend a course of action for the directors of CD Limited.

(10 marks)

(b) Calculate an estimated company value, share price and P/E ratio for CD Limited using Modigliani and Miller's theory of capital structure, assuming the company does borrow and invest.

(6 marks)

(c) Discuss the relevance of the figures you have just calculated in answer to requirement (b) above in placing a value on (i) a small parcel of shares, for example the shareholding of one employee, and (ii) the entire company.

(9 marks)

Note: A report format is NOT required in answering this question.

(Total = 25 marks)

Question 3 – EQU

EQU plc is a listed company whose shares are mainly owned by large financial institutions. It currently owns and operates a theme park, called 'Dragonland', in the south west of England. It covers five square kilometres and contains various rides, gardens and attractions. Customers pay a single entrance fee. The company's accounting year end is 31 July.

The land is leased and the other fixed assets give poor security, so the company is all-equity financed. The venture has been successful and although it was considered risky initially, it has now stabilised, with a constant stream of customers and steady turnover, profitability and cash flows.

The Directors are now considering raising £8 m new finance to be used in full to open a second theme park in Scotland, called 'Phoenixworld'.

The total dividend to be paid by the company on 31 July 2003 will be £1.2 m. The company's shares are already quoted ex div.

The Board meeting

At a Board meeting some concerns were expressed:

The Chairman argued:

> If we want to carry on growing, we need to expand to other sites. I admit that there may be some difficulties in the early years but, basically, Phoenixworld is the same type of business as we have now so the risk should be no different. Therefore the company's cost of equity should not change from its current level, which I think should be about 12% per annum. This seems appropriate for stable earnings such as ours.

> If we go ahead with Phoenixworld, I would expect us not to pay any more dividends after 31 July 2003 until 31 July 2006, at which time a total dividend of £2 m would be declared and this should then grow at 4% per annum indefinitely.

The Chief Executive disagreed:

> Of course Phoenixworld would be more risky. This is a new venture with new capital investment and a different customer base. Earnings are therefore bound to be more volatile. This means that the cost of equity will be higher. I think the cost of equity for the company would rise to 15% per annum if Phoenixworld goes ahead. Instead, we should stay at one site and invest £3 m in new rides and facilities to expand and increase profitability and dividends. This will be a lower risk option and will therefore generate a more certain dividend stream. The company's cost of equity should then stay at the current level of 12%. If this option is taken, I would expect dividends to increase at 12% per annum from the current level (at 31 July 2003) up to, and including, the dividend on 31 July 2007. I would expect dividends in all future years thereafter to be constant at this level as we will reach the capacity of our site by that time.

Requirements

(a) Using the dividend valuation model, calculate the total value of the share capital of EQU plc at 1 August 2003 if the Chairman's proposal to open Phoenixworld is accepted. This calculation should be carried out for each of the following assumptions:

(i) the Chairman's assumption that the company's annual cost of equity stays at 12%;
(ii) the Chief Executive's assumption that the company's annual cost of equity increases to 15%.

Comment on the differences in the two calculations.

(10 marks)

(b) Using the dividend valuation model, calculate the total value of the share capital of EQU plc at 1 August 2003 if the Chief Executive's proposal to expand Dragonland is accepted.

(4 marks)

(c) Discuss the possible forms of financing the proposed new projects and assess which form of finance is likely to be most appropriate for EQU plc. Describe how each financing method, and each of the projects may affect the company's cost of equity.

(11 marks)

Ignore taxation.

For simplicity, assume that dividends are declared and paid at each accounting year-end.

(Total = 25 marks)

Question 4 – MediCons plc

MediCons plc provides a range of services to the medical and healthcare industry. These services include providing locum (temporary cover for healthcare professionals (mainly doctors and nurses), emergency call-out and consultancy/advisory services to government-funded health organisations. The company also operates a research division that has been successful in recent years in attracting funding from various sources. Some of the employees in this division are considered to be leading experts in their field and are very highly paid.

A consortium of doctors and redundant health service managers started the company in 1989. It is still owned by the same people, but has since grown into an organisation employing over 100 full-time staff throughout the UK. In addition, the company uses specialist staff employed in state run organisations on a part time contract basis. The owners of the company are now interested in either obtaining a stock market quotation, or selling the company if the price adequately reflects what they believe to be the true worth of the business.

Summary financial statistics for MediCons plc and a competitor company, which is listed on the UK Stock Exchange are shown below. The competitor company is broadly similar to MediCons plc but uses a higher proportion of part time staff and has no research capability.

	MediCons plc last year end	**Competitor last year end**
Date	31.3.2000	31.3.2000
Shares in issue (million)	10	20
Earnings per share (pence)	75	60
Dividend per share (pence)	55	50
Net asset value (£m)	60	75
Debt ratio (outstanding debt as % of total financing)	10	20
Share price (pence)	N/A	980
Beta coefficient	N/A	1.25
Forecasts:		
Growth rate in earnings and dividends (% per annum)	8	7
After-tax cash flow for 2000/2001 (£m)	9.2	N/A

Notes

1 The expected post-tax return on the market for the next 12 months is 12% and the post-tax risk-free rate is 5%. The company pays tax at 30%.
2 The treasurer of the company has provided the forecast growth rate for MediCons plc. The forecast for the competitor is based on published information.
3 The net assets of MediCons plc are the net book values of land, buildings, equipment and vehicles plus net working capital.
4 Sixty per cent of the shares in the competitor company are owned by the directors and their relatives or associates.
5 MediCons uses a 'rule of thumb' discount rate of 15% to evaluate its investments.
6 Assume that growth rates in earnings and dividends are constant per annum.
7 The post-tax cost of debt for MediCons plc and its competitor is 7%.

Requirements

Assume that you are an independent consultant retained by MediCons plc to advise on the valuation of the company and on the relative advantages of a public flotation versus outright sale.

Prepare a report for the directors that provides a range of share prices at which shares in MediCons plc might be issued. Use whatever information is available and relevant and recommend a course of action.

Explain the methods of valuation that you have used and comment on their suitability for providing an appropriate valuation of the company. In the report you should also comment of the difficulties of valuing companies in a service industry and of incorporating a valuation for intellectual capital.

(25 marks)

Note: Approximately one-third of the marks are available for appropriate calculation, and two-thirds for discussion.

Question 5 – BiOs

BiOs Limited (BiOs) is an unquoted company that provides consultancy services to the biotechnology industry. It has been trading for 4 years. It has an excellent reputation for providing innovative and technologically advanced solutions to clients' problems. The company employs 18 consultants plus a number of self employed contract staff and is planning to recruit additional consultants to handle a large new contract. The company 'outsources' most administrative and accounting functions. A problem is recruiting well-qualified experienced consultants and BiOs has had to turn down work in the past because of lack of appropriate staff.

The company's two owners/directors have been approached by the marketing department of an investment bank and asked if they have considered using venture capital financing to expand the business. No detailed proposal has been made but the bank has implied that a venture capital company would require a substantial percentage of the equity in return for a large injection of capital. The venture capitalist would want to exit from the investment in 4–5 years' time.

The company is all-equity financed and neither of the directors is wholly convinced that such a large injection of capital is appropriate for the company at the present time.

Financial information

Revenue in year to 31 December 2003	£3,600,000
Shares in issue (ordinary £1 shares)	100,000
Earnings per share	756 pence
Dividend per share	0
Net asset value	£395,0001

Note:

1 The net assets of BiOs are the net book values of purchased and/or leased buildings, equipment and vehicles plus net working capital. The book valuations are considered to reflect current realisable values.

Forecast

- Sales revenue for the year to 31 December 2004 – £4,250,000. This is heavily dependent on whether or not the company obtains the new contract.

- Operating costs, inclusive of depreciation, are expected to average 50% of revenue in the year to 31 December 2004.
- Tax is expected to be payable at 30%.
- Assume book depreciation equals capital allowances for tax purposes. Also assume, for simplicity, that profit after tax equals cash flow.

Growth in earnings in the years to 31 December 2005 and 2006 is expected to be 30% per annum, falling to 10% per annum after that. This assumes that no new long-term capital is raised. If the firm is to grow at a faster rate then new financing will be needed.

This is a niche market and there are relatively few listed companies doing precisely what BiOs does. However, if the definition of the industry is broadened the following figures are relevant:

P/E ratios	
Industry Average	18
Range (individual companies)	12–90
Cost of equity	
Industry average	12%
Individual companies	Not available

BiOs does not know what its cost of equity is.

Requirements

(a) Calculate a range of values for the company that could be used in negotiation with a venture capitalist, using whatever information is currently available and relevant. Make and state whatever assumptions you think are necessary. Explain, briefly, the relevance of each method to a company such as BiOs.

(15 marks)

(b) Discuss the advantages and disadvantages of using either venture capital financing to assist with expansion or alternatively a flotation on the stock market in 2–3 years' time. Include in your discussion likely exit routes for the venture capital company.

(10 marks)
(Total = 25 marks)

Question 6 – AB Telecoms

AB is a telecommunications consultancy based in Europe that trades globally. It was established 15 years ago. The four founding shareholders own 25% of the issued share capital each and are also executive directors of the entity. The shareholders are considering a flotation of AB on a European stock exchange and have started discussing the process and a value for the entity with financial advisors. The four founding shareholders, and many of the entity's employees, are technical experts in their field, but have little idea how entities such as theirs are valued.

Assume you are one of AB's financial advisors. You have been asked to estimate a value for the entity and explain your calculations and approach to the directors. You have obtained the following information.

Summary financial data for the past three years and forecast revenue and costs for the next two years is as follows:

Income Statement for the years ended 31 March

	Actual			Forecast	
	2004	2005	2006	2007	2008
	€ million	*€ million*	*€ million*	*€ million*	*€ million*
Revenue	125.0	137.5	149.9	172.0	198.0
Less:					
Cash operating costs	37.5	41.3	45.0	52	59
Depreciation	20.0	22.0	48.0	48	48
Pre-tax earnings	67.5	74.2	56.9	72	91
Taxation	20.3	22.3	17.1	22	27

Balance Sheet at 31 March

	2004	2005	2006
	€ million	*€ million*	*€ million*
ASSETS			
Non-current assets			
Property, plant and equipment	150	175	201
Current assets	48	54	62
	198	229	263
EQUITY AND LIABILITIES			
Equity			
Share capital (Shares of €1)	30	30	30
Retained earnings	148	179	203
	178	209	233
Current liabilities	20	20	30
	198	229	263

Note: The book valuations of non-current assets are considered to reflect current realisable values.

Other information/assumptions

- Growth in after tax cash flows for 2009 and beyond (assume indefinitely) is expected to be 3% per annum. Cash operating costs can be assumed to remain at the same percent age of revenue as in previous years. Depreciation will fluctuate but, for purposes of evaluation, assume the 2008 charge will continue indefinitely. Tax has been payable at 30% per annum for the last three years. This rate is expected to continue for the foresee able future and tax will be payable in the year in which the liability arises.
- The average P/E ratio for telecommunication entities' shares quoted on European stock exchanges has been 12.5 over the past 12 months. However, there is a wide variation around this average and AB might be able to command a rating up to 30% higher than this;
- An estimated cost of equity capital for the industry is 10% after tax;
- The average pre-tax return on total assets for the industry over the past 3 years has been 15%.

Requirements

(a) Calculate a range of values for AB, in total and per share, using methods of valuation that you consider appropriate. Where relevant, include an estimate of value for intellectual capital.

(12 marks)

(b) Discuss the methods of valuation you have used, explaining the relevance of each method to an entity such as AB. Conclude with a recommendation of an approximate flotation value for AB, in total and per share.

(13 marks)
(Total = 25 marks)

A report format is **not** required for this question.

Answers

Question 1 – Target

(a) $£500{,}000 \times 9 = £4.5\,\text{m}$

(b) $(500{,}000 \times 0.80)/0.06 = £6.667\,\text{m}$

(c) $k_e = 6 + (11 - 6)\,1.2 = 12\%$

$$\frac{400{,}000 \times 1.04}{0.12 - 0.04} = £5.2\,\text{m}$$

(d) $= £2.25\,\text{m}$

(e) $2.25\,\text{m} + 1\,\text{m} - 0.25\,\text{m} = £3\,\text{m}$

Question 2 – CD

(a) **Dividend, investment and financing policies**

These three policies are fundamental to a company's operation. To increase shareholder wealth, the directors must invest in positive net present value projects, so as to safeguard a stream of income in the future. At the same time, they need to finance the investments, either through raising external finance or using internal resources. The second possibility will then impact on the dividend paid, which could disappoint shareholders who were expecting cash in the near future.

In an efficient market, shareholders would understand that dividends might be reduced or cancelled in the short term in order to invest in projects that will boost the present value of the cash that will eventually be paid out. They would therefore be indifferent to the dividend policy in any one particular year. In practice, companies usually feel that the markets do not like a wildly fluctuating dividend and set policies that allow them to retain sufficient cash to undertake small projects that arise without disturbing dividends. Large projects are often funded with additional external finance.

In the current situation, CD is a private company with its main shareholders still being the founders and managers. The dividend payout ratio has been around 50% (reduced slightly last year to 45%) and it therefore seems quite high for a company in the early years of its life. The main shareholders would also be well aware of the investment opportunity being taken if the dividend was reduced this year.

CD is currently all-equity financed and introducing debt finance is likely to lower the overall cost of capital. The gearing level will rise to roughly 21 % (see working below) for Debt: Debt + Equity, which is not excessive and debt is cheaper than equity due to the lower risk to the investor. However, the investment is large and CD may be at risk if the project does not perform according to expectations. It might be sensible to cut the dividend further to reduce the reliance on debt finance.

We would recommend that the directors call a meeting of the shareholders and present the investment details. If the shareholders agree that it is beneficial, it is likely they will agree to a reduced, or cancelled, dividend for 2003 to reduce the external debt finance from its projected R150 m.

Workings

			Rm
Earnings – dividends – bonus shares	(1997–2002)	=	458.2
200 − (3.5 × 26.3)	(2003)	=	108.0
	Retained profits		566.2
	Share capital		3.5
	Shareholders' funds		569.7

Gearing = 150/(150 + 569.7) = 21%

(b) **Valuations**

$$\text{Value if ungeared} = \frac{D_1}{k_e} = \frac{(200 \times 1.05)}{0.14} = \text{R}1,500\,\text{m}$$

$V_g = V_U + D_t$

$= 1{,}500 + (150 \times 0.30)$

$= 1{,}545$

Value of equity = 1,545 − 150 =

$$\text{per share, value} = \frac{1{,}395}{3.5} = \text{R}399$$

$$\text{P/E ratio} = \frac{399}{(200/3.5)} = 7$$

(c) **Relevance for valuations**

Modigliani and Miller's theory has a number of assumptions that do not necessarily hold, in particular:

- full information in the marketplace about the company's operations
- no transaction costs or irrational shareholder behaviour
- all investors have the same view
- no further growth is expected.

We can see the difference the final assumption makes if we assume CD continues to grow its earnings at 5% per annum. This would make V_u = (200 × 1.05)/(0.14 − 0.05) = 2,333. This increases the value of the equity in CD by R833 m to R2,228 m, the share value to R637 and the P/E ratio to 11.1.

However, the model depends on a large number of investors scrutinising the information about the company and being able to buy or sell the shares in a liquid market accordingly. CD, being a private company, is not in this situation so there would have to be a very careful assessment of the investment plans before an accurate valuation could be deduced for the whole company.

A small parcel of shares would not necessarily be worth the same as a large block of shares, as there is significant value attached to control or influence in a company. This can be seen in listed companies when control costs are far more per share than a small parcel, and it is even truer in private companies, in which a small shareholding carries no power at all. The value per share calculated was looking at the entire company and is unlikely to be the value agreed per share for a small parcel.

Question 3 – EQU

(a) Total value if Phoenix World opened

(i) *Constant cost of equity*

$$\text{Value} = \frac{[2/(0.12 - 0.04)]}{1.12^2} = £19.93\,\text{m}$$

(ii) *Increased cost of equity*

$$\text{Value} = \frac{[2/(0.15 - 0.04)]}{1.15^2} = £13.75\,\text{m}$$

The difference in value is entirely due to the change in estimate for the cost of equity. This is because at 15% the shareholders require a greater return for the risk perceived in the company and the cash flows predicted do not exceed this return required by as much.

The new project itself will have a much higher risk profile under the Chief Executive's assumptions as it has raised the average return required across the company's entire operations to 15%.

(b) Dragonland expansion

$$\begin{aligned}
\text{Value} &= \frac{(1.2\,\text{m} \times 1.12)}{1.12} && = 1.2\,\text{m} \\
&+ \frac{(1.2\,\text{m} \times 1.12^2)}{1.12^2} && = 1.2\,\text{m} \\
&+ \frac{(1.2\,\text{m} \times 1.12^3)}{1.12^3} && = 1.2\,\text{m} \\
&+ \frac{[(1.2\,\text{m} \times 1.12^4)/0.12]}{1.12^3} && = 11.2\,\text{m} \\
& && \overline{£14.8\,\text{m}}
\end{aligned}$$

(c) Possible financing and impact on cost of equity

The main forms of finance fall into four categories: issue of shares, bank loans, corporate bond or debenture, or leasing.

1. *Issue of shares*

   Shares can be issued via a rights issue, an offer for sale and or public offer, or a placing. However, the £3m required is too small for an offer for sale or a public offer, which would have higher issue costs than the other two methods anyway. Even a rights issue or a placing is likely to have higher issue costs than debt, and the relative control of shareholders would change unless everyone took up their rights.

   If finance was raised from equity, the company would still be all-equity financed, so there is no change in the financial risk to shareholders. There would be no impact on the cost of equity beyond that identified by the Chief Executive if the company undertook the Dragonland project.

2. *Bank loans*

   A bank loan is with a single bank or a syndicate, and is likely to have much lower set-up costs. The bank will, however, require a charge over the assets for security, which may be a problem given that the assets in the existing site were deemed to be inappropriate, and the company will have to arrange repayment of both capital and interest over an agreed time frame.

   The bank loan would introduce gearing to the company and some financial risk for shareholders. The interest paid will make the earnings and potential dividends more volatile, while the possibility of default leading to liquidation introduces additional risk. The cost of equity will therefore rise above any increase due to the change in business.

3. *Corporate bonds or debenture*

   The issue of corporate bonds to the public, or a debenture with a prospectus, will contain restrictive covenants, which may limit the ability to borrow more. The issue costs are likely to be higher than for a bank loan but less than those for equity, and as with the bank loan the capital and interest will have to be paid over a pre-determined schedule. These will also increase the gearing level of the company and hence the financial risk to shareholders, leading to an increase in the cost of equity over and above any increase due to the nature of the business.

4. *Leasing*

   Leasing allows the company to effectively obtain 100% of the finance for the leased asset and has low initial set-up costs. However, the implicit interest rate charged can be high to compensate for this.

   If the lease is long term it is likely to be regarded as long-term debt which will increase the financial risk perceived by shareholders. As with the other forms of debt, this would therefore increase the cost of equity.

5. *Conclusion*

   Given the high issue costs of new equity, and the absence of any gearing, it would seem appropriate to raise debt-finance, probably in the form of bank loans. Although this will increase the cost of equity, it will be partly offset by the cheaper cost of debt, due to the lower risk to the lender and the tax relief on debt interest.

Question 4 – MediCons

REPORT

To: Directors of MediCons plc
From: Independent Consultant
Date: xx of x 20xx

Valuation of the company

This report looks at possible valuations of the company and discusses their suitability, as well as looking at some of the difficulties in valuing a business accurately.

1. *Valuation*

In the appendix, I have outlined three valuations which give the following results:

	Per share	*Total value*
Net assets	£6.00	£60m
Earnings multiple	£12.75	£127.5m
Dividend stream	£11.88	£118.8m

A company is usually bought as a source of future cash streams, rather than to access and sell the assets, so the asset value, which simply looks at the book value of tangible net assets, is not particularly relevant unless it is the intention to liquidate the company. This is clearly not the case here, and is likely to severely underestimate the value of a service company which might have few tangible assets, but a high-income stream generated by intangible assets. Foremost amongst these are the skills of its staff (or intellectual capital) which generates the company's reputation, but it is very difficult to put any kind of objective value on such an intangible asset (except by comparing the difference between an asset valuation and income-based valuations). In the case of MediCon, the income valuations appear to be about double the net asset valuation.

The earnings multiple approach assumes that last years' earnings were fairly typical and that the market will view MediCon in a similar light to its competitor. Subject to these limitations, it gives a quick and easy approximation for the value of the company if floated on the stock exchange. A single buyer of the company may not be prepared to pay as much due to the lack of a liquid market in the shares; conversely another company may be prepared to pay more if it can see synergistic gains to be made on acquisition.

The dividend valuation model assumes constant growth in dividends (at 8%) forever and it's more appropriate for minority shareholdings who would be unable to alter the dividend policy. However, it is useful to see that it is in a similar range to the earnings multiple approach.

2. *Other methods*

Other methods exist for estimating a value, but they will not give any more accuracy; rather they lend comfort to the current range of values and give assurance that we are in the right area. One such is to try and estimate the cash flow for the period over which it is expected to grow often 5–10 years, and discount to a present value.

3. *Flotation or sale*

To make a sale requires a potential buyer to be identified or to come forward. If none has emerged so far, advisers may be able to make enquiries, but as it is likely that a buyer would be a company in the same or similar industry, most of the possible candidates are probably already well aware of MediCon's plans. Therefore, if no offer has been forthcoming, a flotation seems the more likely option.

A flotation will incur higher costs than an outright sale and the market would be concerned if existing shareholders realised all their investment. It will therefore be necessary to issue new shares for cash, whilst an outright sale would buy all the existing shares, paying cash or new shares in the new parent company.

4. *Conclusion*

A current valuation would appear to be around £120m to £125m or £12 to £12.50 per share. A public flotation would enable you to keep control of the company as you will have to maintain your shareholding, while any declared interested parties in an outright sale may be prepared to buy your shares at a higher price, in cash, for the synergy they anticipate.

Appendix

(i) Net asset value $= \dfrac{£60\,\text{m}}{10\,\text{m}} = £6.00$ per share

(£60 m for the entire company)

(ii) *Earnings multiple*

Competitor's P/E ratio $= \dfrac{980}{60} = 16.3$

As MediCon's forecast growth in earnings and dividends are greater, approximate MediCon's P/E ratio as 17.

Value = £0.75 × 17 = £12.75 per share (£127.5 m for the entire company)

(iii) *Dividend valuation model*

Ungearing competitor's beta:

$$\beta_u = \frac{1.25 \times 80}{[80 + (20 \times 0.7)]} = 1.064$$

Regear at MediCon's Gearing level:

$1.064 = \beta \times 90/[90 + (10 \times 0.7)]$

so $\beta = 1.15$

and $K_e = 5 + (12 - 5)1.15 = 13\%$

$$\text{Value} = \frac{(0.55 \times 1.08)}{(0.13 - 0.08)} = £11.88 \text{ (£118 m for the entire company)}$$

Question 5 – BiOs

(a) **Valuation of company**

The true value of a business will be the cash flows it produces, discounted to their present value. However, identifying the cash flows is difficult and a number of different estimates can be made.

Asset valuation

An asset valuation assumes that the company is broken up and the assets and liabilities realised. We are told that the market values of these are approximately £395,000.

As the owners, or those they are contemplating sharing the company with, have no intention of closing the company down, this valuation is less relevant. It is likely to be substantially less than its value as a going concern as it takes no account of assets not included in the balance sheet, or capable of being sold separately, such as goodwill and reputation. For a professional services company such as BiOs this is likely to form a substantial part of the value of the company.

PE multiple valuation

The PE multiple approach compares the price of similar companies to their earnings and then applies a similar multiple, with suitable adjustments, to BiOs. The main problems come in finding companies that are similar, as no two companies are identical, and in making suitable adjustments to take account, for example, of the fact that BiOs is unlisted.

Using different PE ratios will clearly give different values:

Industry average	$18 \times 7.56 \times 100{,}000 = £13.6m$
Low	$12 \times 7.56 \times 100{,}000 = £9.1m$
High	$20 \times 7.56 \times 100{,}000 = £15.1m$

As these are listed companies, shareholders are likely to value them more highly than BiOs as the liquid market in their shares makes them less risky. This would suggest a value of perhaps £10 m, though the prospect of listing on the stock market in the medium term may reduce the discount applied.

Cash flow valuation

A cash flow valuation attempts to estimate cash flows accurately before discounting them, but clearly has to abandon this at some point and make some assumption about the longer term. This is often to assume a constant perpetuity of cash flows at the same level as the last year of the detailed analysis. Here, we are told that growth will be 30% for the first two years after 2004 and then 10% thereafter.

The cash flows, are, therefore:

2004:	$£4.25m \times 0.50 \times 0.70$	$= £1.488m$
2005:	$£1.488m \times 1.30$	$= £1.934m$
2006:	$£1.934m \times 1.30$	$= £2.514m$ rising at 10% thereafter

As BiOs does not know what its cost of equity is, we will have to use the industry average of 12%, although BiOs' cost is likely to be higher than that of listed companies.

$$PV = 1.488/1.12 + 1.934/1.12^2 + (2.514/(0.12 - 0.10))/1.12^2 = £103.1m$$

This is much higher than the other valuations, but is largely due to the value of the tail. The value of the first three years is £4.7m and assuming a constant level of cash flows after 2006 gives a total value of £19.6m.

It is, therefore, very sensitive to the assumption about the long-term growth rate. Without justification for the 10%, it might be more realistic to assume no long-term growth. If we also increase the cost of equity for the increased risk in a private company shareholding to 15%, this would reduce the value to:

$$1.488/1.15 + 1.934/1.15^2 + (2.514/0.15)/1.15^2 = £15.4m$$

Summary

In summary, a wide range of values can be produced, depending on the assumptions built in:

Assets	£395,000
PE multiple range	£9.1–£15.1 m
PE average	£13.6 m
PE likely BiOs	£10 m

Detailed cashflow projections

Growth estimates given	£103.1 m
First three years only	£4.7 m
Constant tail and 15% discount rate	£15.4 m

We would, therefore, need to do substantial work on the assumptions built into these valuations. However, at this stage a tentative estimate, ignoring the asset valuation, might be in the range £10–£16 m.

(b) **Venture capital or flotation**

The main factors to consider in anticipating flotation in two to three years' time are

- The value of the company would appear to be very low for a main listing, and even on the small side for listing on the AIM.
- It may take some time to achieve as the exchange will control the number of new companies listing through a queuing system.
- The finance will be raised and ownership sold into the indefinite future. Venture capital is likely to be temporary and therefore consideration needs to be given to the likely exit route for the investors.
- The investors in a stock market company are likely to be far less involved in the company than venture capitalists, who may well want to participate in board decisions.

Overall, it is important the owners decide on their longer-term objectives as it will be a major influence on the choice of longer-term expansion finance.

Question 6 – AB Telecoms

(a)

Calculations

Methods that could be considered are:

- Asset value
- Market capitalisation
- Dividend/earnings valuation model
- NPV

Each method is calculated as follows:

Asset value

The balance sheet for 2006 shows net assets of £233 m. However, this entity clearly has substantial intellectual capital, which the value of tangible assets in the balance sheet does not reflect. An estimate of the value of an intangible asset can be attempted as follows. This method involves taking the excess returns on tangible assets and uses this figure as a basis for determining the proportion of return attributable to intangible assets.

1. *Calculation of average pre-tax earnings for three years:*
   (€67.5 m + €74.2 m + €56.9 m)/3 = €66.2 m
2. *From the balance sheet the average year end tangible assets over the last three years is calculated as:*
   (€198 m + €229 m + €263 m)/3 = €230 m

3. *The return on assets is calculated by dividing earnings by average assets as follows:*
   (€66.2 m/€230 m) × 100 = 28.8%

4. *The industry's return on assets for this same three years is 15% (as per the scenario)*

5. *Multiply the industry average pre-tax return on assets by the entity's average tangible assets to show what the average telecoms entity would earn from that amount of tangible assets:*
   €230 m × 15% = €34.5 m

   Subtract this from the entity's pre-tax earnings: €66.2 m − €34.5 m = €31.7 m. This figure shows how much more AB earns from its assets than the average telecommunications company.

6. *The after tax premium attributable to intangible assets is calculated as follows:*

(i)	Three-year average income tax rate	=	30%
(ii)	Excess return	=	€31.7 m
(iii)	Multiply (i) by (ii)	=	€9.5 m
(iv)	(ii)−(iii)	=	€22.2 m

7. *The NPV of the premium is calculated by dividing the premium by the entity's cost of capital as follows:*
   €22.2 m/0.08 = €277.5 m ≈ €277 m

If the NPV of the estimated value of intellectual capital is added to the value of net tangible assets we get €263 m + €277 m = €540 m, less current liabilities gives a net figure of €510 m.

Examiner's Note:

This estimate is based on the method shown in the CIMA Study System. Candidates would have gained credit for any valid attempt to place a value on intellectual capital.

Market capitalisation

If we use the industry average P/E of 12.5 the potential value is €497.5 m. If AB can command a rating up to 30% higher, this value rises to €646.7 m.

Examiner's Note:

€497.5 is calculated as €56.9 (2006 pre-tax earnings) less €17.1 (taxation) multiplied by 12.5 (industry average P/E)

Dividend/earnings model

There is insufficient information to use the DVM, although earnings could be used as a proxy. However, as the future growth rate is not constant the simplified model cannot be used. The NPV approach would give broadly similar results.

NPV

Year:	*2007*	*2008*
	€ million	*€ million*
After tax profit	50	64
Add: Depreciation	48	48
Cash flow	98	112
DF @ 10%	0.909	0.826
DCF	89	93

DCF of cash flows for 2009 and beyond are €112 m × 1.03 × 0.826/(0.10 − 0.03) = €1.361 m

NPV = €89 m + €93 m + € 1,361 m = € 1,543 m

Examiner's Note:

The calculations here use the industry average cost of capital. An acceptable alternative would use 8%, the earnings yield (reciprocal of P/E ratio of 12.5). In this case the NPV would be €2,164 m.

	Total	*Per share*
	€m	*€*
Asset value	233	7.7
Asset value including intellectual capital	455	15.17
Market capitalisation	497 – 647	16.57 – 21.57
NPV	1,543	51.43

(b)

Discussion of methods and recommendation

Asset value

Asset value has little relevance except in specific circumstances such as a liquidation or disposal of parts of a business. Asset value is of even more limited usefulness in an entity such as AB, which earns a substantial proportion of its income from intellectual capital that generally does not feature in the balance sheet.

Market capitalisation

The P/E basis of valuation has the advantage that it bases value on the future earnings of the entity. In a listed entity the P/E ratio is used to describe the relationship between the share price (or market capitalisation) and earnings per share (or total earnings). It is calculated by dividing the price per share by the earnings per share. Market capitalisation is the share price multiplied by the number of shares in issue. Market capitalisation is not necessarily the true value of a entity as it can be affected by a variety of extraneous factors but for a listed entity it provides a benchmark that cannot be ignored in, say, a take-over situation.

In the case of an unlisted entity, a P/E ratio that is representative of similar quoted entities might be used as a starting point for arriving at an estimated market value, based upon the present earnings of the unlisted entity. The potential market capitalisation would be the entity's latest earnings multiplied by the benchmark P/E ratio.

AB is an unlisted entity so does not have a market capitalisation or a quoted P/E ratio. Applying the industry average P/E provides a benchmark but not a very good one. As noted in the scenario, there is a wide variation around this average. Also, although not stated, the definition of the industry is likely to be very broad. A better approach might be to find an entity similar to AB and apply its P/E. Again, this is very rough and ready. As AB is unlisted there are arguments for both lowering and raising the P/E as compared with either a proxy entity or the industry average. The Financial Advisor's estimate is that AB could command a rating 30% higher than the industry average. It is not clear how this estimate was made, as an argument could be made for lowering the P/E ratio to reflect the higher risk and lower liquidity of such entities. It would be more appropriate to use the NPV method and adjust the discount rate – as discussed below.

NPV/Earnings method

Forecasting cash flows and discounting at a specific risk adjusted discount rate is the theoretically correct valuation method. The valuation here uses the industry average cost of equity. Using an industry average suffers from the problems noted above. Also, the cost of equity will include an element of return for financial risk if entities have debt in their capital structure. Many entities included in the industry average will have substantial debt finance.

What is needed here is an exercise to calculate a more accurate cost of capital. As with using the P/E ratio approach, discussed above, finding a proxy entity may be more reliable than using an industry average.

Recommendation

As shown in the summary table in part (a), the likely market value ranges from €233 m (net tangible assets) to € 1,543 m (NPV). The NPV valuation is substantially higher than any of the others. While this method is theoretically correct, the reliability of the results does of course depend on the accuracy of the forecast cash flows and the discount rate used. Using growth in perpetuity (although a sensible simplification for examination purposes) is unrealistic.

None of the figures produced by this exercise is wholly reliable, neither is it expected to be as this is simply an estimate based on incomplete information. The main recommendation must be to conduct a more detailed evaluation involving other advisors such as the entity that will be responsible for the flotation. It needs also to be established what percentage of their shareholding each director wishes to sell on flotation and how many new shares will need to be reissued. The calculations have been made on the current number of shares in issue to the directors/founding shareholders.

However, if a recommendation has to be made, a flotation value in the region of €600 m or €20 per share would be conservative.

Examiner's Note:

Any sensible recommendation, or argument for not making one on the evidence available, would gain credit.

A secondary recommendation would be to split the shares in readiness for a flotation. The share prices produced by all valuation methods, except asset value, are 'heavy' – that is buyers would not get many shares for their money. More shares would need to be in issue to allow a reasonably liquid market in them.

6

Mergers, Acquisitions and Buyouts

Mergers, Acquisitions and Buyouts

6

Synergy

Synergy represents a benefit to the entity and its shareholders which comes about because two entities are now operating together. Ultimately, this means some reduction in costs or increase in revenues.

Synergy could be a one-off cost saving such as:

- Selling one of the head office sites
- Selling other duplicated assets.

It could also be a cost saving or revenue boost which is felt every year, such as:

- Cross-selling to the other entity's customers
- Production economies of scale
- Storage, distribution and marketing rationalisation
- Elimination of overlapping jobs
- Sharing of assets
- Elimination of a competitor
- Possibly cheaper financing costs.

More generally, any transfer of skills or sharing of resources (from warehouses to customer lists and goodwill) is likely to lead to synergy.

In income-based valuations,

- One-off synergy should be added to the total value as a 'bonus' on top of the income stream which can be produced by the entity.
- Ongoing synergy should be included in the annual income before valuing the income stream.

Synergy makes no difference to asset-based valuations. This is because cost savings or revenue boosts are irrelevant, and surplus assets are already included in the list of all the assets being valued.

Studies tend to suggest that a predator often overestimates synergy and underestimates the costs of reorganising the merged entity. In the excitement of a contested bid, this can lead to them offering too much for the target's shares and hence reducing the wealth of their own shareholders.

Forms of consideration for acquisitions

The main forms of consideration for acquisitions are in cash, shares or loan stock:

	Advantages for purchaser	*Advantages for vendor*
Cash	no sharing of control	certainty of consideration
Shares	no liquidity problems	no tax on capital gains on sale share in future profits
Loan stock	less of an immediate liquidity problem but no sharing of control	a guaranteed income stream without suffering immediate tax on capital gains

Hostile bids and defence strategies

A friendly bid is when the management of the target entity view it favourably and recommend it to their shareholders.

A hostile bid is when the management of the target entity are against it. The potential purchaser (or predator) therefore approaches the shareholders directly. In a hostile bid, the predator is unlikely to have as much detailed operational information on which to base the bid.

In a hostile bid, there are a number of defence strategies the management of the target can use to stop the predator taking over the entity.

To discourage any interest, the management might use:

(a) a clear strategic plan to demonstrate the benefits of the current management team
(b) poison pills, to make the entity unattractive if taken over
(c) strategic shareholdings, where the managers or associates control a number of shares.

If the predator expresses interest, the management might:

(d) dispose of the assets attracting their attention (Crown Jewels)
(e) persuade a more friendly predator to bid for them (White Knight)
(f) launch a management buyout themselves
(g) try to take over the predator (Pac Man)
(h) try to have it referred to the competition authorities.

If a full bid is launched, the management of the target entity will circulate a defence document to shareholders, explaining why they should stay with the present management.

Management buyouts (MBOs) and venture capitalists

An MBO is where the managers of a business, possibly only part of an entity, buy it from the shareholders. In the past this has often meant taking on very high levels of debt (a highly leveraged buyout) but the growth of venture capital has reduced the amount of long-term interest-bearing loans needed. Venture capitalists will look for high capital growth and will often have identified an exit route before investing.

Questions

Question 1 – Company A (Practice Question)

Company A has earnings of £1 m and a P/E ratio of 7.5. It is considering a bid for company B, which has earnings of £0.5 m and a P/E ratio of 6. It estimates that the P/E ratio after acquisition will change to 7.

What is the maximum A can realistically offer B if:

(a) there is no expected synergy?
(b) A expects annual post-tax synergy of £0.25 m?

Question 2 – PR

PR plc is listed on the London Stock Exchange. The directors have made a bid for its main UK competitor, ST plc. ST plc's directors have rejected the bid. If the bid eventually succeeds, the new company will become the largest in its industry in Europe. However, it will still be smaller than some of its US competitors. The directors of PR plc are aware that the company must continue to expand if it is to remain competitive in a global market and avoid being taken over by a larger US company.

Relevant information is as follows:

	PR plc	*ST plc*
Share price as at today (21 May 2002) (pence)	671	565
Shares in issue (million)	820	513
P/E ratios as at today	14	16
Debt outstanding (market value) (£ billion)	2.2	1.8

Other information:

The average P/E for the industry is currently estimated as 13.

- The average debt ratio for the industry (long-term debt as proportion of total funding) is 30% based on market values.
- 40% of PR plc's debt is repayable in 2005; 30% of ST plc's in 2006.
- PR plc's cost of equity is 13% net of tax.
- PR plc has cash available of £460 m following the recent disposal of some subsidiary companies. ST plc's cash balances at the last balance sheet date (31 December 2001) were £120 m.

Terms of the bid

PR plc's directors made an opening bid one week ago of 10 PR plc shares for 13 ST plc shares. They are aware that they might have to raise the bid in order to succeed and also may need to offer a cash alternative. Their advisers have told them that, typically, 50% of shareholders might be expected to accept the share exchange and 50%, the cash alternative.

Requirements

Assume you work for PR plc's financial advisers. You have been asked to write a report advising the directors of PR plc. Your report should cover the following issues:

(a) A discussion of the implications that the current share prices of the two companies have for the bid. Recommend terms of a revised share exchange.

(8 marks)

(b) The advantages and disadvantages of offering a cash alternative and how the cash alternative might be financed, based on your revised bid terms recommended in answer to (a) above. Your discussion should include an evaluation of the impact of the proposed finance on the merged group's financial standing. Assume a rights issue is not appropriate at the present time.

(17 marks)
(Total = 25 marks)

Question 3 – AB plc

AB plc is a firm of recruitment and selection consultants. It has been trading for 10 years and obtained a stock market listing 4 years ago. It has pursued a policy of aggressive growth and specialises in providing services to companies in high-technology and high-growth sectors. It is all-equity financed by ordinary share capital of £50m in shares of £0.20 nominal (or par) value. The company's results to the end of June 2002 have just been announced. Profits before tax were £126.6m. The Chairman's statement included a forecast that earnings might be expected to rise by 4%, which is a lower annual rate than in recent years. This is blamed on economic factors that have had a particularly adverse effect on high-technology companies.

YZ plc is in the same business but has been established much longer. It serves more traditional business sectors and its earnings record has been erratic. Press comment has frequently blamed this on poor management and the company's shares have been out of favour with the stock market for some time. Its current earnings growth forecast is also 4% for the foreseeable future. YZ plc has an issued ordinary share capital of £180m in £1 shares. Pre-tax profits for the year to 30 June 2002 were £112.5m.

AB plc has recently approached the shareholders of YZ plc with a bid of 5 new shares in AB plc for every 6 YZ plc shares. There is a cash alternative of 345 pence per share. Following the announcement of the bid, the market price of AB plc shares fell 10% while the price of YZ plc shares rose 14%. The P/E ratio and dividend yield for AB plc, YZ plc and two other listed companies in the same industry immediately prior to the bid announcement are shown below. All share prices are in pence.

2002				
High	**Low**	**Company**	**P/E**	**Dividend yield %**
425	325	AB plc	11	2.4
350	285	YZ plc	7	3.1
187	122	CD plc	9	5.2
230	159	WX plc	16	2.4

Both AB plc and YZ plc pay tax at 30%.

AB plc's post-tax cost of equity capital is estimated at 13% per annum and YZ plc's at 11% per annum.

Assume you are a shareholder in YZ plc. You have a large, but not controlling, shareholding and are a qualified management accountant. You bought the shares some years ago and have been very disappointed with their performance. Two years ago you formed a 'protest group' with fellow shareholders with the principal aim of replacing members of the Board. You call a meeting of this group to discuss the bid.

Requirement

In preparation for your meeting, write a briefing note for your group to discuss. Your note should:

(a) Evaluate whether the proposed share-for-share offer is likely to be beneficial to shareholders in both AB plc and YZ plc. You should use the information and merger terms available, plus appropriate assumptions, to forecast post-merger values. As a benchmark, you should then value the two companies using the constant growth form of the dividend valuation model.

(13 marks)

(b) Discuss the factors to consider when deciding whether to accept or reject the bid and the relative benefits/disadvantages of accepting shares or cash.

(8 marks)

(c) Advise your shareholder group on what its members should do with their investment in YZ plc, based on your calculations/considerations.

(4 marks)
(Total = 25 marks)

Question 4 – TDC

TDC Inc. is a transport and distribution company listed on the New York Stock Exchange. On 14 November 2003, the directors made a bid for a competitor, UED plc, that is based in the UK. UED plc's directors are considering the bid, but have indicated the terms are inadequate and would have to be improved if they were to feel able to recommend it to their shareholders.

The merger would create the fourth largest company in the industry worldwide, but it would still be substantially smaller than the three largest companies. TDC Inc. has suffered from slow growth over the past few years and has long been rumoured by market professionals to be a likely target of a hostile bid from one of the three larger companies, or even a reverse takeover by a smaller company. The bid for UED plc is therefore being seen by the market as defensive.

	TDC Inc.	*UED plc*
Market data		
Common stock/share price as at today (18 November 2003)	US$11.36	425 pence
Common stock/share price on 18 October 2003	US$12.45	305 pence
Common stock/shares in issue	120 m	145 m
P/E ratio as at today	11	13.5

Accounting data		US$m	£m
Forecast profit after tax for the current financial year		98.5	45.5
Net asset values at last balance sheet date (30 June 2003)		825.2	230.5
Including cash balances of		125.5	65.2
Debt outstanding (market value)		250	75
	[Repayable	2007	2008]

Other information:

The average P/E for the industry is currently estimated as 10 in the UK and 13 in the USA.

The average debt ratio for the industry internationally (long-term debt as proportion of total funding) is 15% based on market values.

TDC Inc's cost of equity is 12% net of tax.

The US$/£ exchange rate today is 1.53.

Terms of the bid
TDC Inc's directors have made an opening bid of 1 TDC Inc. common stock for 2 UED plc shares. No cash alternative has been offered so far.

Requirement

Assume you are the Financial Manager with TDC Inc. Write an internal memorandum for the Board that:

(a) discusses how the recent price movements of the two companies' shares might impact on the bid negotiations;

(6 marks)

(b) recommends revised bid terms that might be acceptable to the directors and shareholders of UED plc and also to your own Board. Your recommendation should be fully evaluated;

(12 marks)

(c) evaluates the strategic implications of making a hostile bid compared with an aggressive investment programme of organic growth.

(7 marks)
(Total = 25 marks)

Question 5 – RD

RD plc has made a takeover bid for LO plc. RD plc's share price has been performing well in recent months as the market believes its Managing Director, Mr Jones, has the ability to improve dramatically the company's earnings. The acquisition of LO plc, an erratic performer in recent years, seems to be a sensible move in commercial terms. However, the market does not react to the terms of the bid as Mr Jones expected and he finds RD plc's share price falling.

A summary of the financial data before the bid is as follows:

	RD plc	*LO plc*
Number of shares in issue (million)	5	15
Earnings available to ordinary shareholders (£m)	2.5	7.5
P/E ratio	12.5	7.5
Mr Jones estimated financial data post-acquisition		
Estimated market capitalisation	£125 m	
Estimated share price	£8.33	
Estimated EPS	£0.67	
Estimated equivalent value of one old LO plc sh	£5.55	

The offer is 10 RD plc shares for 15 LO plc shares. At the time of the bid announcement, no information is released other than the bid terms and the comment by Mr Jones that he hopes to 'turn LO round'. The expected rate of return on RD plc's equity capital is 15% per annum constant.

Requirements

(a) (i) To suggest how Mr Jones might have calculated post-acquisition values

(ii) to write a short report suggesting a probably post-acquisition share price and advising shareholders in both RD plc and LO plc on whether the bid should proceed

(15 marks)

(b) It is later announced that the proposed merger is expected to result in immediate administrative savings of £5m. Sales of redundant assets by the end of the first year are expected to realise £10m. Net income is expected to increase by £7.5m per annum for the foreseeable future as a result of a more aggressive marketing policy for LO plc's business.

Note: You should assume all figures are net of tax.

You are required to explain how this new information would affect your estimate of a probable post-acquisition share price, and comment on how it might affect LO plc's bargaining position.

(10 marks)
(Total = 25 marks)

Question 6 – PCO plc

PCO plc operates in oil and related industries. Its shares are quoted on the London International Stock Exchange. In its retailing operations the company has concentrated on providing high quality service and facilities at its service stations rather than competing solely on the price of petrol. Approximately 75% of its Revenue and 60% of its profits are from petrol, the remainder coming from other services (car wash and retail sales from its convenience stores which are available at each service station).

The company has been highly profitable in the past as a result of astute buying of petroleum products on the open market. The company does not enter into supplier agreements with the major oil companies except on very short-term deals. However, profit margins are now under increasing pressure as a result of intensifying competition and the cost of complying with environmental legislation.

The managing director of the company is assessing a possible acquisition that would help the company increase the percentage of its non-petroleum revenue and profits. OT plc specialises in oil distribution from the depots owned by the major oil companies to their retail outlets. Its shares have been quoted on the UK Alternative Investment Market for the past 2 years. It operates a fleet of oil tankers, some owned and some leased. PCO plc has used its services in the past and knows it has an up to date and well-managed fleet. However, a bid for OT plc would almost certainly be hostile and, as the directors and their families own 40% of the shares, a successful bid is far from assured.

Extracts from PCO plc's Balance Sheet at 31 December 2003

Assets Employed	£m
Cash and marketable securities	105.00
Accounts receivable and inventories	95.00
Less current liabilities	(75.00)
Working capital	125.00
Property, plant and equipment	160.00
Less long-term liabilities:	
Secured loan stock 7% repayable 2009	(80.00)
	205.00
Shareholders' equity	
Stated capital	
(Authorised £50 m)	
Issued	40.00
Accumulated profits	165.00
Net Assets Employed	205.00

PCO plc's financial advisors have produced estimates of the expected NPV and the first full year post-acquisition earnings of PCO plc and OT plc:

PCO plc plus OT plc	*Estimated post-acquisition earnings in first full year following*	*Estimated NPV of combined organization*
	£70 million	£720 million
		acquisitions:

Summary financial statistics

	PCO plc	*OT plc*
Last year end	31 December 2003	31 December 2003
Shares in issue (millions)	40	24
Earnings per share (pence)	106	92
Dividend per share (pence)	32	21
Share price (pence)	967	1020
Book value of fixed assets and current assets less current liabilities (£ million)	285	145
Debt ratio (outstanding debt as % of total market value)	17.0	14.0
Forecast growth rate % (constant, annualised)	5	9
Beta coefficient	0.9	1.2

Requirements

(a) Calculate, for PCO plc and OT plc *before* the acquisition:

(i) The current market value and P/E ratio
(ii) The cost of equity using the CAPM, assuming the return on the market is 8% and the return on the risk free asset is 4%
(iii) The prospective share price and market value using the dividend valuation model.

(6 marks)

(b) Discuss and advise on the following issues:

(i) The price to be offered to the target company's shareholders. You should recommend a range of terms within which PCO plc should be prepared to negotiate,
(ii) The most appropriate form of funding the bid and the financial effects (assume cash or share exchange are the options).
(iii) The business implications (effect on existing operation, growth prospects, risk and so on).

(19 marks)

Marks are split roughly equally between sections of part (b) of the question.

(Total = 25 marks)

Question 7 – FS

FS provides industrial and commercial cleaning services to organisations throughout a country in the European Union. Its shares have been listed for 15 years and, until two years ago, the entity followed a policy of aggressive growth, mainly by acquisition.

However, in the last two years, there have been few suitable takeover opportunities and, as a consequence, growth has slowed. The market has downgraded FS's shares and they are currently trading at €3.57, the lowest price for five years. The market as a whole has declined in value, but not to the same extent as FS's shares.

FS's bank has recently informed FS's directors of a possible takeover opportunity of another of its clients, MT. This is a large private entity in the same industry as FS. MT's directors have indicated to the bank that if the price is right they may be prepared to sell the entity. MT's directors have made their financial forecasts and other strategic documentation available to the bank on a strictly confidential basis, requesting that this information only be released to a serious potential bidder. After much discussion between the bank and the two companies, MT agrees that FS should have the information.

MT's results for the past three years and the directors' estimates for the current year are as follows:

Year to 30 June	*Revenue €million*	*Earnings €million*
2003	925	55.5
2004	1,020	62.7
2005	1,150	71.5
2006 (forecast)	1,350	88.9

From 2007 onwards, growth in earnings and dividends is likely to fall to 4% per annum, according to MT's directors. MT has paid a dividend of 50% of its earnings for the past 10 years.

Summary balance sheets as at 30 June 2005 for both FS and MT are as follows:

	FS *€million*	*MT* *€million*
TOTAL ASSETS		
Non-current assets	1,944	1,040
Current assets*	796	680
	2,740	1,415
EQUITY AND LIABILITIES		
Equity		
Share capital (Shares of €1)	420	
(Shares of 50 cents)		220
Retained earnings	1,080	680
	1,500	900
Non-current liabilities		
(Secured bonds, 6% 2015)	750	
(Unsecured bonds, 7% 2010)		300
Current liabilities	490	215
	1,240	515
	2,740	1,415
* Includes cash of	250	65

FS's revenues and earnings for the year ended 30 June 2005 were €2,250 m and €128.5 m respectively.

After thoroughly examining the information on MT, financial managers in FS have identified a number of savings and potential synergies that would arise if the takeover were to go ahead. These synergies are estimated to have a net present value of €200 m. However, the FS directors believe MT's forecast earnings are over-optimistic and think earnings growth for 2006 onwards is likely to be in the range 2% to 4%. The bank advisers disagree, but they are in a delicate situation trying to balance the interests of two clients.

FS's cost of equity is 8.5%. MT has not provided information on its cost of capital, but the two entity's asset betas are likely to be the same. FS's equity beta is quoted as 1.1. The expected risk-free rate of return is 3% and the expected return on the market is 8%. Assume that the debt beta for both companies is 0.2 and that FS's debt is trading at par.

Ignore tax in your calculations.

Requirements

Assume you are a Financial Manager with FS. Advise the directors of FS on

(i) the appropriate cost of capital to be used when valuing MT. Accompany your comments with a calculation of the cost of equity for MT.

(6 marks)

(ii) a bidding strategy; that is the initial price to be offered and the maximum FS should be prepared to offer for the shares in MT. Use whatever methods of valuation you think appropriate and accompany each with brief comments on their suitability in the circumstances here. In calculations of value that require a discount rate, use the cost of equity you have calculated in (i) above. Your answer should consider the interests of both groups of shareholders.

(13 marks)

(iii) the most appropriate form of consideration to use in the circumstances. Assume the choice is either a share exchange or cash. Your answer should consider the interests of both groups of shareholders.

(6 marks)
(Total = 25 marks)

Question 8 – VCI

VCI is a venture capital investor that specialises in providing finance to small but established businesses. At present, its expected average pre-tax return on equity investment is a nominal 30% per annum over a five-year investment period.

YZ is a typical client of VCI. It is a 100% family owned transport and distribution business whose shares are unlisted. The company sustained a series of losses a few years ago, but the recruitment of some professional managers and an aggressive marketing policy returned the company to profitability. Its most recent accounts show revenue of $105 m and profit before interest and tax of $28.83 m. Other relevant information is as follows:

- For the last three years dividends have been paid at 40% of earnings and the directors have no plans to change this payout ratio;
- Taxation has averaged 28% per annum over the past few years and this rate is likely to continue;
- The directors are forecasting growth in earnings and dividends for the foreseeable future of 6% per annum;
- YZ's accountants estimated the entity's cost of equity capital at 10% some years ago. The data they worked with was incomplete and now out of date. The current cost could be as high as 15%.

Extracts from its most recent balance sheet ***at*** *31 March 2006* are shown below.

	$ million
ASSETS	
Non-current assets	
Property, plant and equipment	35.50
Current assets	4.50
	40.00
EQUITY AND LIABILITIES	
Equity	2.25
Share capital (Nominal value of 10 cents)	18.00
Retained earnings	20.25
Non-current liabilities	15.00
7% Secured bond repayable 2016	4.75
Current liabilities	19.75
	40.00

Note: The entity's vehicles are mainly financed by operating leases.

YZ has now reached a stage in its development that requires additional capital of $25m. The directors, and major shareholders, are considering a number of alternative forms of finance. One of the alternatives they are considering is venture capital funding and they have approached VCI. In preliminary discussions, VCI has suggested it might be able to finance the necessary $25m by purchasing a percentage of YZ's equity. This will, of course, involve YZ issuing new equity.

Requirements

(a) Assume you work for VCI and have been asked to evaluate the potential investment.

(i) Using YZ's forecast of growth and its estimates of cost of capital, calculate the number of new shares that YZ will have to issue to VCI in return for its investment and the percentage of the entity VCI will then own. Comment briefly on your result.

(9 marks)

(ii) Evaluate exit strategies that might be available to VCI in five years' time and their likely acceptability to YZ.

(6 marks)

Note: Use sensible roundings in your calculations.

(Total for Requirement (a) = 15 marks)

(b) Discuss the advantages and disadvantages to an established business such as YZ of using a venture capital entity to provide finance for expansion as compared with long-term debt. Advise YZ about which type of finance it should choose, based on the information available so far.

(10 marks)

(Total = 25 marks)

A report format is **not** required for this question.

Answers

Question 1 – Company A

(a)	Value combined = (1 m + 0.5 m) × 7	= 10.5 m
	Value of A alone = 1 m × 7.5	= 7.5 m
	Maximum bid	£3 m
(b)	Value combined = (1 m + 0.5 m + 0.25 m) × 7	= 12.25 m
	Value of A alone	= 7.5 m
	Maximum bid	= £4.75 m

This therefore gives A some leeway in its bid (£1.75 m).

Question 2 – PR

REPORT

To: Directors of PR plc
From: Adviser
Date: xx of x 2002

Bid for ST plc

This report will discuss the implications for the bid of the current share prices, and the advantages and disadvantages of a cash bid and how it could be financed.

(a) *Current share prices*

The bid terms are 10 PR shares for 13 ST shares. At today's prices, the PR shares would be worth £67.10 and the ST shares £73.45. It is therefore unlikely that the bid will be accepted at today's prices, and it would have to be increased to roughly 17 PR shares for 20 ST shares.

However, the share prices are based on the market expectations of the gain to the respective shareholders, and in particular a bid at this level may not represent good value to the existing shareholders of PR. The benefits of the acquisition need to be assessed carefully to decide what it is worth paying.

The earnings of ST are approximately £181 m (£5.65/16 × 513m), which gives an approximate value at your cost of equity (13%) of £1.4 billion (valued as a perpetuity). Given that the current market capitalisation of ST is £2.95 billion, the market has already built in a substantial premium to allow for any operating synergy. Only if the cost savings and revenue increases are likely to exceed £1.5 billion in present value terms (or £200 m per annum in post-tax earnings), should the directors consider increasing their bid.

(b) *Cash alternative*

The main advantage of a cash offer is that the benefits of the merger in the future operations all accrue to those that remain as shareholders in PR plc. The disadvantage is that the cash has to be found to fund the payments required.

If the bid of 17 PR shares for 20 ST shares is accepted, each ST share is being valued at 17 × £6.71/20 = £5.70. We are assuming that 50% × 513 m × 50% = £1,462 m. The two companies have total cash of £580 m, leaving £882 m to be raised.

This is best financed through long-term debt finance, although we need to examine the impact on the group's capital structure. If we do not allow for any synergy over and above that reflected in ST's share price, and assume that the market takes no account of the change in the capital structure, the equity after merger = £5.5 billion + £2.9 billion = £8.4 billion, and the debt will be £4.9 billion approximately (including the £882 m raised). This gives gearing of 37%, which is higher than the industry average but not excessive.

However, this ignores any extra synergy not anticipated by the market (which would increase equity and reduce gearing) and the impact of increased gearing from PR's perspective, which might increase the cost of equity from 13% and reduce the equity value, hence increasing the ratio.

In addition, £1.4 billion of debt is repayable within four years, which will decrease the gearing to 30% (using the same equity value). Much will therefore depend on the earning potential of the merged entity and how much can be generated to pay off this debt without having to refinance.

Question 3 – AB plc

(a) **Share-for share offer**

	AB	*YZ*	*Combined*
Profit after tax (£m)	88.62	78.75	167.37
EPS (p)	35.45	43.75	41.84
P/E ratio	11	7	
Share price (pre bid)	£3.90	£3.06	£3.82
MV of company (£m)	974.8	551.3	1,526.1
No. of shares (million)	250	180	400

This assumes that there is no operating synergy and so no increase in the combined earnings; it is unlikely a bid would be launched if substantial synergy was not envisaged.

On these assumptions, even though the EPS increases for a shareholder in AB, the share value decreases from £3.90 to £3.82. A shareholder in YZ who held 6 shares had a value of £18.36 but will now have 5 shares in the combined entity worth £19.10. There is therefore a transfer of wealth from the existing AB shareholders to the YZ shareholders. This would partly explain the 10% fall in the AB share price and the 14% increase in YZ's. However, AB clearly feel there are substantial savings to be made as they are offering cash of £3.45 per YZ share.

This gives a combined market value of £167.37 m × 11 = £1,841 m or £4.60 per share. Original AB shareholders gain 70 pence per share and original YZ shareholders [(5 × 4.60) − (6 × 3.06)]/6 = 77 pence per original share.

This would suggest that AB is slightly undervalued, but that YZ is hugely undervalued in the marketplace. It is possible that the market does not believe YZ's growth estimates, given its poor performance to date.

The dividend valuation model estimates the share value for each company as:

$$AB = \frac{(0.3545 \times 1.04)}{(0.13 - 0.04)} = £4.10 \text{ per share}$$

$$YZ = \frac{(0.4375 \times 1.04)}{(0.11 - 0.04)} = £6.50 \text{ per share}$$

(b) **Factors to consider**

In considering whether to accept or reject the bid, and whether to take shares or cash, we need to consider the following:

The market does not appear to believe the growth rate predicted by YZ.
In the short term, target companies tend to gain most.
YZ share price is near its lowest level for the year, suggesting that AB are buying when our price is depressed.
If we reject the bid, will AB improve the terms?
Cash may give rise to a tax charge.
We do not know what AB's future dividend policy will be.

(c) **Recommendations**

It is difficult to make a definite recommendation, as it will depend on shareholders' views of the future. We could sell for cash, at a higher price than our shares are currently worth. Alternatively, we could accept shares if we feel the AB management will revitalise the company.

A final possibility would be to reject the bid and continue to push for the Board of YZ to be replaced. Some of the valuations considered suggest that we are very undervalued by the market.

Question 4 – TDC

MEMORANDUM

To: Directors of TDC Inc.
From: Financial Manager
Date: xx of x 2003

Bid for UED plc

This memo will discuss the impact of the recent price movements, recommend revised terms and evaluate the strategic implications of a hostile bid as against organic growth.

(a) *Impact of recent price movements*

In the last month our share price has fallen 9% from $12.45 to $11.36 while UED's has risen by 40% from £3.05 to £4.25. Even though the bid was only made four days ago, it appears the stock market had already anticipated it.

The market would appear to think that our management can get better growth in the earnings than UED and have allowed for this benefit in the price. Additionally, it is likely that they are aware bidders usually pay more than the target company appears to be worth in order to gain control.

Our share price has fallen, which suggests that the market feels we are likely to offer more than it will be worth to us, thus decreasing shareholders' wealth.

We will need to offer a cash alternative at some stage, which is likely to mean raising more finance, probably debt; cash stands at \$125 m, which is probably not enough to cover those that want the cash alternative, and UED's cash may be spent by the time we acquire it.

(b) *Recommended revised terms*

The current bid terms are 1 TDC share for 2 UED share; based on today's prices, the TDC share is worth \$11.36 while 2 UED shares are worth \$13 at today's exchange rate. The bid needs to be increased to be successful; without allowing for any other changes in share prices (which is unlikely) it would need to increase to 4 TDC shares (worth \$45.44) for 7 UED shares (worth \$45.50).

Using our own cost of equity and assuming 100% payout ratio, we can calculate the growth which the market has already assumed in the current price:

$$6.50 = \frac{[6.50/13.5 \times (1+g)]}{(0.12-g)}$$

which gives $g = 4.3\%$ per annum

Therefore, we should only raise our bid to that recommended above if we feel that we can achieve in excess of this growth rate. At these terms, all of the benefits of the 4.3% growth will accrue to the existing shareholders of UED.

A cash alternative will also need to be offered, as many UK shareholders may not want American shares. This may require raising additional debt finance; if all the shareholders required the cash alternative we would need to raise an additional [(6.50 × 145 m) − 225 m] or 717 m.

Thus for the combined group, market values might be:

Equity = 1,363 + 943	= 2,306
Debt = 717 + 365	= 1,082
	\$3,388 m

The gearing in this worst-case scenario would rise to 32%, which is more than double the industry average, which may mean that shareholders will feel interest cover will be at risk.

These calculations are approximations based on a number of assumptions, and using the current market valuations and exchange rate. The asset value per share is \$6.88 for TDC and \$2.43 for UED; given that they are in the same industry it would seem that UED's assets are either undervalued or much older than TDC's and probably need replacing. This may affect the amount we are prepared to offer for the company.

(c) *Strategic implications of a hostile bid*

The advantages of making a hostile bid as opposed to organic growth include:

- It reduces the competition, and allows a large increase in market share quickly.
- Allows some diversification of risk, unless the companies are identical.
- Will achieve the company's strategic aims more quickly than organic growth.

However, disadvantages include:

- Evidence suggests that hostile bid purchases tend to overpay for the business.
- It is expensive to integrate two businesses and it is particularly difficult after a hostile bid when the people who work in the two organisations are probably against the change.

Question 5 – RD

(a) **Post-acquisition values**

(i) *Mr Jones' estimate*

Mr Jones has used RD's P/E ratio to deduce a value from the combined earnings:

12.5 × £10 m = £125 m
Share price = £125 m/15 m = £8.33 per share
EPS = £10 m/15 m = £0.67

Value of one old LO share = £8.33 × 10/15 = £5.55

(ii)

REPORT

To: Shareholders
From: Management Accountant
Date: xx of x 20xx

Acquisition of LO plc by RD plc

Assuming that no synergy arises, the value of the combined group will be the sum of the values of the parts.

Value = (12.5 × £2.5 m) + (7.5 × £7.5 m) = £87.5 m

The share price will then be, assuming the terms of 10 RD shares for every 15 LO is taken up, £87.5 m/15 m = £5.83.

Before the acquisition, RD's share price was £0.50 × 12.5 = £6.25, so each RD shareholder will lose 42p per share, a total of £2.1 m from this group being transferred in value to the old shareholders of LO. Without any synergy, it would seem likely that RD's shareholders will not proceed on these terms, while LO's shareholders will gain and will want it to go ahead. As the bidder has already made a bid, it is unlikely that it can be retracted, and RD's shareholders must hope that the 'turnaround' of LO will generate substantial savings.

(b) **New information**

Value without synergy	= £87.5 m
Admin. savings	= £5 m
Assets sale = 10/1.15	= £8.7 m
Income increase = 7.5/0.15	= £50 m
Market capitalisation	= £151.2 m

Share price = £151.2 m/15 m = £10.08 per share.

Existing shareholders in RD thus gain £3.83 per share or a total of £19.15 m. As the total synergy has a value of £63.7 m, the main part of the gain (£44.55 m) is still going to the current LO shareholders. It appears that LO's performance has been erratic in the past and LO's shareholders may not have many other options available to them. RD should therefore try to restructure the deal so that the majority of the synergistic gains accrues to the RD shareholders.

If the synergy could be achieved by LO combining with a number of companies, it would raise its value as they could approach other possible purchasers. This would have the effect of increasing their share of the savings achieved.

Question 6 – PCO plc

(a) **Values before the acquisition**

	PCO	*OT*
Current market value	$9.67 \times 40 = £386.8\,m$	$10.20 \times 24 = £244.8\,m$
PE ratio	$967/106 = 9.1$	$1020/92 = 11.1$
Dividend valuation		
Cost of equity	$4 + (4 \times 0.9) = 7.6\%$	$4 + (4 \times 1.2) = 8.8\%$
Share price	$(32 \times 1.05)/(0.076 - 0.05)$ = 1292 pence	
Prospective market value	$12.92 \times 40 = £516.8\,m$	

Note that the value for OT cannot be calculated in the dividend valuation model as the prospective growth rate exceeds the cost of equity.

(b) (i) *Price to be offered*

- As a going concern which has its shares traded on a public exchange, the asset valuation of £145m is likely to be some way below any income valuation.
- The total increase in value as a group has been estimated as 720m − 387m − 245m = £88m.
- PCO should not offer more than 245 + 88 = £333m but will have to offer more than the current value of £245m.
- The value of the synergy will need to be split between the two groups of share holders. A possible offer would be to split it in proportion to the original market values. This would mean offering $245 + (88 \times 245/631) = £279\,m$.

This would give an offer price of £11.62 per share.

(ii) *Form of funding*

Cash

- PCO does not have sufficient cash to fund the acquisition and would have to raise debt finance. Allowing for the £105m in cash, it would have to raise £174m (assuming a price of £279m).
- If PCO has to repay OTs £40m debt, the finance raised will have to increase by this amount. If they do not have to repay it, then it will still be in the consolidated balance sheet. In either case, debt will rise to 80 + 174 + 40 = £294m which exceeds shareholders' funds in the balance sheet.

Shares

- A share for share exchange would need to be calculated to ensure that each original group gains by the agreed amount.

- If we wish £279 m to be the value of the bid, this gives a gain of £34 m to OT shareholders and £54 m to PCO shareholders.

  If X = number of new shares issued, then:
  $720 \times 40/(40 + X) = 387 + 54$ giving X = 25.306 m shares
  This gives an exchange of 1.0544 PCO shares for every OT share.

- Unfortunately, such an offer may well be rejected as on current share prices, it would mean losing on the exchange for the OT shareholders:
  24 m × £10.20 = £244.8 m becomes 25.306 m × £9.67 = £244.7 m
- The management will, therefore, have to make very clear the benefits of the acquisition for shareholders, and specify the value of £88 m.
- As soon as this becomes widely known, the share prices of each company will, in theory, move towards the post-merger values of £441 m and £279 m, which give share prices of £11.025 and £11.625. This equates to a correct exchange of 1.0544 PCO shares for every OT share, and the gain of £88 m has been apportioned by market forces before the acquisition takes place.
- In practice, the share prices would be different, due to the risk of the deal not going through, as well as because of market speculation and the imperfect information held by the market.
- Issuing another 25 m or so new shares would need approval to increase the authorised share capital as it only has leeway of another 20 m. This might be one way to encourage the share price to rise if investors anticipated a bid, thus making any eventual offer appear more attractive.

(iii) *Business implications*

- It is likely to be a hostile bid, which will involve extensive costs for advisors.
- Market activity and speculation may drive the share price of OT so high that a bid offer becomes unattractive or PCO increases its bid so that virtually all the gains pass to the OT shareholders.
- Given the nature of the businesses, there may be some reduction in petrol delivery costs but it is difficult to see this being worth £88 m and the disadvantage is that PCO will lose a degree of flexibility in its suppliers.
- A rights issue of equity rather than debt might be more appropriate if a cash purchase is intended. Alternatively, a choice of cash or shares could be given to help keep the gearing down.
- Other possible acquisition targets should be considered and analysed before settling on OT as there may be more synergy available through other combinations.

Question 7 – FS

(i) In an investment appraisal, theory suggests that the rate to use should reflect only the business risk of the investment. This means using the asset beta in the CAPM, if this model is being used to calculate a discount rate. In a takeover where the target is a substantial size, relative to the bidder, there is a stronger argument for using the equity beta, especially if the bid is being financed by a combination of debt and equity.

There are arguments for using the cost of equity of either the bidder or the target. On the one hand, the rate should reflect the risk of the cash flows, which suggests using the target's rate. However, how the assets are managed could also influence the risk of cash flows, which implies the bidder's rate should be preferred. Unless the two entities are very dissimilar in terms of business risk and capital structure, the rates are likely to be similar. If there is a wide disparity, the question should be asked whether the takeover is in the interests of shareholders who, presumably, invest in the bidder because they are happy with the level of risk they are taking on.

The cost of equity for FS is given in the question, but can be 'proved' using the CAPM formula: Rf + ß(Rm − Rf) = 3% + 1.1(8% − 3%) = 8.5%. To calculate the cost of equity for MT it is necessary to calculate the asset beta or return on assets of FS. This is most easily done by ungearing FS's equity beta and re-gearing using MT's debt ratio.

Step 1 – Calculate market value for FS

There are 420 m shares in issue and the market price is €3.57. The market value is therefore €1,499.4 m – say €1,500 m, which is the same as the book value.

Step 2 – De-gear the beta

$$ßu = ßg\left(\frac{VE}{VE} + VD\right) + ßd\left(\frac{VD}{VD} + VE\right)$$

$$= 1.1\left(\frac{1,500}{(750 + 1,500)}\right) + 0.2\left(\frac{750}{(750 + 1,500)}\right)$$

$$= 0.73 + 0.07$$

$$= 0.8$$

Return on assets is, therefore, 3% + 0.8 (8% − 3%) = 7%

Step 3 – Calculate ßg for MT

$$ßg = ßu\left(\frac{VD}{VE}\right)(ßu - ßd)$$

$$= 0.8 + \left(\frac{300}{900}\right)(0.8 - 0.2)$$

$$= 0.8 + 0.2$$

$$= 1.0$$

Strictly, it is market values that should be used, but these are not readily available. FS's market and book values of equity are the same, therefore using MT's book value of equity and debt seems an acceptable approximation.

Step 4 – Calculate Re for MT

If MT's equity beta is 1, then the expected cost of equity for MT is the same as for the market, which is 8% (3% + 1(8% − 3%)).

(ii) The first step is to attempt to place a value, or range of values, on MT. There are four methods that can be considered: asset value, earnings (or market) value based on an estimated P/E ratio, dividend-based value using the DVM and shareholder value using net present value of future cash flows. These last two methods could also be combined with a calculation of a discount rate using the CAPM. Each method is considered in turn, ignoring, in the first instance, the estimated €200 m synergy savings.

Asset value

There is €900 m (€1,415 − €515) in net assets at book values as at 30 June 2005. This would rise to €944.45 m at 30 June 2006 (€900 + retained earnings in 2005/06 of €44.45 [€88.9 × 50%]) taking the MT directors' earnings forecast), assuming current assets and liabilities do not change significantly. If the FS's directors' most cautious earnings estimate were taken (2% growth), then retained earnings would be €36.47 m (€71.5 × 1.02 × 50%) and the net asset value €936.47 m.

Market value using estimated P/E

We can calculate a range of values here by applying FS's P/E ratio of 11.7 to MT's 2005 earnings, forecast 2006 earnings of MT's figures and FS's more cautious estimate (to nearest €million):

Using 2005 earnings	837 = (71.5 × 11.7)
Using MT's 2006 forecast	1,040 = (88.9 × 11.7)
Using 2% growth on 2005	853 = (71.5 × 1.02 × 11.7)

An adjustment could be made for the following factors:

- MT is unlisted; there are arguments for both lowering and raising the P/E for this.
- There will be aspects of MT that are different from FS, not least that FS has been 'downgraded' by the market because of slower growth.

On balance, there is insufficient information to make any reasoned adjustment. An industry P/E ratio could be sought and applied, but the two points above would still need to be considered.

Examiner's note:

Any sensible adjustment by candidates would gain credit.

Cash flows using CAPM

We do not have enough information to calculate a NPV of the entity using forecast cash flows, but this is the theoretically correct method. An exercise should be carried out to forecast cash flows for the next 5–10 years and calculate a more accurate discount rate.

Examiner's note:

This method was not implied by the question, as sufficient information was not available, but credit would be given to candidates who provided sensible comments.

Dividend valuation model

There are a number of possible valuations using this model, depending on which 2006 forecast is more acceptable.

If we take MT's 2006 forecast as accurate, then any calculation of g would make the model unworkable. The growth between 2005 and 2006 is 24%; the average growth over the last three years can be calculated as follows:

Historic growth rate

$$88.9 = 55.5(I + g)3$$

$$I + g = \sqrt[3]{1.6018}$$

$$I + g = 1.17$$

$$g = 17\%$$

This exceeds the cost of equity, which would make the dividend valuation model unusable.

Notes:

1. Using a simple average is also close to 17% and would gain credit.
2. The super-growth version of the DVM could be used, but this is time-consuming and not expected here. Also, earnings will be affected by any changes in the tax rate, but this is unlikely to have a significant effect on dividend growth *percentage.*

Assuming FS's more cautious forecast of between 2% and 4% growth over 2005 and using the constant growth version of the model (Po = D1 /ke − g) we would get:

DO (in 2005) is €71.5 m × 50% = €35.75 m

Value assuming

2% growth	4% growth
= 35.75 × 1.02/0.08 − 0.02	35.75 × 1.04/0.08 − 0.04
= €608 m	€930 m

Using 2% growth provides a value less than the asset value and unlikely to be indicative of the market value of the entity at all.

The range of values, to the nearest €million, excluding the estimated value of the synergies that would arise from the acquisition is therefore as follows:

All figures in €millions

Asset values	936−944
Market values using FS P/E	837−1,040
Dividend valuation model values	608−930

The relatively high value given by net assets, compared to the other methods of valuation, suggests MT would command a significantly higher P/E ratio than FS and that the MT directors' earnings forecast may not be over-optimistic after all, especially when synergistic benefits are taken into account.

Bidding strategy

This is likely to be an agreed bid, so there is no reason why FS cannot ask for more information before making its initial offer. However, given that MT have already made available 'financial forecasts and other strategic documentation', they may not be prepared to supply anything more before an initial bid is received.

FS should assume a two-stage bid; an initial offer that is not so low that MT will refuse further negotiations and a second 'final' offer. The maximum FS should be prepared to pay depends on what it genuinely believes is the growth rate for MT and whether the estimated synergies are realistically achievable. A suggestion is therefore an initial bid of (say) around €950 m with a maximum bid of (say) €1,250 m. MT of course will not be aware of the estimated value of synergies, although they may have done their own sums and made an educated guess of what their entity is worth to FS.

It is notable that this bid has been 'engineered' by the entity's bank. Clearly, the bank has a vested interest. FS should revisit its corporate objectives and strategies and look at the acquisition from first principles: does the operational and strategic fit make sense in the context of the entity's objectives?

> **Examiner's note:**
>
> Any sensible figures used by candidates will gain credit, for example adding the estimated synergy value at each stage of the valuations rather than at the summary stage, or using MT's forecasts, rather than FS's in the DVM, but the test here is to understand the difficulties of valuation and the key role of non-symmetric information and negotiation in the bidding process.

(iii) *Methods of financing*

CASH

According to the latest balance sheet FS has cash at bank of €250 m, plus (possibly) the €65 m cash MT has in its balance sheet. Even assuming these cash balances are still available post-takeover €315 m is insufficient to purchase MT. FS therefore will need to raise new debt to finance the cash purchase (and will need short-term financing to cover the total payment in advance of acquiring MT and its cash balances). The main advantages of debt are the tax relief available on interest payments and the fact that the EPS of FS's shareholders will not be diluted, as compared with an issue of shares or a rights issue. The tax benefit is a genuine one, but the EPS dilution argument is spurious. The dilution will b e short term provided the acquisition is financially sound and the investment is a positive NPV, the EPS effect is immaterial. However, this message needs to be fully explained and quantified to shareholders and the market.

The potential disadvantages to consider about new debt are the effects on gearing and the implications for cost of capital and credit rating.

In respect of MT's shareholders, the benefits are that they know exactly what they are getting, but the disadvantage could be an immediate tax liability on the gain.

SHARES

Assuming MT accepted a price of around €284 (maximum bid as above divided by number of shares in issue – 1,250/440) this would suggest a share exchange of approximately 1 FS for 1.25 MT. FS would need to issue approximately 350 m shares. The entity's gearing, and probably cost of capital, would fall, but these are unlikely to be significant issues.

It also implies that MT's shareholders will own around 45% of the equity of the new entity.

The key factor will be whether MT's shareholders will accept FS shares and what they might do with them afterwards. The reason for the sale of the entity might be that the shareholders want to liquidate some of their investment. If they accept FS shares they might wish to sell them immediately (and accept a tax liability on the gain).

This has two possible consequences for FS:

1. If large numbers of FS shares are offered for sale on the market, this would depress the share price unless there are many willing buyers.
2. If one or a group of MT shareholders sells to one large third party buyer, this could form the platform for a bid for FS.

Other factors that could be considered are the administrative costs and difficulties of issuing new equity and control – although this is probably not an issue here.

A choice of cash or shares might be popular with MT's shareholders, but creates uncertainty for FS in terms of forecasting gearing and cash required after MT's shareholders have decided what they will accept.

Question 8 – VCI

(a) (i) **Calculations**

Calculation of dividends and retained earnings:

	$ million
Revenue	105.00
Profit before interest and tax	28.83
Interest (15.0 × 7%)	1.05
Profit after interest before tax	27.78
Tax at 28%	7.78
Earnings	20.00
Dividends at 40%	8.00
Retained earnings	12.00

Valuation assuming constant growth of 6%

Value = D1/(Ke−g)

Ke @	10%	15%
	($8.00 m × 1.06)/(0.10 − 0.06)	($8.00 m × 1.06)/(0.15 − 0.06)
	$212 m	$94 m
Value per share $ (22,500,000 shares in issue)	9.42	4.19
Shares to issue to VCI	2,653,928 ($25 m/9.42)	5,966,587 ($25 m/4.19)
Total shares in issue after new issue	25,153,928	28,466,587
Percentage owned by VCI	10.6 (2.654/25.154 × 100)	21.0 (5.967/28.467 × 100)

The calculations suggest YZ would need to issue between approximately 2.7 and 6 m new shares depending on the valuation accepted. This would result in VCI owning between around 11% and 21% of YZ. Even 21% is not a particularly high percentage, assuming this does not give VCI the highest single shareholding. If this were the case, then YZ is vulnerable to the level of control VCI could exert on its management.

(ii) **Exit strategies**

- Sell back to YZ shareholders, perhaps via a MBO. As founding shareholders they may value the business more highly than a third party investor. This is an advantage for VCI and provides VCI with a good base to negotiate a higher price. This might be a disadvantage to YZ shareholders, who also might not be in a position to raise the finance.

- Push YZ to apply for a stock market listing – YZ is too small for a main market listing, so it would have to be on the secondary market – and then sell on the open market. This can be an administratively lengthy and expensive process. Also, YZ may not wish to make available the percentage of shares necessary to allow a market in its shares. However, there would be many advantages of a listing at this stage in YZ's development.
- If VCI is seeking a quick sale, it may be easier to sell to a ready buyer, for example a trade sale, although this might infer a lower price for this speed and ease of disposal. YZ may not be happy with the new shareholder unless it has some right of veto built into the initial deal with VCI.

Some comment that VCI is unlikely to achieve its required rate of return given YZ's growth rate would gain credit.

Some calculations are also possible, for example at the 15% cost of equity, \$25m buys VCI a 21% stake in the company. If the pre-tax earnings for the year to 31 March 2007 are \$27.78m × 1.06 = \$29.45m, less 21% of this figure is VCI's, that is \$6.18m. This would be a 6.18/25 = 25% return, less than the 30% sought. At the 10% cost of capital share valuation, VCI would only attract 11% of the earnings, \$3.24m, and a return of 13%.

(b) **VCI financing versus long-term debt**

Advantages

- Money appears to be readily available.
- VCI may bring useful management expertise and, possibly, take a seat on the board (could also be seen as a disadvantage/interference by YZ).
- Reduces rather than increases gearing.

Disadvantages

- VCI may want more control than management wish to give and may push for higher risk strategies than YZ is comfortable with to allow for its required rate of return.
- It may ask for a seat on the board (which could be an advantage, as noted above).
- VCI may eventually sell shares to an unwanted (to YZ) buyer, or push for an early flotation.
- No tax advantages on dividend payments, compared with debt.
- Difficulty of valuing shares: in the circumstances here we are valuing only part of the entity and estimates of value might need to be adjusted for a part-sale. Any adjustment will inevitably be subjective, but in some ways it is no different from flotation where founding shareholders issue less than 50% in order to retain control.
- There may be higher set up fees.

YZ has high gearing based on book values and appears dangerously illiquid, with a current ratio of less than 1. Borrowing from a bank is likely to be difficult and expensive in these circumstances. However, although YZ is 'well established', which meets one of VCI's investment criteria, it has lower growth than would normally be expected by venture capitalists. New finance from either route might therefore be problematic. Putting its finances in order might be a pre-requisite for additional funding from any source.

Part 4

Investment Decisions and Project Control

7

Investment Appraisal Techniques

Investment Appraisal Techniques

7

Appraisal methods

Payback period

The payback period is the time taken to recoup the initial investment (in cash terms).

Advantages	*Disadvantages*
Use cash	No account of time value of money
Emphasises liquidity	Ignores cash flows after payback period
Simple	

Accounting rate of return (ARR)

$$\text{ARR} = \frac{\text{Average annual profit}}{\text{Investment}}$$

Although normally calculated on initial investment, longer projects may be assessed based on average investment. This is the net book value halfway through the project's life.

Advantages	*Disadvantages*
Similar approach to ROCE	No account of time value of money
Uses accounting figures	Needs a target percentage
	Percentages are relative and misleading in comparisons

Net present value

NPV = present value of cash inflows − present value of cash outflows

Advantages	*Disadvantages*
Takes account of time value of money	Estimates of discount rate
Theoretical link to shareholders wealth	Not easily understood
Looks at cash and considers whole project	Does not build in all risks
Builds risk into discount rate	

Internal rate of return

This is the return the project gives, on a discounted cash-flow basis. It can be calculated by finding the discount rate which would completely absorb the returns from the project and give an NPV of zero.

This can be estimated using two discount rates and their NPVs, using the formulae

$$IRR = r_1 + (r_2 - r_1)\frac{(NPV_1)}{NPV_1 - NPV_2}$$

Advantages	*Disadvantages*
Takes account of time value of money	Can have multiple IRR (up to as many as changes in sign of cash flow)
Does not rely on exact estimate of cost of capital	Percentage is relative No direct connection to shareholders wealth Not designed for comparing projects

Conflict between NPV and IRR

When choosing between two mutually exclusive projects, you may get conflicting results with NPV and IRR. Where this is the case choose the project with the higher NPV.

Alternatively, a modified IRR can be used, which compounds all future cash flows to the final year at the cost of capital. It then calculates the IRR based on the initial investment and the single final value representing all other cash flows.

Asset replacement

- Identify all the cash flows associated with purchasing the asset, the initial cost, maintenance charges and scrap value.
- Calculate the present value of the cash flows.
- Calculate the Annual Equivalent Cost of holding the asset over its entire life:

  $$AEC = \frac{NPV}{CDF}$$

  where CDF = cumulative discount factor
- Repeat this for each possible length of asset life. The optimum replacement cycle will be that which has the lowest annual equivalent cost.

Capital rationing

Single period capital rationing occurs when there is inadequate funding to finance all of the initial investment needed to undertake all positive net present value projects, but finance is freely available in subsequent years.

Projects can either be divisible, that is the whole or any fraction of the project can be undertaken, or indivisible, that is only the whole project can be undertaken.

A summary of possible situations and approaches is as follows:

Divisible projects	Maximise NPV per £ invested (using profitability index).
Indivisible projects	Consider, by trial and error, the NPV of the different possible combinations.

Questions

Question 1 – ZX Rationing

The company is considering three other investment opportunities. The initial capital investment required, the NPVs and duration of these three projects are as follows:

	Initial investment £m	*NPV* £m	*Duration Years*
Project 1	3.85	0.85	3
Project 2	4.25	0.90	4
Project 3	2.95	0.68	2

However, resource constraints mean that the company cannot invest in all three projects. It wishes to restrict investment to £7.5 m.

Notes:

- The projects are not divisible.
- The company has used its cost of capital of 14% to evaluate all three investments.
- Any surplus cash could be invested in the money market at 6%.
- Assume all rates in this part of the question are net of tax.

Requirement

Discuss and recommend, with reasons, which project(s) should be undertaken.

(15 marks)

Question 2 – Expansion

The directors of XYZ plc wish to expand the company's operations. However, they are not prepared to borrow at the present time to finance capital investment. The directors have therefore decided to use the company's cash resources for the expansion programme.

Three possible investment opportunities have been identified. Only £400,000 is available in cash and the directors intend to limit their capital expenditure over the next 12 months to this amount. The projects are not divisible (i.e. cannot be scaled down) and none of them can be postponed. The following cash flows do not allow for inflation which is expected to be 10% per annum constant for the foreseeable future.

Expected net cash flows (including residual values)

Project	Initial Investment	Year 1	Year 2	Year 3
	£	£	£	£
A	−350,000	95,000	110,000	200,000
B	−105,000	45,000	45,000	45,000
C	−35,000	−40,000	−25,000	125,000

The company's shareholders currently require a return of 15% nominal on their investment for any project of a similar risk to the current operations.

Ignore taxation for any projects of a similar risk to the current operations.

Requirements

(a) (i) Calculate the expected net present value and profitability indexes of the three projects, and

(ii) comment on which project(s) should be chosen for investment, assuming the company can invest surplus cash in the money market at 10% (*Note:* You should assume that the £400,000 expenditure limit is the absolute maximum the company wishes to spend).

(12 marks)

(b) Discuss whether the company's decision not to borrow, thereby limiting investment expenditure, is in the best interests of its shareholders.

(13 marks)
(Total = 25 marks)

Question 3 – RST

RST is a publicly owned and funded health organisation based in the Far East. It is reviewing a number of interesting possibilities for new development projects in the area and has narrowed down the choice to the five projects detailed below. RST is aware that government budget restrictions may be tighter in a year's time and so does not want to commit to a capital budget of more than $30m in Year 1. In addition, any project cash inflows in Year 1 may be used to fund capital expenditure in that year. There is sufficient capital budget remaining in Year 0 to enable all projects to be undertaken. Under government funding rules, any unused capital in Year 0 cannot be carried over to Year 1 and no interest may be earned on unused capital. No borrowings are permitted.

RST assesses capital projects at a hurdle rate of 15% based on the equity beta of health-based companies in the private sector.

	Cash outflows		*Cash inflows*
	Year 0	*Year 1*	
Project	*$ million*	*$ million*	*$ million*
A	9	16	4 from Year 1 in perpetuity
B	10	10	4 from Year 2 in perpetuity
C	10	12	5 in Years 1 to 10
D	8	5	6 in Years 3 to 7
E	9	8	2 in Years 1 to 5; 5 in Years 6 to 15

Notes:

- the projects are not divisible
- each project can be undertaken only once
- ignore tax.

Requirements

(a) Advise RST on the best combination of projects based on an evaluation of each project on the basis of both:

(i) NPV of cash flows;
(ii) a profitability index for use in this capital rationing analysis.

(15 marks)

(b) Discuss

(i) whether or not capital rationing techniques based on NPV analysis are appropriate for a publicly owned entity such as RST.

(5 marks)

(ii) as a publicly owned entity, what other factors RST should consider and what other analysis it should undertake before making a final decision on which project(s) to accept.

(5 marks)
(Total = 25 marks)

Question 4 – CD Furniture

CD is a furniture manufacturer based in the UK. It manufactures a limited range of furniture products to a very high quality and sells to a small number of retail outlets worldwide.

At a recent meeting with one of its major customers it became clear that the market is changing and the final consumer of CD's products is now more interested in variety and choice rather than exclusivity and exceptional quality.

CD is therefore reviewing two mutually exclusive alternatives to apply to a selection of its products:

Alternative 1

To continue to manufacture, but expand its product range and reduce its quality. The net present value (NPV), internal rate of return (IRR) and modified internal rate of return (MIRR) for this alternative have already been calculated as follows:

NPV	=	£1.45 m using a nominal discount rate of 9%
IRR	=	10.5%
MIRR	=	Approximately 13.2%

Alternative 2

To import furniture carcasses in 'flat packs' from the USA. The imports would be in a variety of types of wood and unvarnished. CD would buy in bulk from its US suppliers, assemble and varnish the furniture and re-sell, mainly to existing customers. An initial investigation into potential sources of supply and costs of transportation has already been carried out by a consultancy entity at a cost of £75,000.

CD's Finance Director has provided estimates of net sterling and US$ cash flows for this alternative. These net cash flows, in *real* terms, are shown below.

Year	*0*	*1*	*2*	*3*
US$m	−25.00	2.60	3.80	4.10
£m	0	3.70	4.20	4.60

The following information is relevant:

- CD evaluates all its investments using nominal Sterling cash flows and a nominal discount rate. All non-UK customers are invoiced in US$. US$ nominal cash flows are converted to Sterling at the forward rate and discounted at the UK nominal rate;
- For the purposes of evaluation, assume the entity has a three-year time horizon for investment appraisals;
- Based on recent economic forecasts, inflation rates in the US are expected to be constant at 4% per annum. UK inflation rates are expected to be 3% per annum. The current exchange rate is £1 = US$1.6.

Note: Ignore taxation.

Requirements

Assume that you are the Financial Manager of CD.

(i) Calculate the net present value (NPV), internal rate of return (IRR) and (approximate) modified internal rate of return (MIRR) of alternative 2.

(12 marks)

(ii) Briefly discuss the appropriateness and possible advantages of providing MIRRs for the evaluation of the two alternatives.

(4 marks)

(iii) Evaluate the two alternatives and recommend which alternative the entity should choose. Include in your answer some discussion about what other criteria could or should be considered before a final decision is taken.

(9 marks)
(Total = 25 marks)

A report format is **not** required for this question.

Answers

Question 1 – ZX rationing

Possible combinations	*Investment*	*NPV*
1 and 3	£6.8 m	£1.53 m
2 and 3	£7.2 m	£1.58 m

Therefore, as profits are indivisible, we should invest in projects 2 and 3; this will leave £0.3 m excess cash which can be put to the money market for the short term. This is not a long-term option, however, as the return is below that required by shareholders.

As all three projects have positive NPVs, it would be sensible to look for additional funds, or to lift its restrictions, so that all can be undertaken for the additional £3.55 m.

The company has used 14% to assess all three projects, but they might have different risk characteristics which would suggest different required returns.

If the projects had been divisible, the decision would be different:

Project	*NPV/£ invested*
1	0.22
2	0.21
3	0.23

This would suggest that projects 3 and 1 should be undertaken, with the remaining finance of £0.7 m used to do approximately 16% of project 2, giving an overall NPV of £1.68 m.

Question 2 – Expansion

(a)

(i) *PV of future cash flows*

In £'000	*A*		*B*		*C*	
t_1	$95 \times 1.1/1.15$	= 91	$45 \times 1.1/1.15$	= 43	$(40) \times (1.1/1.15)$	= (38)
t_2	$110 \times (1.1/1.15)^2$	= 101	$45 \times (1.1/1.15)^2$	= 41	$(25) \times (1.1/1.15)^2$	= (23)
t_3	$200 \times (1.1/1.15)^3$	= 175	$45 \times (1.1/1.15)^3$	= 39	$125 \times (1.1/1.15)^3$	= 109
		367		123		43
t_0 Investment		(350)		(105)		(35)
NPV		17		18		13
Profitability Index		1.05		1.17		1.37

(ii) *Decision*

As the shareholders require 15%, it is not worthwhile putting money on deposit at 10% (it would have a negative NPV).

It should therefore be returned to the shareholders in the form of dividends or share buybacks. In practice this may seem unlikely, and it is likely that shareholders would require a substantially lower return on a bank deposit, as it is lower risk, leading to a zero NPV: shareholders would then be indifferent as to the amount on cash put in deposit.

Possibilities	*Investment*	*NPV*
A and C	£385,000	£30,000
B and C	£140,000	£31,000

(other possibilities of A, B or C alone will obviously give less)

So invest in projects B and C.

(b) **The interests of the shareholders**

A company has to balance its investment decisions against the financing decision, either using external finance or internal funds, possibly impacting on the dividend policy.

If we assume shareholders' best interests to mean maximising shareholder wealth via the share price, the company would want to undertake all positive NPV projects if it had sufficient finance. This, in theory in an efficient market, would increase the share price; however, raising external finance will involve issue costs which will reduce shareholder value, and reducing the level of dividends might reduce the share price if shareholders were relying on this cash stream.

Whether the company has arrived at the right compromise in committing the expenditure to £400,000 and not borrowing will depend on a number of factors:

- The volatility of the company's operating cash flow; if these are highly volatile, additional gearing will put the returns to shareholders at risk and thus increase the risk perceived and the cost of equity while decreasing the value.
- The current level of gearing, as the company may not be able to manage additional interest payments easily, and it may not be able to raise more if it has no further assets for security.
- The need to respond flexibly to situations as they arise may be important in the industry; debt financing is often long term with structural repayments and interest, which can then affect the operational choices.
- The tax position as debt interest is allowable for tax purposes but a nil tax paying position (possibly due to losses carried forward) would make additional debt finance less attractive.

Question 3 – RST

(a)

Evaluating projects is on the next page.

Selecting projects:

Consider all possible combinations of projects within the $30m capital constraint in year 1:

				Cumulative NPV $m	Net cash outflow in year 1 $m
Ranking by NPV:	C, B, A, E, D	Accept:	C, B, A	12.90	29
Ranking by PI:	C, D, E, B, A	Accept:	C, D, E, B	15.22	28
Best combination	C, D, E, B			15.22	28

Conclusion: accept projects B, C, D and E on the basis of capital rationing analysis
Justification: This is the combination of projects which offers the highest overall NPV return.

(b)

(i) Discussion of whether such analysis is appropriate for public bodies:

- Publicly-owned bodies may be subject to absolute spending constraints, unlike private entities who could normally borrow to fund an attractive project that falls outside its capital spending budget for the year. Effective allocation of capital is therefore, arguably, even more important for publicly-owned bodies than for private entities.
- The key objective of a private entity is to maximise shareholders' wealth and NPV calculations are a useful measure of the increase in shareholders' wealth created by a project; however, publicly-owned bodies will have other priorities and objectives and so a model of capital rationing based on maximising NPV may not be appropriate.

(ii) Discussion of what other factors should be considered and analysis undertaken:

- Sensitivity analysis of the impact of changes in key underlying variables to the outcome.
  - Consideration of non-financial factors such as:
  - government or self-imposed targets and priorities on such issues as type of patient care to be provided or geographic locations that are in greatest need of improved health care;
  - environmental issues;
  - staffing issues.

Evaluating projects:

Project A

		$m	*d.f.*	*NPV*
Outflows	Year 0	−9	1.000	−9.00
	Year 1	−16	0.870	13.92
Inflows	Years 1 to inf	4	6.667 (W1)	26.67
Year 1 net outflow:		**−12**		

***Profitability index against year 1 net cash flow:* (W6)** **0.31**

- second figure is based upon discounted year 1 cash flows ***or 0.36***

Project B

		$m	*d.f.*	*NPV*
Outflows	Year 0	10	1.000	−10.00
	Year 1	10	0.870	−8.70
Inflows	Years 2 to inf	4	5.797 (*W*2)	23.19
				4.49
Year 1 net outflow:		**−10**		

Profitability index against year 1 net cash flow: ***0.45 or 0.52***

Project C

		$m	*d.f.*	*NPV*
Outflows	Year 0	−10	1.000	−10.00
	Year 1	−12	0.870	−10.44
Inflows	Years 1–10	5	5.019 (*W*3)	25.10
				4.66
Year 1 net outflow:		**−7**		

Profitability index against year 1 net cash flow: ***0.67 or 0.77***

Project D

		$m	*d.f.*	*NPV*
Outflows	Year 0	−8	1.000	−8.00
	Year 1	−5	0.870	−4.35
Inflows	Years 3–7	6	2.534 (*W*4)	15.20
Year 1 net outflow:		**−5**		**2.85**

Profitability index against year 1 net cash flow: ***0.57 or 0.66***

Project E

		$m	*d.f.*	*NPV*
Outflows	Year 0	−9	1.000	−9.00
	Year 1	−8	0.870	−6.96
Inflows	Years 1–5	2	3.352	6.70
	Years 6–15	5	2.495 (*W*5)	12.48
Year 1 net outflow:		**−6**		

Profitability index against year 1 net cash flow: ***0.54 or 0.62***

Workings:

W1:	6.667 = 1/0.15
W2:	5.797 = (1/0.15)/1.15
W3:	5.019 = af (t = 10, r = 15)
W4:	2.534 = 4.160 − 1.626
	= af (t = 7, r = 15) − af (t = 2, r = 15)
W5:	2.495 = 5.847 − 3.352
	= af (t = 15, r = 15) − af (t = 5, r = 15)
W6:	0.31 = 3.75/12
	Or: 0.36 = 3.75/(12/1.15)

Question 4 – CD Furniture

(i) **Calculations of NPV, IRR and MIRR for alternative 2**

Forward rates

Spot	= 1.6
1 year forward	= 1.616 (1.6 × (1.04/1.03))
2 years forward	= 1.631 (1.615 × (1.04/1.03))
3 years forward	= 1.647(1.631 × (1.04/1.03))

Calculation of NPV

Year:	*0*	*1*	2	3
All figures in millions				
US$ cash flows	−25.00	2.60	3.80	4.10
Inflated at 4% per annum	−25.00	2.70	4.11	4.61
Converted to £ at	1.600	1.616	1.631	1.647
£	−15.63	1.67	2.52	2.80
£ cash flows		3.70	4.20	4.60
Inflated at 3% per annum		3.81	4.46	5.03
Total cash flows £	15.63	5.48	6.98	7.83
DF @ 9%	1	0.917	0.842	0.772
DCFs	−15.63	5.03	5.88	6.04

NPV = £1.32 m

Calculation of IRR

DF @ 14%		1	0.877	0.769	0.675
DCFs	−15.63	4.81	5.37	5.29	

NPV = £20.16 m

IRR by interpolation is calculated as follows:

$$9\% + \left[\frac{1.32}{(1.32 + 0.16)} \times (14\% - 9\%)\right]$$

$$\approx 9\% + 4.5\% = 13.5\%$$

However, the spread between the two rates is a long way apart for the result to be interpreted with accuracy.

Calculation of MIRR

		At 9% reinvestment rate	
Year	*Cash flow*	*Factor*	*£m*
1	5.48	1.1881	6.51
2	6.98	1.090	7.61
3	7.83	1	7.83
Total			21.95

MIRR = 15.63/21.95 = 0.712
From tables this is 12%

(ii) **Comments on MIRR**

The process for calculating MIRR is:

- An outflow in year 0 and a single inflow at the end of the project life is assumed.
- Cash flows after the initial investment are converted to a single cash inflow by assuming that the cash flows are reinvested at, usually, the cost of capital.
- MIRR is calculated by dividing the outflow by the single inflow, using PV tables and interpolation to arrive at the discount rate, or MIRR.

MIRR is intended to address some of the deficiencies of IRR, for example:

- It eliminates the possibility of multiple rates of return.
- It addresses the reinvestment issue.
- MIRR rankings are consistent with the NPV rule, which is not always the case with IRR.

However, there are weaknesses:

- If the reinvestment rate is greater than the cost of capital, then MIRR will underestimate the project's true return.
- The determination of the life of the project can have a significant effect on the actual MIRR if the difference between the project's IRR and the entity's cost of capital is large.
- The MIRR, like IRR, is biased towards projects with short payback periods.
- It does not appear to be understood or used extensively in practice.
- In the case here, we are evaluating two mutually exclusive projects. The argument for using MIRR is therefore weak.

Examiner's note:

The above discussion of MIRR was more than expected from a candidate, but some indication of an understanding of the key criteria for MIRR was expected.

(iii) **Recommendation**

Summary:

	Alternative 1	*Alternative 2*
NPV	£1.45 m	£1.32 m
IRR	10.5%	13.5%
MIRR	13.2%	12.0%

On the basis of NPV and MIRR the choice is for alternative 1. On the basis of IRR, alternative 2 is more advantageous. The main points to consider in respect of these criteria are:

- Theoretically, NPV is superior as shareholder wealth will increase by this amount. This criterion alone should recommend alternative 1.
- IRR has certain technical difficulties, although in reality these have little significance. Its advantage is that is it more easily understood by non-finance managers. This is not an argument for using it in preference to NPV.
- MIRR overcomes some of the technical difficulties of IRR, as explained below, but is little used and more difficult to understand.

Other criteria to consider are:

- Has a real evaluation of the market/customer requirements been carried out? Only one customer has been consulted as far as we know.
- Cash flows beyond three years need to be estimated – also, how has the FD made his estimates?
- What is the effect on other stakeholders if alternative 2 was chosen, for example employees and local suppliers?
- Is the investment consistent with the entity's objectives?
- Theory of interest rate parity has its weaknesses in practice. Some sensitivity analysis of the effect of different forward exchange rates, and therefore discount rate for alternative 2, could be attempted.
- Payback could also be considered. The information in the question is insufficient to make comparisons between the two alternatives.

The recommendation on purely financial grounds is marginal, so if using NPV as the main criterion the choice should be for alternative 1, but other criteria, including non-financial considerations, should be taken into account before a final decision is made.

8

Advanced Investment Appraisal Techniques

Advanced Investment Appraisal Techniques

8

Relevant costs in a net present value

In making investment decisions, relevant costs are crucial. We need to identify ***future, incremental cash flows*** so that we can assess the impact on the business of undertaking the project compared with not doing so:

Future. Ignore 'sunk' costs (i.e. costs already incurred) as they will not change no matter what decision is taken.

Incremental. Only include the extra cash flows incurred or earned by undertaking the project (including all the knock-on results).

Cash. Only include additional cash flows for the company as a whole, so exclude depreciation (include the full cash expense) and absorbed overheads.

Inflation

If the cash flows are not yet inflated by their specific inflation rates, then we need to calculate the actual cash payment or receipt that will take place.

The cost of capital must also include an allowance for general inflation (the money cost of capital):

$$(1 + m) = (1 + i_g) \times (1 + r)$$

where

m = money cost of capital
i_g = general inflation rate (e.g. RPI)
r = 'real' cost of capital (i.e. excludes inflation)

An alternative approach is not to include inflation but to then exclude the general inflation expected from the cost of capital (i.e. deduce r above, given m and i_g).

Taxation

There are two effects caused by tax for our purposes – tax on operating cash flows and capital allowances.

Assume tax on operating cash flows arises with a 1-year delay unless told otherwise.

Assume capital allowances are taken as soon as possible, that is assume the asset is purchased on the last day of the year, unless told otherwise. Therefore, the capital allowance is obtained immediately and the tax saved 1 year later.

Working capital

Remember that the cash flows to include are the amounts needed to take the working capital up (or down) to the level required for the forthcoming year. Working capital does not attract any tax relief so should be calculated after the tax impacts.

Uncertainty

All investment appraisal projects have to deal with uncertainty; cash flows have to be forecast, tax rates estimated for the whole project and discount rates have to be estimated.

Such uncertainty can be allowed for by using:

An increased discount rate – to reflect the amount of risk associated with the cash flows.

Certainty equivalents to reduce the value of the cash flows.

Sensitivity analysis to look at how the NPV of the project changes when one factor is changed and hence identify the crucial estimates.

To calculate the sensitivity of a cash-flow estimate:

$$\%\ \text{Sensitivity} = \frac{\text{NPV}}{\text{PV cash flow considered}}$$

To calculate the sensitivity to sales volume, use contribution as the denominator in the above formula.

To calculate the sensitivity to the discount rate, calculate the IRR.

Remember it can only deal with one changing variable at a time and the result does not indicate the likelihood of the variable changing, it only quantifies the amount by which the variable can change.

Expected values can be used if probabilities are estimated; alternatively the various possible outcomes can be calculated and the probability of each assessed.

Capital investment real options

Traditional NPV only includes predictable cash flows. In some situations this may exclude considerable benefits or costs, often of a strategic nature, which cannot be estimated, such as options on timing or abandonment and other market benefits.

It can be very difficult to value these options, but the NPV clearly does not take account of all the project consequences and needs to be balanced against these more qualitative factors.

Post-implementation audits

As estimates are used in the assessment of projects, it is sensible to monitor performance against estimates, and to introduce greater realism into future estimates.

? Questions

Question 1 – Rock (Practice Question)

Rock Ltd invests £100,000, and proposes to make exclusive rocking chairs for 10 years. The company will plan to make 250 chairs per annum, earning a contribution of £151 per chair. Fixed costs are expected to be £17,500 per annum and the scrap value of machinery after 10 years is forecast at £10,000.

Ignore tax and writing down allowances, and use a discount rate of 15%.

Calculate the NPV and the sensitivity to the:

- initial investment
- volume
- contribution
- fixed costs
- scrap.

Question 2 – X training

All of the 100 accountants employed by X Ltd are offered the opportunity to attend six training courses per year. Each course lasts for several days and requires the delegates to travel to a specially selected hotel for the training. The current costs incurred for each course are:

Delegate costs

	£ per delegate per course
Travel	200
Accommodation, food and drink	670
	870

It is expected that the current delegate costs will increase by 5% per annum.

Course costs

	£ per course
Room hire	1,500
Trainers	6,000
Course material	2,000
Equipment hire	1,500
Course administration	750
	11,750

It is expected that the current course costs will increase by 2.5% per annum.

The Human Resources Director of X Ltd is concerned at the level of costs that these courses incur and has recently read an article about the use of the Internet for the delivery of training courses (e-learning). She decided to hire an external consultant at a cost of £5,000 to advise the company on how to implement an e-learning solution. The consultant prepared a report which detailed the costs of implementing and running an e-learning solution:

	Notes	£
Computer hardware	(1)	1,500,000
Software licences	(2)	35,000 pa
Technical Manager	(3)	30,000 pa
Camera and sound crew	(4)	4,000 per course
Trainers and course material	(5)	2,000 per course
Broadband connection	(6)	300 per delegate per annum

Notes

1. The computer hardware will be depreciated on a straight-line basis over 5 years. The scrap value at the end of the 5 years is expected to be £50,000.
2. The company would sign a software licence agreement which fixes the annual software licence fee for 5 years. This fee is payable in advance.
3. An employee working in the IT Department currently earning £20,000 per annum will be promoted to Technical Manager for this project. This employee's position will be replaced. The salary of the Technical Manager is expected to increase by 6% per annum.
4. The company supplying the camera and sound crew for recording the courses for Internet delivery has agreed to hold its current level of pricing for the first 2 years but then it will increase costs by 6% per annum. All courses will be recorded in the first quarter of the year of delivery.
5. The trainers will charge a fixed fee of £2,000 per course for the delivery and course material in the first year and expect to increase this by 6% per annum thereafter. The preparation of the course material and the recording of the trainers delivering the courses will take place in the first quarter of the year of delivery.
6. All of the accountants utilising the training courses will be offered £300 towards broadband costs which will allow them to access the courses from home. They will claim this expense annually in arrears. Broadband costs are expected to decrease by 5% per annum after the first year as it becomes more widely used by Internet users.

X Ltd uses a 14% cost of capital to appraise projects of this nature.

Ignore taxation.

Requirements

As the Management Accountant for X Ltd,

(a) Prepare a financial evaluation of the options available to the company and advise the directors on the best course of action to take, from a purely financial point of view. (Your answer should state any assumptions you have made.)

(16 marks)

(b) (i) Using the annual equivalent technique, calculate the breakeven number of delegates per annum taking each of the six e-learning courses that is required to justify the implementation of the e-learning solution. (Note that you should assume that the number of delegates taking the e-learning courses will be the same in each of the 5 years.)

(6 marks)

(ii) Comment on the implementations of the breakeven number you have calculated in your answer to **(b)** (i).

(3 marks)
(Total = 25 marks)

Question 3 – HS and IT

HS and IT are both manufacturing companies which trade in similar industries. However, HS is a much larger company with more diversified markets, and trades internationally. By comparison, IT trades solely in its domestic market. Comparative data on these two companies is as follows:

	HS	IT
Sales revenue	US$2.5 billion	US$1.2 m
Gross profit margin	28%	17%
Debt: equity	40%	10%
Shares in issue	200 m	2,000
Number of shareholders	Many	Few
Share price	US$12.60	Not available

Requirement

Compare and evaluate the usefulness or impact of the following variables in the investment appraisal process for these two companies:

1 The use of weighted average cost of capital (WACC) as a discount rate.
2 The use of certainty equivalents compared with using an adjusted discount rate in evaluating the cash flow.
3 The use of payback or accounting rate of return compared with DCF techniques.
4 The influence and effects of taxation on their investment decisions.

(Each item carries up to 7 marks to a maximum of 25 for all four.)

(Total = 25 marks)

Question 4 – SS

SS Ltd is an Internet service provider and also stores and transmits client data over the Internet via its server infrastructure. SS Ltd generates approximately £100,000 in contribution each year from these services to clients.

Because of technical advances in information technology, the existing server infrastructure will shortly become obsolete, and the company is considering what to do. The maintenance of this server infrastructure costs £24,000 per annum and is paid in advance at the beginning of each year. The server infrastructure has been fully written off but has a scrap value of £3,000. A technical consultant hired at a cost of £5,000, prepared a report outlining that two possible replacement server infrastructures are available on the market. The details of each alternative are as follows:

	Alternative 1	*Alternative 2*
Initial cost	£100,000	£100,000
Estimated useful life	3 years	5 years
Scrap value	£5,000	£3,000
Annual maintenance costs (in advance)	£24,000	£30,000
Annual contributions	£100,000	£105,000

SS Ltd incurs 30% tax on corporate profits. Writing down allowances are allowed at 25% each year on a reducing balance basis. At the end of the server infrastructure's life, a balancing charge or allowance will arise equal to the difference between the scrap proceeds and the tax written down value. Corporation tax is to be paid in two equal instalments: one in the year that profits are earned and the other in the following year.

SS Ltd's after-tax nominal (money) discount rate is 12%.

You can assume that all cash flows occur at the end of each year unless otherwise stated.

Requirements

(a) Calculate for each alternative the net present value and annual equivalent cost. Advise senior management which server infrastructure to purchase, stating any assumptions you have made.

(15 marks)

(b) (i) Briefly explain the purpose and limitations of sensitivity analysis in relation to investment appraisal.

(4 marks)

(ii) Calculate the sensitivity of your recommendation to changes in the contribution generated by Alternative 1, and discuss its relevance to the decision.

(6 marks)
(Total = 25 marks)

Question 5

Assume that you have been appointed finance director of Breckall plc. The company is considering investing in the production of an electronic security device, with an expected market life of 5 years.

The previous finance director has undertaken an analysis of the proposed project; the main features of his analysis are shown below.

He has recommended that the project should not be undertaken because the estimated annual ARR is only 12.3%.

Proposed Electronic Security Device Project

£'000

Year→	*0*	*1*	*2*	*3*	*4*	*5*
Investment in depreciable fixed assets	4,500					
Cumulative investment in working capital	300	400	500	600	700	700
Revenue		3,500	4,900	5,320	5,740	5,320
Materials		535	750	900	1,050	900
Labour		1,070	1,500	1,800	2,100	1,800
Overhead		50	100	100	100	100
Interest		576	576	576	576	576
Depreciation		900	900	900	900	900
		3,131	3,826	4,276	4,276	4,726
Taxable profit		369	1,074	1,044	1,014	1,044
Taxation		129	376	365	355	365
Profit after tax		240	698	679	659	679

Total initial investment is £4,800,000.

Average annual after-tax profit is £591,000.

All of the above cash-flow and profit estimates have been prepared in terms of present-day costs and prices, as the previous finance director assumed that the sales price could be increased to compensate for any increase in costs.

You have the following additional information available:

(a) Selling prices, working capital requirements and overhead expenses are expected to increase by 5% per year.
(b) Material costs and labour costs are expected to increase by 10% per year.
(c) Tax depreciation allowances are allowable against profits at 25% per year on a reducing balance basis.
(d) Taxation on profits is at a rate of 35% payable one year in arrears.
(e) The fixed assets have no expected salvage value at the end of 5 years.
(f) The company's real after-tax weighted average cost of capital is estimated to be 8% per year, and nominal after-tax weighted average cost of capital 15% per year.

Assume that all receipts and payments arise at the end of the year to which they relate, except those in year 0, which occur immediately.

Requirements

(a) Estimate the NPV of the proposed project. State clearly any assumptions that you make. **(13 marks)**

(b) Calculate by how much the discount rate would have to change to result in a NPV of approximately zero. **(4 marks)**

(c) Describe how sensitivity analysis might be used to assist in assessing this project. What are the weaknesses of sensitivity analysis in capital investment appraisal? Briefly outline alternative techniques of incorporating risk into capital investment appraisal. **(8 marks)**

(Total marks = 25)

Answers

Question 1 – Rock

			15%	
t_0	Invt	(100,000)	1	(100,000)
t_{10}	Scrap	10,000	0.247	2,470
t_1–t_{10}	Cont	37,750	5.019	189,467
t_1–t_{10}	FC	(15,000)	5.019	(87,833)
	NPV			4,104

$$\text{Initial investment} = \frac{4,104}{100,000} = 4.1\%$$

i.e. the initial investment can increase 4.1% before the NPV becomes zero

$$\text{Volume:} \frac{4,104}{189,467} = 2.2\%$$

i.e. volume or contribution can fall 2.2% before the NPV becomes zero

$$\text{Fixed costs} = \frac{4,104}{87,833} = 4.7\%$$

i.e. fixed costs can increase 4.7% before the NPV becomes zero

$$\text{Scrap} = \frac{4,104}{2,470} = 166\%$$

i.e. the scrap proceeds have to turn negative before the NPV becomes zero!

Question 2 – X training

(a) **External training versus e-learning**

External training courses

	t_0	t_1	t_2	t_3	t_4	t_5
Delegates		548,100	575,505	604,280	634,494	666,219
Courses		72,263	74,069	75,921	77,819	79,764
		620,363	649,574	680,201	712,313	745,983
DF(14%)		0.877	0.769	0.675	0.592	0.519
PV		544,058	499,522	459,136	421,689	387,165

Total PV of costs = £2,311,570

e-learning

	t_0	t_1	t_2	t_3	t_4	t_5
Hardware	1,500,000					(50,000)
Licence	35,000	35,000	35,000	35,000	35,000	
Manager		30,000	31,800	33,708	35,730	37,874
Crew		24,000	24,000	25,440	26,966	28,584

Trainers		12,000	12,720	13,483	14,292	15,150
Connection		30,000	28,500	27,075	25,721	24,435
	1,535,000	131,000	132,020	134,706	137,709	56,043
DF (14%)	1	0.877	0.769	0.675	0.592	0.519
	1,535,000	114,887	101,523	90,927	81,524	29,086

Total PV of costs = £1,952,947

Therefore, on the basis of these calculations X Ltd should undertake the e-learning option.

Assumptions:

- The delegate and course costs for external training are the current costs and will increase, by the appropriate inflation rate, by next year.
- The consultant's fee is unavoidable and is a sunk cost.
- The Technical Managers' salary is the amount that will be paid in the first year and will inflate thereafter.
- The recording costs are assumed paid at the end of the year, even though the recording takes place in the first quarter.
- As the e-learning investment lasts 5 years, the external training has been evaluated over the same period.

(b) (i) *Breakeven*

If the company changes to e-learning, the fixed costs will be considerably higher. This will only be worthwhile if the variable cost saving more than covers the additional fixed costs.

	Fixed cost (PV)	*Variable costs (PV)*	
External training	259,048	2,052,524	(delegates)
e-learning	1,858,536	94,411	(broadband)
Difference	1,599,488	1,958,113	
Annual equivalent (divide by 3.432)	466,051	570,546	
		or £5,705	per delegate

Breakeven number of delegates = 466,051/5,705 = 81.7 or 82 delegates,

(ii) *Interpretation*

The company needs at least 82 of the 100 accountants to take up the e-learning in order to make it viable. As this is a high proportion of the 100, it would be sensible to make sure that the accountants were happy to take it up before going ahead.

Question 3 – HS and IT

1. WACC as a discount rate

The WACC represents the overall return required from the company's current operations, and should strictly only be used for investment appraisal if the project has the same business risk and is financed in the same proportions as the existing business.

However, in a big company, such as HS, a new investment may not be very large compared with the existing operations, so, if no new finance is raised, the WACC might be used as an approximation. IT, being a smaller company, might be looking at relatively larger projects and would need to use an adjusted discount rate, as discussed below, in order to assess the investment accurately.

2. **Certainty equivalents**

   Certainty equivalents take account of the risk of the project by reducing the cash flows to those which are reasonably certain, and using a risk-free rate to discount them. The difficulty is in assigning the probabilities, which are highly subjective, to these cash flows. HS might have the expertise available to undertake this, but it is unlikely that IT will.

   An adjusted discount rate is a rate which reflects the risk attached to this particular project. Again, this can lead to a subjective risk premium, but one way round this is to look for a company in the same line of business as the project. The cost of capital can then be adjusted for any differences in gearing. This is a more straightforward method and is likely to be used by IT.

3. **Payback and accounting rates return (ARR)**

   Payback period and ARR do not use discounted cash flows and are therefore not as theoretically valid as net present value for maximising shareholders' wealth. However, it is difficult to be accurate with a method such as NPV, and so a large company such as HS will probably look at a variety of methods. Often this will be NPV and the payback period. A smaller company, such as IT, will tend to rely on one method, such as payback period.

   Payback is easy to use and understand and is a useful screening process to eliminate investments with higher risk. However, it ignores the cash flows after the payback period and so does not give a complete picture.

   ARR, by using profits which spread the investment cost over the entire project, and by not discounting, can distort the result, often making the investment appear less viable.

   If HS uses a number of methods, it is likely to come to a more informed decision than IT, but this links to its more numerous shareholders and the need for a more structured approach to corporate governance.

4. **Taxation impact on investment decisions**

   Tax is a cash flow and also affects the profits generated, so it will have an impact on the investment decision whichever method is used. The impact it has will depend on the extent to which the tax cash flows change. HS is likely to have more scope for relieving taxes as it is a large company, trading internationally, and might be able to take advantage of double taxation treaties, transfer pricing and management charges, and the lower tax rates in some other countries. It might also have tax advisers, although they can be expensive.

Question 4 – SS

(a)

Alternative 1

	t_0	t_1	t_2	t_3	t_4
Contribution		100,000	100,000	100,000	
Maintenance	(24,000)	(24,000)	(24,000)		
	(24,000)	76,000	76,000	100,000	
Tax		(11,400)	(11,400)	(11,400)	
			(11,400)	(11,400)	(11,400)
Investment	(100,000)			5,000	
Tax re: CA's		3,750	2,813	7,687	
			3,750	2,813	7,687
	(124,000)	68,350	59,763	92,700	(3,713)
DF (12%)	1	0.893	0.797	0.712	0.636
PV	(124,000)	61,037	47,631	66,002	(2,361)

NPV = £48,309 so annual equivalent = 48,309/2.402 = £20,112 per annum

Alternative 2

	t_0	t_1	t_2	t_3	t_4	t_5	t_6
Contribution		105,000	105,000	105,000	105,000	105,000	
Maintenance	(30,000)	(30,000)	(30,000)	(30,000)	(30,000)		
	(30,000)	75,000	75,000	75,000	75,000	105,000	
Tax		(11,250)	(11,250)	(11,250)	(11,250)	(11,250)	
			(11,250)	(11,250)	(11,250)	(11,250)	(11,250)
Investment	(100,000)					3,000	
Tax re: CA's		3,750	2,813	2,109	1,582	4,296	
			3,750	2,813	2,109	1,582	4,296
	(130,000)	67,500	59,063	57,422	56,191	91,378	(6,954)
DF (12%)	1	0.893	0.797	0.712	0.636	0.567	0.507
	(130,000)	60,278	47,073	40,884	35,737	51,811	(3,526)

NPV = £102,257 so annual equivalent = 102,257/3.605 = £28,365 per annum

On the basis of these calculations, Alternative 2 will generate the most for the company.

(b)

(i) *Sensitivity analysis*

Sensitivity analysis attempts to identify those variables in which a small change in the estimate would lead to the decision-maker changing their mind. This might mean turning a positive NPV to a negative one, or the ranking of investments changing. Those estimates, which are crucial, can then be re-examined to ensure we are confident about them before deciding to invest.

To calculate the change needed in each variable, we alter one at a time to see how far it must move to give a negative NPV or to change the ranking. Those in which the change needed is small (say less than 10%) will be the crucial estimates.

There are two main limitations of the method. Firstly, only one input is altered at a time even though there might be a much more dramatic impact if a number of estimates proved incorrect at the same time. Secondly, the method gives information on the impact of a change in estimate, but does not attempt to predict how likely this might be.

(ii) *Changes in alternative 1 contribution*

PV of current alternative 1 contribution:	100,000 × 2.402 = 240,200
	(15,000) × 2.402 = (36,030) (tax)
	(15,000) × 2.145 = (32,175) (tax)
	£171,995

To change the choice from Alternative 2 to Alternative 1, Annual Equivalent of Alternative 1 must increase to £28,365.

This would give an overall NPV of 28,365 × 2.402 = £68,133

This is an increase in NPV of 68,133 − 48,309 = £19,824

The contribution must increase by 19,824/171,995 = 11.53% for this to happen (or by £11,526 pa).

Question 5

- This question is intended to test the candidate's ability to recognise relevant cash flows in the appraisal of capital projects, and make appropriate adjustments for price level changes in the calculation of an estimated NPV. Additionally, the candidate's knowledge of sensitivity analysis and the treatment of risk is tested.

(a) It is not appropriate to leave the cash flows in terms of present-day prices and to discount such cash flows at the real cost of capital. This would understate the entity's tax liability, as capital allowances are based upon original rather than replacement cost, and do not change in line with changing prices. The cash flows should be adjusted by the appropriate estimate of price change.

Revised estimates of revenue, expenses and tax liability (£'000)

Year	*1*	*2*	*3*	*4*	*5*
Sales (5% rise per year)	3,675	5,402	6,159	6,977	6,790
Less:					
Materials (10% rise per year)	588	907	1,198	1,537	1,449
Labour (10% rise per year)	1,177	1,815	2,396	3,075	2,899
Overheads (5% rise per year)	52	110	116	122	128
Tax depreciation allowances	1,125	844	633	475	1,423*
	2,942	3,676	4,343	5,209	5,899
Taxable income	733	1,726	1,816	1,768	891
Taxation (35%)	256	604	636	619	312

* This includes the balance of the written-down value of the fixed assets at the end of year 5, as there is no expected salvage value.

Interest is ignored, as the cost of finance is encompassed within the discount rate.

	Cash-flow estimates (£'000)						
Year	*0*	*1*	*2*	*3*	*4*	*5*	*6*
Inflows							
Revenue	–	3,675	5,402	6,159	6,977	6,790	–
Outflows							
Materials	–	588	907	1,198	1,537	1,449	–
Labour	–	1,177	1,815	2,396	3,075	2,899	–
Overheads	–	52	110	116	122	128	–
Fixed assets	4,500						
Working capital	300	120	131	144	156	(851)*	–
Taxation	–	–	256	604	636	619	312
	4,800	1,937	3,219	4,458	5,526	4,244	(312)
Net cash flows	(4,800)	1,738	2,183	1,701	1,451	2,546	(312)
Discount factors at 15%**	1.000	0.870	0.756	0.658	0.572	0.497	0.432
Present values	(4,800)	1,512	1,650	1,119	830	1,265	(135)

* Assuming that working capital is released at the end of the project.

** This discount rate, being the market rate, is assumed to incorporate 'inflation effects'. Fifteen per cent will only be appropriate as a discount rate if the project's systematic risk is similar to the systematic risk of the company as a whole.

Expected NPV is £1,441,000. On this basis it is recommended that the investment should be undertaken.

(b) Calculat ing the IRR will p roduce an NPV of zero. This can be achieved by 'trial and error'.

Year	*Cash flow*	*20% Discount*	*PV*	*27% Discount*	*PV*
0	(4,800)		(4,800)		(4,800)
1	1,738	.833	1,448	.787	1,368
2	2,183	.694	1,515	.620	1,353
3	1,701	.579	985	.488	830
4	1,451	.482	699	.384	557
5	2,546	.402	1,023	.303	771
6	(312)	.335	(105)	.238	(74)
			765		5

The discount rate would have to change from 15% to approximately 27% to produce a net present value of zero. This is a change of approximately 80%.

(c) Capital investment appraisal involves a large number of estimates of future cash flows. These estimates, and the estimate of an appropriate discount rate, are subject to varying margins of error. Sensitivity analysis is the process by which each individual element of cash flow (for example revenues, labour costs, overheads), and the discount rate, are taken in turn to see the extent to which that element can vary, with all other elements held constant, before expected net present value becomes zero.
This allows management to ascertain which elements the proposed investment is most sensitive to. These elements should be re-examined in order to see whether the cash-flow estimates can be improved in accuracy.

The weaknesses of sensitivity analysis include:

1. In sensitivity analysis each element is varied individually. It is, however, likely that interrelationships exist between many of the elements, and two or more elements will, in reality, vary simultaneously.
2. Sensitivity analysis takes no account of the probabilities of events occurring.
3. No indication is given as to the correct reaction of the financial manager to a particular level of sensitivity, or whether decisions should be altered because of the level of sensitivity.

Other traditional techniques of incorporating risk include using the probability distribution of a range of estimates to calculate expected net present value, finding the standard deviation of the probability distribution, decision trees, certainty equivalents, and simulation.

These measures of risk normally apply to individual projects in isolation. Considering a project in its broader portfolio context will produce a more appropriate measure of risk. The direct measurement of systematic risk through the use of a risk-adjusted discount rate generated by the capital asset pricing model is often considered to be an appropriate way of incorporating risk into capital investment appraisal. (The certainty equivalent technique may be applied in conjunction with the CAPM.)

9

Financing and Appraisal of International Investments

Financing and Appraisal of International Investments

9

Techniques for dealing with cash flows denominated in a foreign currency

Two methods exist to calculate net present value of international investment decisions. One method converts the foreign currency into the domestic one and discounts the cash flows at the domestic opportunity cost of capital. This method requires a forecast of foreign exchange rates. The second method discounts foreign investments at the foreign country's cost of capital and converts the result into the domestic currency using the spot rate of exchange. An ability to use both methods and an understanding of the difficulties with each is required.

A knowledge of interest rate parity and purchasing power parity theories and the relationship between spot and forward rates is required, together with an ability to use the theories to calculate exchange rates given certain assumptions.

Short-term hedging strategies

Entities use hedging techniques to manage their exposure to fluctuations in exchange rate, although a valid strategy is not to hedge, avoiding the cost of using a particular hedging technique but increases risk. The choice of strategy will depend on the entity and its perception of the current and future economic environment. Methods include:

- Forward contracts
- Money market hedging
- Futures
- Options
- Matching
- Leading and lagging.

Identifying financing requirements

Decisions on how to finance international operations are influenced by the availability of finance for investment in particular countries and the types and levels of risk involved.

Questions

Question 1 – GH

GH plc is *a* UK-based retailing company that operates in the USA and UK. The company is evaluating the potential for expansion into Europe, starting in France. A detailed assessment of the costs and likely incremental revenues of opening stores in two major French cities has been carried out. The initial cost of the investment is FFr80m. The nominal cash flows, all positive and net of all taxes, are summarised below.

	Year 1	*Year 2*	*Year 3*
Cash flow (FFr million)	35.50	42.50	45.00

The company's treasurer provides the following information:

- The expected inflation rate in France is 4% each year and in the UK 3% each year.
- Real interest rates in the UK and France are the same. They are expected to remain the same for the foreseeable future.
- The current spot rate is FFr8.5 to £1 sterling.
- The risk-free annual rate of interest in France is 6% and in the UK 5%. These nominal rates are not expected to change in the foreseeable future.
- The company's post-tax weighted average cost of capital (WACC) is 15%, which it uses to evaluate all investment decisions.

The expansion will be financed by a combination of internal funds generated in the UK and long-term fixed interest rate debt raised in France. The company plans to purchase in France the majority of its goods for resale.

Requirements

(a) Calculate the £ Sterling net present value of the project, using both the following methods:

(i) by discounting annual cash flows in £ sterling;
(ii) by discounting annual cash flows in FFr, using an adjusted discount rate; and explain, briefly, the reasons why the two methods give almost identical answers.

(9 marks)

(b) Assume that the company's management is considering purchasing from outside France a substantial proportion of its goods to be sold in the French stores. Approximately 50% of total goods for resale might be purchased in the Far East and a further 25% in the UK. Discuss how a decision to change buying patterns might affect the evaluation and funding of the investment.

(8 marks)

(c) Assume that inflation in France turns out to be higher than forecast for the whole period of evaluation, with corresponding impact on the other economic factors. Inflation in the UK is slightly less than forecast. Discuss how the financial returns on the investment might be affected, and advise on a funding strategy that could minimise the impact of such inflationary effects.

(8 marks)

Note: Parts (b) and (c) are independent – that is, part (c) is not dependent upon the answer to part (b).

(Total = 25 marks)

Question 2 – KH

KH is a large food and drink retailer based in the United States of America. To date, the company has operated only in the US but is planning to expand into South America by acquiring a group of stores similar to those operated in the US. Projected cash flows in the US and South America for the first three years of the project, in real terms, are estimated as follows:

	Year 0	*Year 1*	*Year 2*	*Year 3*
Cash flows in USA:				
In US$'000	−10,000	−300	−400	−500
Cash flows in the South American country:				
In SA Currency'000	−1,000,000	+250,000	+350,000	+450,000

US$ cash flows are mainly incremental administration costs associated with the project. SA currency cash flows are cash receipts from sales less all related cash costs and expenses.

The exchange rate for the South American country's currency is extremely volatile. Inflation is currently 40% a year. Inflation in the US is 4% a year. Best estimates by KH's treasurer suggest these rates are likely to continue for the foreseeable future. The current exchange rate is SA currency 30 to US$1.

The following information is relevant:

- KH evaluates all investments using nominal cash flows and a nominal discount rate
- SA currency cash flows are converted into US$ and discounted at a risk-adjusted US rate
- All cash flows for this project will be discounted at 20%, a nominal rate judged to reflect its high risk
- For the purposes of evaluation, assume the year 3 nominal cash flows will continue to be earned each year indefinitely.

Note: Ignore taxation.

Requirements

Assume that you are the Financial Manager of KH. Prepare a report to the Finance Director that evaluates the proposed investment. Include in your report the following:

(a) Calculation of the net present value of the proposed investment and a recommendation as to whether the company should proceed with the investment, supported by your reasons for the recommendation.

(12 marks)

(b) Discussion of the main political risks that might be faced by the company and provision of advice on management strategies that could be implemented to counter those risks.

(13 marks)

(Total = 25 marks)

Question 3 – TMC

TMC is a large cosmetic and toiletries retail organisation based in a country within the European common currency zone. Its current turnover is approximately Euro 1.4 billion and it has an asset base of Euro 750 m.

The company is evaluating opening up to 10 new retail outlets in a country in Asia, to be financed by its existing cash or other highly liquid assets. It proposes to operate these new retail outlets itself for the first two years of operation. After that time, and subject to satisfactory commercial and financial performance, each outlet will be offered as a franchise to either the outlet manager/employees or to a third party.

Forecast nominal cash flows for the first two years of operation for a single outlet are as follows:

	Year 0 Asian $m	*Year 1* Asian $m	*Year 2* Asian $m
Initial investment	−15		
Pre-tax operating cash flows		4.5	5.5
Exchange rate information is as follows:			
Spot rate as at today Euro/Asian $		0.65	
Forecast inflation rates (% per annum)			
European common currency area		1.50	
Asian country		3.50	

Estimated cash flows beyond year 2 depend on the type of operation. If the company continues to operate the outlet, it assumes zero growth per year on year 2's post-tax Euro operating cash flows until the end of year 10. Cash flows beyond year 10 are ignored. If the outlet is franchised, there will be a one-off taxable payment by the franchisee at the beginning of year 3 of Asian $500,000 plus an annual payment in perpetuity of Asian $3.2 m (both figures in time 3 money), commencing at the end of year 3.

Additional information

- Corporate taxes in the Asian country are 30% per annum, payable or refundable the year in which the liability to tax arises. In the European country, they are 35% payable or refundable the following year. Double taxation agreements are in force between the two countries. Both countries allow 100% writing-down allowance for investments of this type.
- TMC uses 9% as the discount rate in its investment appraisals.
- All operating cash flows may be assumed to occur at the end of each year. The initial capital investment will be made at the beginning of year 1 and written off over 5 years.
- TMC evaluates international investments by converting the foreign currency cash flows to Euros and applying its domestic cost of capital.

Requirement

Evaluate the proposed investment and recommend whether it should proceed. You should include in your evaluation some discussion of the risks that might be associated with the two alternative methods of operation being considered after year 2 and advise on how these risks might be managed.

(Total = 25 marks)

Notes: Up to 10 marks are available for calculations. A report structure is not required for this question.

Question 4 – AB overseas

AB plc manufactures products for children. The company's turnover and earnings last year were £56 m and £3.5 m respectively. Its shares are not listed but they occasionally change hands in private transactions. AB plc's weighted average cost of capital (WACC) is 13% net of tax. The directors believe that an appropriate gearing ratio (debt to debt + equity) for a company such as AB plc is 30%, which is the industry average. Currently, AB plc's gearing ratio is slightly higher than this at 35%. Its debt comprises two secured long-term bank loans and a permanent overdraft, secured by a floating charge on the company's current assets. The current cost of debt to a company such as AB plc is 10% before tax.

The company is considering expansion outside the UK, in particular in an Eastern European (EE) country where its products have become popular. The EE government has offered AB plc a financing deal to establish a manufacturing operation. The financing would take the form of an EE marks 30 m 6-year loan at a subsidised rate of only 2.5% each year interest. The current exchange rate is EE marks 20 to the £ sterling.

Interest would be payable at the end of each year and the principal repaid at the end of 6 years. The exchange rate of EE marks to the £ would be fixed at the current rate for the whole 6-year period of the loan. The marginal corporate tax rate in both countries is 25%.

Requirements

(a) Calculate the company's present cost of equity and the present value of the EE government subsidy implicit in the loan. Comment briefly on the method used and any assumptions you have made in your calculations.

(7 marks)

(b) Discuss the relevance of both the cost of equity you have calculated in answer to (a) above and the WACC given in the scenario, to the company's investment decision. Include comment on an alternative discount rate that could be used appropriately in the scenario's circumstances.

(6 marks)

(c) (i) Discuss the advantages and disadvantages of using the EE government subsidy in AB plc's international investment decision.
(ii) Recommend alternative methods of financing that might be suitable for AB plc in the circumstances of the scenario.

(12 marks)
(Total = 25 marks)

Answers

Question 1 – GH

(a)

(i)

	t_0	t_1	t_2	t_3
In FFm	(80)	35.50	42.50	45.00
X/R(W1)	8.500	8.583	8.666	8.750
In£m	(9.41)	4.14	4.90	5.14
DF (15%)	1	0.870	0.756	0.658
PV	(9.41)	3.60	3.70	3.38

NPV = £1.27 m

(ii)

	t_0	t_1	t_2	t_3
FFm	(80)	35.50	42.50	45.00
DF (W2)	1	0.861	0.742	0.639
PV	(80)	30.57	31.54	28.76

NPV in FFm = 10.87
At X/R of 8.500 = £1.27 m

W1:
- t_1 X/R = 8.50 × 1.04/1.03 = 8.583
- t_2 X/R = 8.583 × 1.04/1.03 = 8.666
- t_3 X/R = 8.666 × 1.04/1.03 = 8.750

W2:
- UK risk premium (CAPM) = 15−5 = 10%
- FF risk premium = 10% × 1.04/1.03 = 10.097
- FF return required = 6% + 10.097% = 16.1%

These give identical answers as the exchange rates have been estimated using PPP, which links inflation rate differences to interest rates and to exchange rates. The second method adjusts the discount rate to 16.1% and keeps the exchange rate constant at 8.5.

(b) In theory, purchasing power parity says that there will be no effect on the cost to the business, as any change in exchange rates exactly matches the difference in inflation rates in the two countries. However, in practice, there might be substantial impacts on the company because:

- legal restrictions may be imposed on the purchase of goods from the Far East;
- the French revenues will not be matched by costs in the same currency, which means that other hedging techniques may need to be put in place;
- the discount rate may need to be adjusted to allow for the additional risks of dealing in different currencies;
- there might be additional costs, such as transport costs and additional taxes;
- as the French currency is forecast to depreciate against sterling, purchases from theUK might become progressively more expensive.

(c) **Funding strategy**

If inflation rises, interest rates will rise and if PPP and interest rate parity hold, the French currency will depreciate more rapidly than forecast. This means that in sterling terms the NPV will be lower unless the company can raise its prices in line with inflation. It will also be affected by the rate at which the costs in France rise and the source of the goods used.

As finance is to be partly through a French loan, it will be an advantage if the French currency depreciates as it will become cheaper to service the loan as well as the ultimate repayment.

Question 2 – KH

REPORT

To: Finance Director
From: Financial Manager
Date: 30 May 2001

Investment in South America

(a) *Calculation and assessment of viability*

	t_0	t_1	t_2	t_3
SAm (real)	(1,000)	250	350	450
SAm (nominal)	(1,000)	350	686	1,235
X/R (W1)	30	40.38	54.36	73.18
In US$m	(33.33)	8.67	12.62	16.88
US cash flows (nominal)	(10)	(0.31)	(0.43)	(0.56)
US$m	(43.33)	8.36	12.19	16.32
DF (20%)	1	0.833	0.694	0.579
PV	(43.33)	6.96	8.46	9.45
		NPV of above		= (18.46)
	t_4 onwards = 16.32/0.20 × 0.579			= 47.25
				$28.79 m

WI: t_1 X/R = 30 × 1.40/1.04 = 40.38
t_2 X/R = 40.38 × 1.40/1.04 = 54.36, etc.

It would therefore seem to be a viable project and the calculations suggest we should go ahead. However, it needs a substantial cash injection at the start of the project and the risk, as looked at later in this report, needs considering carefully.

(b) *Political risks faced and management strategies*

The main political risks faced are as follows:

- repatriation of profits and dividends may be restricted;
- there might be Government interference in the market, ranging from dictating prices or imposing high taxes to expropriating assets;
- there may not be developed capital markets making it difficult to raise finance locally or to hedge currency risks;
- depending on the country under consideration, there might be poor infrastructure with little political will to improve it, social unrest and corruption.

Strategies could be developed to mitigate these to some extent, such as:

- assess the extent of the risks by research, discussions with experts and visits;
- purchase in depth analysis of the political and economic prospects that give scores for political risk;
- involve the Government as far as possible, without compromising ethical standards, and try to get commitments on areas such as repatriation of funds;
- take out insurance, where available, against events such as war and riots (although this may be very expensive);
- ensure that purchases are made in the local currency if at all possible.

Conclusion

The political risk should be considered as part of the overall strategic decision-making process, and those residual risks which cannot be mitigated need to be balanced against the strategic benefits.

Question 3 – TMC

First two years:

In A$'000s

	t_0	t_1	t_2	t_3
Operating cash flow		4,500	5,500	
Tax		(1,350)	(1,650)	
Investment and tax (15,000)	(15,000)	4,500		
	(15,000)	7,650	3,850	
X/rate	0.650	0.637	0.625	0.613
In Euro'000s	(9,750)	4,873	2,406	
Extra tax on op CFs			(143)	(172)
Extra credit on CAs			546	
	(9,750)	4,873	2,809	(172)
DF(9%)	1	0.917	0.842	0.772
PV	(9,750)	4,469	2,365	(133)

NPV for first 2 years = Euro (3,049,000)

Alternative 1

Post-tax Euro operating CF in year 2 = 2,406 − 172 = 2,234

Ignoring the fact that European tax is payable a year in arrears (i.e. the final tax at t_{11}),

PV = 2,234 × (6.418 − 1.759) = 10,408,000

NPV for first 2 years	= (3,049,000)
NPV	Euro 7,359,000

Alternative 2

PV of fee = 500,000 × 0.625 × 0.65 × 0.842	= E171,000
PV of payments = (3,200,000 × 0.613 × 0.65)/ 0.09 × 0.842	= E11,929,000
NPV for first 2 years	= (3,049,000)
NPV	= E9,051,000

This also ignores the time lag in the European tax.

Assessment and risks

- Both alternatives, on the basis of these estimates, are viable, with Alternative 2, giving a franchise, giving the most benefit to the company.
- Both assessments are very dependent on the forecasts of cash flows after year 2. These need examining very carefully as the net present value over the first 2 years is negative. It would be sensible to conduct sensitivity analysis on these important cash flows.
- As the investment is overseas, the cash-flow estimates are subject to exchange rate fluctuations, and over 10 years these could be substantial. Hedging is a possibility in the short term but it is unlikely that arrangements could be made for 10 years.
- There is some commercial risk in Alternative 2 in which a franchise is offered as the reputation of the company will depend on the competence of the franchise.
- There may be some credit risk if the franchise is offered as the company is relying on the franchise to make regular payments.
- Political risk will probably be increased by operating in another country. The tax arrangements, particularly the 100% first-year allowances, would impact on the viability if withdrawn; any change in allowing repatriation of profits could also cause problems. However, these risks are reduced if the country has a stable government as there are unlikely to be sudden major changes.
- Overall, the investment changes the risk profile of the company and would be expected to increase the overall risk to an investor and hence the cost of equity. However, as a large company, it is likely that many of its investors are well diversified institutions and so only interested in systematic risk. As such, the overseas venture may be welcomed by them as reducing or diversifying, part of the systematic risk, and the value of the company might rise accordingly.

Question 4 – AB overseas

(a) **Cost of equity**

Given by $(0.65 \times K_e + (0.35 \times 10 \times 0.75) = 13$

$$\text{So } K_e = 16\%$$

This calculation assumes that the gearing ratio stays at 35%.

Value of subsidised loan given by the loan cash flows (net of tax) discounted at the opportunity cost of capital (in this case the cost of a new commercial loan):

	£	*DF at 7.5%*	*PV*
t_0	1,500,000	1	1,500,000
$t_1 - t_6$	(28,125)	4.694	(132,019)
t_6	(1,500,000)	0.6480	(972,000)
	Net PV	£395,981	

This has used the current commercial cost of debt to discount, which assumes that by using this loan we have not had to raise a commercial loan. However, it might have been funded from a mix of finance sources, or internally, which would alter the opportunity cost used to discount. The higher the rate, the higher the savings and the benefit (so at the WACC of 13% PV = £667,556).

(b) **Discount rate relevance**

Neither the current cost of equity nor the current WACC are entirely relevant to the investment decision. As the investment is likely to carry a higher business risk than AB's normal operations and the financing structure appears likely to change, AB will need to use a discount rate which has been adjusted to reflect the risk of the project.

One alternative is to find, if possible, a company that operates in the same sector and use its beta, adjusted for the difference in gearing between the companies, to devise a cost of equity via CAPM. However, it will be difficult to find a company that reflects the risk of the operations in the Eastern European country.

(c) **Financing**

1. *Government subsidy*

The advantages of the EE Government subsidy include:

- cheaper finance than commercial rates
- no security is needed for the loan
- the overseas Government will want to help make the project a success.

The disadvantages include:

- the exchange rate may alter, making the repayment of interest and capital more expensive in sterling terms;
- commercial rates may change, making the subsidised loan look less attractive;
- the company is then tied into the loan and the project for 6 years;
- the company will need to establish how trustworthy the foreign Government is, in terms of honouring its commitments.

2. *Alternative methods*

These might include:

Leasing
Finance leases to acquire the main assets for the investment might be available, although there might be some difficulty, given that the assets leased will be overseas.

Equity
£1.5 m is too small for a new issue of shares, but a rights issue would be possible. This rather depends on whether the existing private investors have sufficient funds and the willingness to invest in the project.

Long-term loans
The company already has two loans and an overdraft and its gearing is higher than the industry average (and higher than it would like). Further loans would increase the gearing further and might be considered too risky, especially as it is into a new market.

Venture capital
Venture capitalists might be interested in providing finance, but will require a very high return for the risk envisaged, and are likely to want a sizeable portion of the company's equity. This therefore may not be acceptable to the current owners.

Recommendations

No obvious alternative presents itself unless the existing shareholders have excess funds available for investment. The company itself has no cash (as it runs a permanent overdraft) and the best option may be to accept the foreign Government's offer (subject to the reservations in (c) 1).

Part 5

Case Studies and Exam Papers

10

Case Study Questions

Case Study Questions 10

Section A of the examination paper will contain a compulsory case-study type question. Pre-seen material will have set the scene, but most of the relevant detail required to answer the case study requirements will be contained within the unseen material. The compulsory case study question takes up 50% of the exam and requires careful planning. The main problem is likely to be poor time management causing you to write very little, or nothing at all, on parts which could have given you easy marks.

The 20 minutes extra reading time at the start of the exam is particularly valuable here. Remember that you cannot write in the answer booklet or use your calculator, but you can use the time profitably to read the question and note in the margin your approach.

You need to break the requirements down into separate questions for timing purposes, but at the same time you don't want to be continually re-reading the scenario.

One approach would be as follows:

Read through all the requirements carefully; they are likely to cover a number of technical areas. Notice any parts that you can answer immediately, or that you have any ideas about and put some notes down on those.

Then scan the scenario quickly. Are there headings which help you find information; what industry and type of entity is involved; are there any sections which are only relevant to one requirement?

Get an idea of where the information needed for each requirement is in the scenario (the information for calculating the cost of capital, for example, is likely to be grouped together) and mark it in the margin.

Then go back to the requirements and start working through them, reading the detail in the scenario as you need it. Watch your time carefully in the 3 hours of the actual exam, particularly in the case study question. Even if you haven't finished one requirement, go on to the next if the time is up. You can always come back if you have more time, but it's more important to get the easier marks at the beginning of each question than to make that final point!

It is important to note that calculations not specifically requested in the question are often possible, and incorporating additional appropriate ratios and numerical analysis into the question may earn credit.

The case-study questions that follow cover a number of syllabus topic areas. They are adapted from the case-study questions set under the previous syllabus, but reflect the type of material likely to be presented as the unseen elements of the case. On the following questions, be very strict with your time and see if you manage to make a reasonable attempt at all the requirements.

Questions

Question 1 – KL Group

Background of company
KL Group plc provides a range of products and services for sale in the United Kingdom and overseas. Its shares are listed on the London Stock Exchange and are widely held, although institutions hold the majority of shares. The company is structured as a group of wholly owned subsidiaries. Each subsidiary specialises in a particular product or service.

Financial data

Key data for the year to 31 December 2001 is as follows:

Sales revenue	£850 m
Earnings	£105 m
Shares in issue	250 m
Share price as at today (21 May 2002)	331 pence
Weighted Average Cost of Capital (WACC) for the Group	14% (nominal net of tax rate)

Company objectives

The company has two stated objectives:

1. to increase operating cash flow and dividends per share year on year by at least 5%;
2. to increase the wealth of our shareholders whilst respecting the interests of our employees, customers and other stakeholders and operating to the highest ethical standards.

Future plans

The directors are considering establishing a new subsidiary company, KL15, to process industrial waste. The subsidiary will require a factory. The directors have identified that the factory used by a long-established subsidiary, KL3, is currently operating at only 50% capacity. This factory could be converted for use by the new subsidiary at a cost of £1.3 m. KL3's annual net (after-tax) earnings are £1.5 m. This subsidiary's operations would cease immediately after the decision to proceed with KL15 is taken as it will take some months to convert the factory.

However, the company is aware that the government is reviewing the environmental controls currently in operation for waste processing and it is possible that tougher regulations will be introduced. Industry spokesmen are attempting to argue that current controls are adequate. Nevertheless, the directors of the KL Group plc wish to consider the situation should these tougher controls be introduced, and two alternative methods of equipping the new subsidiary have been proposed by the company's technical advisers.

The company has sufficient cash available from a recent disposal to finance the capital costs of the new subsidiary under either alternative.

Alternative 1

This alternative will equip the factory to process waste to the highest environmental standards that the government regulations might impose. This would require the purchase of very expensive, specialised machinery from the USA. This machinery would have to be ordered and delivery time is approximately 6 months, which would coincide with completion of the factory conversion. The cost of this machinery is currently US$12 m but the price of the equipment is likely to rise by 5% over the next 6 months. If an order is placed immediately (year 0), together with a 50% deposit, the supplier will hold today's price. The balance of the purchase price is payable 6 months after installation. The current exchange rate, US$ to £1 sterling, is 1.45. Inflation in the USA is forecast to be 4% over the next 12 months. In the UK it is forecast to be 2.5%.

This equipment is not likely to need replacement for at least 8 years.

Forecast revenues for KL15 under this equipment alternative are as follows. The probabilities are based on forecasts of the economy in the UK and the main overseas trading areas where the KL Group plc hopes to sell its services.

	Year 1 (6 months of operating)			**Year 2**			**Year 3**		
Revenues (£m)	0.5	2.5	3.5	8.5	10.5	12.5	10.5	13.5	16.0
Probability	0.4	0.5	0.1	0.4	0.5	0.1	0.4	0.5	0.1
Expected revenues (£m)		1.8			9.9			12.55	

The probabilities of sales for year 2 or 3 and beyond are assumed to be independent of the achievement of the previous year's sales.

The costs are as follows:

- Cash operating costs are expected to have a fixed element of £1.5 m each year starting as soon as the factory starts work, plus a variable element of 30% of sales revenue. A full year's fixed costs will be charged to production in year 1.
- Redundancy payments of £1.2 m will be necessary for staff from the KL3 subsidiary. These would be payable immediately.
- The costs of the factory conversion will be incurred during the 6 months following the decision to proceed but, for simplicity, it can be assumed that these are paid at the end of year 1.
- The availability of capital allowances and other tax reliefs mean that no tax is likely to be payable until year 4. For year 4 onwards a rough estimate suggests 20% of annual net cash flows (revenue less cash operating costs) will be payable in tax.

Alternative 2

To plan for a continuation of, or modest improvement to, current regulations and produce accordingly. This alternative has greater flexibility as there is a much larger market, worldwide, for processing waste at a lower and therefore much cheaper specification. The capital cost to the KL Group plc would also be much lower at £2.5m. Equipment for this alternative is readily available in the UK and can be bought when the factory conversion is completed. However, the equipment is likely to need to be replaced in 6 years' time from the date of purchase.

The revenues shown below are forecast using similar methods as used in Alternative 1. However, sales will be made to a wider range of customers, many in developing countries.

	Year 1 (6 months of operating)			**Year 2**			**Year 3**		
Revenues (£m)	3.5	4.5	5.5	4.5	6.5	7.5	8.5	9.5	11.5
Probability	0.2	0.6	0.2	0.2	0.6	0.2	0.2	0.6	0.2
Expected revenues (£m)		4.5			6.3			9.7	

Costs are as follows:

- Fixed cash operating costs will be £1.2m each year; variable costs will be 15% of sales revenue.
- With this alternative, there will be fewer redundancies from KL3 and the associated costs will be only 20% of those for Alternative 1.
- Costs of factory conversion are as Alternative 1.
- Tax relief will be similar to Alternative 1, that is, no tax will be payable until year 4 when tax will become payable at 20% of annual net cash flow (revenue less cash operating costs).

Requirements

(a) Calculate net present values for the new subsidiary (KL15) under the two alternatives, using whatever assumptions you think are appropriate. Include brief comments on your assumptions.

(15 marks)

(b) Assume you are the company's financial manager. Write a report to the directors that:

(i) discusses how the new subsidiary and the two alternatives might contribute to the attainment of the Group's objectives. Refer to the figures you have calculated in answer to part (a) where appropriate.

(10 marks)

(ii) analyses and discusses the various types of risk and limitation involved in each alternative.

(10 marks)

(iii) recommends which, if either, of the alternatives should be chosen. Your recommendation should take into account all aspects of your evaluation as discussed in parts (b) (i) and (b) (ii) of this question.

(5 marks)

You should provide any additional calculations that you consider appropriate to support your discussion and analysis.

(Total for part (b) = 25 marks)

(c) Option pricing theory was originally developed to apply to share prices. The theory can also be applied to capital investment options, sometimes known as 'real options'.

Discuss the option features involved in the KL Group plc's decision and explain, briefly, the benefits of including such options in the investment appraisal process.

(10 marks)
(Total = 50 marks)

Question 2 – Dobbs

Background

Dobbs plc is an international publishing company based in the United Kingdom. It has recently sold a subsidiary that publishes technical journals, a field the company considered to be noncore business. The sale raised £30m in cash. The directors are evaluating what they consider to be a very promising acquisition opportunity and the cash raised from the sale of the subsidiary would be used as part of the financing arrangement.

Potential investment in a new subsidiary

Alice Jain Inc. is an American publisher that has two main divisions. One division publishes books, mainly 'blockbuster' type fiction, and the other publishes 'lifestyle' magazines. Both divisions have seen strong growth over the past 5 years as a result of changes in the public's magazine-buying habits and also because of two high-selling authors whom the company contracted before they became popular. These contracts have between 3 and 5 years to run before they are re-negotiated. Many industry observers think Alice Jain Inc. has been successful because of good luck rather than good judgement and that with stronger management the company could become a major international publisher.

Alice Jain Inc. is privately owned (i.e. it does not have a listing on a stock market). There are approximately 50 shareholders although 60% of the shares are owned by the husband and wife partnership that started the business 25 years ago. Dobbs plc's directors have already made an informal approach to Alice Jain Inc's directors and believe they will be receptive to an offer if terms can be agreed. No announcement has yet been made to the press or to Dobbs plc's shareholders about their intentions.

On the basis of industry information and private sources, Dobbs plc's directors forecast the following cash flows from Alice Jain Inc.:

Year	1	2	3	4
Net cash flows ($m)	35.5	43.5	46.5	52.5

Notes:

1. The spot $US/£ exchange rate is 1.45. Forecast economic data relevant to the USA and the UK is as follows:

	USA	*UK*
Risk-free rates for each year (%)	3.5	4.5
Inflation rates for each year (%)	2.5	3.2

   Assume the theory of interest rate parity applies when forecasting exchange rates.

2. The cash flows are in real terms. Dobbs plc evaluates all its investment decisions at its domestic, post-tax cost of capital, which is a nominal 11%. It evaluates international investments by converting the foreign currency cash flows to sterling and applying its domestic cost of capital of 11%. The cost of capital for Alice Jain Inc. is not known. Dobbs plc's Finance Director has used the capital asset pricing model to assist in the calculation of a discount rate based on the published information about a quoted British company with a similar commercial and financial profile to Alice Jain Inc. He has calculated that the proxy company's nominal, post-tax cost of capital is 13%.
3. When evaluating investments, Dobbs plc ignores cash flows beyond 4 years and terminal values.

Financing of the acquisition

Dobbs plc's directors are considering offering Alice Jain Inc's shareholders either shares in Dobbs plc or a cash alternative. The two majority shareholders are likely to take 50% shares,

50% cash as there are tax advantages to a share exchange. This will use up most of the cash from the sale of the subsidiary. The cash for the remaining shareholders will have to be raised by Dobbs plc increasing its borrowing. The 'worst case' scenario is that the remaining shareholders (i.e. those except the two major shareholders) will all opt for cash.

Finance Director's concerns

Dobbs plc's long-term debt to equity ratio is relatively high compared with other publishing companies of similar size. The Finance Director thinks some of the cash raised from the sale of the subsidiary should be used to purchase a small British publishing company at an approximate cost of £15 m. The remaining cash should then be used to repay some of Dobbs plc's outstanding debt.

The other directors disagree and believe the financial risk of investing in Alice Jain Inc. will be justified by substantial value enhancement strategies that can be put in place following the acquisition.

Summary financial information on bidder and target companies

	Dobbs plc £m	*Alice Jain Inc.* $m
Income statement for 12 months to 31 December 2002		
Turnover	251.5	75.8
Operating profit	65.6	20.9
Finance costs	12.0	2.0
Profit before tax	53.6	18.9
Taxation	15.0	7.0
Balance sheet at 31 December 2002		
Fixed assets	195.0	45.0
Net current assets	75.0	25.0
Total assets less current liabilities	270.0	70.0
Long-term debt	125.0	15.0
Net assets	145.0	55.0
Ordinary share capital		
Ordinary shares of £1	45.0	
Common stock of $1		15.0
Total reserves	100.0	40.0
Equity shareholders' funds	145.0	55.0

Current share price for Dobbs plc is 885 pence. High and low share prices for the past 12 months were 925 pence and 755 pence respectively. No share price is available for Alice Jain Inc.

Assume you are a financial manager with Dobbs plc.

Requirements

(a)

(i) Calculate the present value of the investment/acquisition's cash flows and explain your method of evaluation, including your choice of discount rate.
(ii) Calculate the number of shares Dobbs plc might need to issue and the amount of debt that might need to be raised in the 'worst case' scenario. Include brief comments to explain your calculations.

(Total for part (a) = 16 marks)

(b) Write a report to the directors of Dobbs plc, evaluating the potential acquisition. You should include in your report:

  (i) a recommendation, with reasons, of whether the investment should proceed and at what price;
  (ii) advice on strategies for enhancing the value of the combined company following the acquisition;
  (iii) discussion of the Finance Director's recommendation to acquire a smaller company and repay some debt;
  (iv) advice on Dobbs plc's directors' responsibilities to ensure fair and equal treatment for all shareholders in accordance with current take-over regulation.

Use additional calculations to support your arguments wherever relevant and appropriate.

Note: Marks are distributed roughly equally between these four sections of the report.

(Total for part (b) = 34 marks)
(Total = 50 marks)

Question 3 – C&C

Background to company

C&C Airlines plc operates a small fleet of aeroplanes from an airport in the United Kingdom. Its business is aimed at low-budget travellers on short-haul flights. The company was formed in 1990 by a group of private investors who continue to own the company. Two of these investors take an active role in the management of the company as executive directors.

The shareholders' objective is long-term capital growth. They have taken relatively low dividends out of the company since its incorporation. The strategy has been to accept low, or no, profits, and build the brand name and market share in its niche market. Their 'exit strategy' is eventually to sell a majority holding in the company following either a stock market flotation or private sale of shares to another company.

Assets and revenue

C&C Airlines plc currently owns 12 planes, mainly Boeing 737s. It has bought all of them second-hand from the major airlines. The company's total net assets are currently, and realistically, valued at £130 m. It is all-equity financed. The revenue in the last full financial year was £85 m. The forecast revenue for the current year is £98 m. Profits after tax are forecast as £18 m.

Proposed investment

The company's directors are examining a proposal for a strategic move into the long-haul market. The initial investment involves the purchase of a 5-year-old Boeing 757, which will be used to fly to and from the Caribbean. Negotiations to buy this plane are already underway. C&C Airlines plc plans to operate the plane for 3 years and replace it at the end of this time with a newer model.

When fully loaded, this type of plane will carry 220 passengers. The company estimates an average return fare of £300 per passenger on this route. All income will be received in £ sterling. The company's estimates of average passenger loading are as follows:

	Probability of load being achieved	
Load	*Year 1 (%)*	*Years 2–3 (%)*
100% (all seats taken)	10	15
80% full	50	60
50% full	30	20
40% full	10	5

The plane is expected to make 6 return trips every week and be operational 48 weeks of the year.

The capital costs of the purchase of the plane are US$30m. To date, C&C Airlines plc has spent £500,000 on market research and purchase negotiations. Other financial data associated with the venture are

- Capital allowances are available at 25% on a reducing balance of the total capital cost.
- The estimated resale value of the plane 3 years after purchase, in nominal terms, is $16m.

Cash operating costs (per annum)

Sterling-denominated costs such as maintenance, insurance, crew wages, salaries and training	£2.9m
US$-denominated fuel costs	US$4.2m

Overheads and other costs (per annum)

Administration and office space (These costs include a £50,000 re-allocation of current head office costs.)	£0.3m
Advertising and promotion	£0.35m

Estimates of increases in income and costs

The figures given above are all in nominal terms as at today. Because this is an increasingly competitive market, the company is unlikely to be able to increase fares in line with inflation. The best estimate is an annual increase of 2%. Operating costs (excluding fuel) are expected to increase by the annual UK rate of inflation (3%). Forecasting fuel costs is very difficult but best estimates are that they will rise by 5% each year over the next 3 years. Assume these inflationary increases commence in the first year of operations. Overheads and other costs are expected to be held constant in nominal terms.

Currency and inflation rates

- current spot exchange rate is US$1.53/£1
- estimated per annum inflation rates are as follows:
  - UK 3%
  - USA 4%

Inflation rates in the UK and USA are expected to remain at these levels.

Allowing for risks

The company evaluates investments by discounting cash flows at 9% per annum nominal and applying certainty equivalents to net after-tax cash flows. The estimates for the proposed investment are shown below:

Year	*Certainty equivalent*
1	0.90
2	0.85
3	0.80

The company's new Finance Director would prefer to use a risk-adjusted discount rate. A competitor company to C&C Airlines plc has a quoted equity beta of 1.3 and a debt:equity ratio (based on market values) of 1:4. This is unlikely to change in the foreseeable future. The post-tax return on the market is expected to be 12% and the risk-free rate 5%. Assume a debt beta of 0.15.

Assumptions:

- Capital costs are paid immediately but all other cash flows occur at year-end.
- Taxation at 30% is paid or repaid at the end of the year in which the liability/repayment arises (i.e. no time lag).
- The plane is acquired and becomes operational immediately.

Requirements

(a) Calculate the discount rate to be used in the investment decision using the CAPM and comment, briefly, on the limitations of using the CAPM in the circumstances here.

(5 marks)

(b) Calculate the £ sterling NPV of the proposed investment in the new plane using: the discount rate calculated in (a) above, rounded to the nearest 1%; and a discount rate of 9% per annum nominal and adjusting for the company's estimated certainty equivalents, and recommend, briefly, whether to proceed with the investment, based solely on your calculations above.

NPV should be calculated in sterling, converting US$ cash flows to sterling. Assume the theory of purchasing power parity applies when calculating exchange rates.

(Total for part (b) = 20 marks)

(c) Assume you are the assistant to the Finance Director. On his behalf, draft a report to the Board that critically evaluates the following:

(i) the major economic forces that might impact on, or influence, the success of the investment;
(ii) commercial aspects of the investment that involve the greatest uncertainty and risk; strategies for managing the risks discussed in parts (c)(i) and (c)(ii).

The report should conclude with a recommendation of a course of action.

(Total for part (c) = 25 marks)
(Total = 50 marks)

Question 4 – Hi-Clean

Background

The Hi-clean Group is a UK-based unlisted company that imports, assembles and distributes laundry and cleaning equipment for hotels and restaurants and for public sector departments, such as hospitals, prisons and the armed forces. The company was formed in 1985 with £24m start-up capital in ordinary shares of £1. No other capital has been raised since then, except from the venture capital company explained below.

The company has seen growth in turnover and post-tax profits of around 20% each year over the past 3 years in all sectors of its customer base, although sales to the public sector now account for a much higher proportion of the total than 5 years ago: 38% in 2004 compared with 18% in 2000.

Details on major shareholder

A venture capital company owns 20% of the company's shares, bought 3 years ago for £25m. The venture capital company also provided a £25m loan with equity warrants attached. The loan carries a variable rate of interest, LIBOR + 3%, and is repayable in 2006. The warrants allow for the venture capital company to buy 1 share at 400 pence for every £10 of debt at the time the loan is repaid. This shareholder is looking to exit from its investment in Hi-clean in 2–3 years time. Unless Hi-clean has obtained a share listing by then, the venture capital company has indicated it is unlikely to exercise its warrants. The venture capital company's usual required return is an average of 50% per annum (dividends plus capital gain as percentage of initial investment) over a 5-year investment period.

Although the venture capital company has a seat on the Hi-clean Group Board, it has taken a very 'hands-off' approach and had little involvement in the company's direction or management.

Forecast results for the year to 31 December 2004

The accounts department has produced the following full-year forecasts for 2004:

Results by sector

	Public sector £m	*Hotels and restaurants* £m	*Total* £m
Revenue	83.60	136.40	220.00
Direct costs	45.98	68.20	114.18
Gross profit margin	37.62	68.20	105.82
Fixed overheads *	26.53	43.29	69.82
Operating profit	11.09	24.91	36.00

* Fixed overheads are apportioned to operating sectors on the basis of turnover.

Summary group income statement

	£m
Operating profit	36.00
Finance costs	1.75
Profit before taxation	34.25

Taxation	6.17
Profit after tax	28.08
Ordinary dividends	8.43

Summary group balance sheet	£m
Fixed assets (net book value)	124.00
Net current assets	48.00
Loan capital	25.00
Assets less liabilities	147.00
Capital and reserves	
Called up share capital (Ordinary shares of £1)	30.00
(Authorised share capital £35 m)	
Share premium account	18.00
Retained earnings	99.00
Shareholders' funds	147.00

Future funding and request for study

Hi-clean's directors have, for some time, been considering a public listing for the company's shares to raise new finance and provide an exit route for the venture capital company. Assume you are the Financial Manager with Hi-clean. The directors have asked you for a study that includes a forecast of the company's financial situation at 31 December 2005. You have spent the last month obtaining the following information from a variety of sources.

Growth in turnover and profits

You expect growth to continue but not at the high levels seen over the past few years. A complication is that a general election will take place shortly and the outcome will have an effect on Hi-clean's business. If Party A wins, it has promised more money for some public sector departments, which may increase Hi-clean's sales to its public sector customers. However, this increased spending would be paid for by an increase in certain taxes that would adversely impact on some of Hi-clean's private customers. If Party B wins, spending on public services will also increase, but not necessarily in areas serviced by Hi-clean. Opinion polls suggest Party A has a 60% chance of winning and Party B 40%.

Based on your informed opinion about prospects for the economy and the industry, you forecast the following range of sales revenues and probabilities for 2005, by sector, depending on which party wins the election.

		Public sector		*Hotels and restaurants*
If Party A wins:	Revenue £m	102.00	112.00	123.00
	Probabilities	0.55	0.45	1
If Party B wins:	Revenue £m	95.00	110.00	143.00
	Probabilities	0.50	0.50	1

Other information/assumptions

- Corporate tax will be payable at the current percentage level of 18% owing to availability of capital allowances. No capital expenditure is planned for 2005.
- Gross profit margin percentage by sector is expected to remain unchanged irrespective of the election outcome.

- Fixed costs are expected to rise to £71.8 m.
- LIBOR is currently 4%. It is expected to fall to 3% in 2005.
- Average P/E ratio and cost of equity capital for listed companies in this industry are currently 11 and 9% respectively. It is difficult to forecast how P/E ratios will move over the next 12 months but market professionals are expecting an upturn in the market generally, so anything between 12 and 15 is not unreasonable.
- The dividend payout ratio has been constant at 30% since 2001.

Requirements

(a) For 2005, calculate forecasts of the following:

(i) turnover, gross margin and operating profits by customer sector;
(ii) a profit and loss account and earnings per share for the Hi-clean Group.

Assume a full-year effect for all the changes forecast for 2005. Provide comments to accompany your forecasts that explain any significant changes between 2004 and 2005.

(10 marks)

(b) As Financial Manager, write a report to the directors of Hi-clean Group. In your report you should:

(i) Calculate a range of potential values as at the end of 2005 for the entire Group and for the venture capital company's shareholding. Base your calculations on the information you have available and assume the Group remains a private, unlisted company. Accompany your calculations with a brief discussion of each valuation method.
(ii) Comment on the reasons for potential differences between the value of the entire company and the value of the venture capital company's shares (that is, why the value of the venture capital company's shares might not be strictly proportionate).

(18 marks)

(c) Based on your forecasts, estimate whether the venture capital company will achieve its target return on investment in Hi-clean and identify exit strategies that might be avail able to the investor in 2006. Evaluate how the venture capital company's situation might affect Hi-clean's future financial strategy.

(10 marks)

(d) Identify the main risks and opportunities facing the company and advise on methods of managing the risks.

(12 marks)
(Total = 50 marks)

Question 5 – JHC Group

Background of company

JHC Group manufactures and distributes a wide range of food products for sale throughout Europe. It also provides advisory services to retailers. Its shares are listed and are widely held, although institutions hold the majority. The company is structured as a group of wholly-owned subsidiaries. Each subsidiary specialises in a particular product or service.

Financial data

Key data for the year to 31 December 2003 is as follows:

Revenue	€1,750 m
Earnings	€215 m
Shares in issue	350 m
Share price as at today	€8.31
Weighted Average Cost of Capital (WACC) for the Group	9% (nominal net of tax rate)

Company objectives

The company has two stated objectives:

- To increase operating cash flow and dividends per share year-on-year by at least 4%, which is 2.5% above the current rate of inflation.
- To increase the wealth of shareholders while respecting the interests of our employees, customers and other stakeholders and operating to the highest ethical standards.

Future plans

The directors are considering establishing a new subsidiary company, SP, to manufacture and distribute health food products. The subsidiary will require a factory. The directors have identified that the factory used by a long-established subsidiary, CC, is currently operating at only 60% capacity. This factory could be converted for use by the new subsidiary at a cost of €2.8 m. CC's annual net (after-tax) earnings are €2.2 m and are expected to remain at this level in nominal terms for the foreseeable future. This subsidiary's operations would cease immediately the decision to proceed with SP is taken as it will take some months to convert the factory.

However, the company is aware that the European parliament is discussing legislation that would introduce more stringent controls on the manufacture of health food products than are currently in operation. Industry spokesmen are attempting to argue that current controls are adequate. Nevertheless, the directors of the JHC Group wish to consider the situation should these tougher controls be introduced and two alternative methods of equipping the new subsidiary have been proposed by the company's technical advisers.

The company has sufficient cash available from a recent disposal to finance the capital costs of the new subsidiary under either alternative.

Alternative 1

This alternative will equip the factory to manufacture to the highest food safety standards that new regulations might impose. It would require the purchase of specialised machinery, which would have to be ordered. Delivery time is approximately 6 months, which would coincide with completion of the factory conversion.

Capital costs
The cost of this machinery is currently €8 m but its price is likely to rise by 5% over the next 6 months. If an order is placed immediately (year 0), together with a 40% deposit, the supplier will hold today's price. The balance of the purchase price is payable 6 months after installation (i.e. 12 months after payment of the initial deposit). This machinery is not likely to need replacement for at least 8 years.

Revenues
Forecast revenues for SP for the first 3 years of operation have been provided by JHC Group's planning department as follows. The probabilities are based on forecasts of the economies of JHC Group's main trading areas.

	Year 1 (6 months of operating)			*Year 2*			*Year 3*		
Revenues (€m)	2.5	4.5	7.4	7.5	12.5	16.5	13.5	18.5	21.5
Probability	0.3	0.5	0.2	0.3	0.5	0.2	0.3	0.5	0.2
Expected revenues (€ m)		4.48			11.80			17.60	

The probabilities of sales for year 2 or 3 and beyond are assumed to be independent of the achievement of the previous year's sales revenues.

Operating and other costs/reliefs

- Cash operating costs are expected to have a fixed element of €2.5 m each year, plus a variable element of 35% of sales revenues. A full year's fixed costs will be charged to production in year 1. Variable costs will be much higher under this alternative because the new regulations are likely to require more expensive ingredients in the products.
- Redundancy payments of €2.1 m will be necessary for staff from the CC subsidiary. These would be payable immediately.
- The costs of the factory conversion will be incurred during the 6 months following the decision to proceed but, for simplicity, it can be assumed that these are paid at the end of year 1.
- The availability of capital allowances and other tax reliefs mean that no tax is likely to be payable until year 4. For year 4 onwards, a rough estimate suggests 20% of annual net cash flows (revenues less cash operating costs) will be payable in tax.

Alternative 2

To plan for a continuation of, or modest improvement to, current controls and regulations. This alternative has greater flexibility, as there is a much larger market, worldwide, for cheaper products.

Capital costs
The capital cost to JHC Group would also be much lower at €4.5 m. Equipment for this alternative is readily available and can be bought when the factory conversion is completed.

However, the equipment is likely to need to be replaced in 6 years' time from the date of purchase.

Revenues
The revenues shown below are forecast using similar methods as used in Alternative 1. However, sales will be made to a wider range of customers, many in developing countries.

	Year 1 (6 months of operating)			*Year 2*			*Year 3*		
Revenues (€ m)	4.5	7.5	9.5	7.1	9.4	11.1	9.5	12.5	15.6
Probability	0.1	0.6	0.3	0.1	0.6	0.3	0.1	0.6	0.3
Expected revenues (€ m)		7.80			9.68			13.13	

Costs are as follows:

- Fixed cash operating costs will be €1.5 m each year; variable costs will be 20% of sales revenue.
- With this alternative, there will be fewer redundancies from CC and the associated costs will be only 20% of those for Alternative 1.
- Costs of factory conversion are as Alternative 1.
- Tax relief will be similar to Alternative 1, that is, no tax will be payable until year 4 when tax will become payable at 20% of annual net cash flow (revenue less cash operating costs).

The revenues and costs for both alternatives are in nominal terms.

Requirements

Assume you are JHC Group's financial manager.

(a) (i) Calculate the net present value for the new subsidiary (SP) under each of the two alternatives. Make, and comment on, appropriate assumptions about cash flows beyond year 3, including terminal values, and the discount rate to use in the evaluation.

(15 marks)

(ii) Explain, without doing any additional calculations, the appropriateness and possible advantages of providing modified internal rates of return (MIRRs) for the evaluation of the two alternatives.

(5 marks)

(b) Write a report to the directors that discusses how the new subsidiary and the two alternatives might contribute to the attainment of the Group's objectives and recommends which, if either, of the alternatives should be chosen. Refer to the figures you calculated in part (a) where appropriate. You should provide any additional calculations that you consider relevant to support your discussion and analysis.

(22 marks)

(c) Discuss the option features involved in the JHC Group's decision and explain, briefly, the benefits of including such options in the investment appraisal process.

(8 marks)

(Total marks = 50)

Question 6 – GAS plc

Description of the business

GAS plc is an international energy entity with a head office in the UK. Through its principal operating subsidiaries based in the UK and elsewhere in Europe, it generates electricity and supplies gas and electricity via energy supply networks across Europe.

GAS plc's strategy is to generate future growth through investment in new power stations, energy supply networks and gas storage assets. Its current focus for new investment is Bustan, a large Asian country that is in urgent need of major improvements in its electricity generation and supply systems to support the recent rapid increase in industrial production.

Group profile

On 31 December 2004, GAS plc had 1,200 m 50 pence ordinary shares in issue and a share price of 335 pence ex-dividend. Shareholders expect a return on equity of 9.4%.

Dividends for GAS plc for the year ended 31 December 2004 were 14 pence a share, maintaining the 5% annual increase in dividends that has been achieved in recent years. For simplicity, dividends should be assumed to be declared and paid on 31 December each year.

Investment project

The new investment in Bustan has been at the planning stage since the beginning of 2004 when the government of Bustan first invited proposals for a large construction project from interested parties.

The project was evaluated over a 10-year period beginning January 2005 and the project net operating cash flows in B$, the local currency of Bustan, were estimated to be as follows:

	B$ *million*
Year 1	20
Year 2	150
Year 3	250
Year 4–10	300

All cash flows should be assumed to arise on 31 December of each year. It should also be assumed that annual cash flows, less tax, are paid across to the UK on the final day of each year.

The cost of the initial investment in plant and other equipment at the beginning of January 2005 was B$700 m and this is subject to depreciation charged in the subsidiary accounts on *a* straight line basis at 5% per annum. An additional B$50 m was required to finance working capital at the beginning of January 2005.

Tax

Bustan charges entity tax at a preferential rate of 20% for the first 10 years of such investment projects, rather than the normal rate of 40%. In Bustan, tax depreciation allowances are calculated on the same basis as accounting depreciation allowances. The tax rate in the UK is 30%, but a double tax treaty allows taxes charged in Bustan to be deducted from UK taxes charged in the same period. Assume that Bustan taxes are payable in the year in which they are incurred and that UK taxes are payable one year in arrears.

Exchange rates

At 31 December 2004, the spot exchange rate was £1 = B$0.7778. The B$ is expected to weaken against the British pound (sterling) in line with the differential in long-term interest rates between the two countries over the life of the project. Long-term interest rates are expected to remain stable at 4.8% per annum in the UK and 10% per annum in Bustan for the foreseeable future.

Financing the project

The total initial investment of B$750 m was funded by GAS plc at the beginning of 2005. The B$700 m investment in plant and equipment was funded by a rights issue and the B$50 m working capital requirement out of surplus cash.

GAS plc evaluated the project on the basis of a realisable residual value of B$350 m for the plant and equipment and that 80% of the investment in working capital would be realised at the end of the project. Both these amounts are to be repaid in full to the UK without any taxes payable in either Bustan or the UK.

Press statements

In June 2004, GAS plc issued a press statement announcing its intention to submit a proposal for the project. On the same day, it announced its plans to use a 1 for 4 rights issue to fund the B$700 m capital investment in the event of the proposal being accepted.

GAS plc's proposal was accepted on 1 January 2005 and a press release issued to announce the acceptance of the proposal and GAS plc's intention to proceed with the project without delay. The press statement also announced GAS plc's intention to temporarily reduce dividend growth rates during the development stage of the project. Revised dividend plans are as follows:

2005–2007	Dividend per share to be frozen at December 2004 levels
2008 onwards	7% per annum growth

Investment criteria

Criterion 1
GAS plc requires overseas projects to generate an accounting rate of return in the overseas country, which is Bustan in this instance, of at least 25% per annum. Accounting rate of return is defined as:

$$\frac{\text{average annual accounting profit before interest and taxes}}{\text{average annual (written down) investment}}$$

Criterion 2
GAS plc also assesses investment projects based on the net present value of the cash flows and applies a risk-adjusted *sterling* discount rate of 10.5% to overseas projects of this nature.

Requirements

(a) Show, by calculation, that the proposed investment project in Bustan met the two minimum investment criteria set by GAS plc.

(18 marks)

(b) Discuss the major risk issues that should have been considered by GAS plc when evaluating the project.

(7 marks)

(c) The board of GAS plc has been concerned about the unusually volatile movements in the entity's share price in 2004 and 2005 and has asked you, an external management consultant, to draft a report to the board of GAS plc that critically addresses the issues detailed below. Assume a semi-strong efficient market applies.

(i) Explain the possible reasons for the unusually volatile movements in GAS plc's share price in the twelve months up to and including 1 January 2005. No calculations are required.

(6 marks)

(ii) Advise what would have been a fair market price for GAS plc's shares in January 2005 following the announcement of the acceptance of the proposal and after adjusting for the proposed rights issue. As part of your answer, calculate GAS plc's share price on each of the bases listed below and discuss the relevance of each result in determining a fair market price for the entity's shares:

- the theoretical ex-rights price *before* adjusting for the project cash flows;
- the theoretical ex-rights price *after* adjusting for the project cash flows;
- directors' dividend forecast issued in January 2005.

(14 marks)

(iii) Advise on how and to what extent directors are able to influence their entity's share price.

(5 marks)

(Total for requirement (c) = 25 marks)

Within the overall mark allocation, up to 4 marks are available for structure and presentation.

(Total = 50 marks)

Question 7 – PM Industries

Background

PM Industries plc (PM) is a UK-based entity with shares trading on a UK Stock Exchange. It is a long established business with widespread commercial and industrial interests worldwide. It had a modest growth and profitability record until four years ago when a new Chief Executive Officer (CEO) was appointed from the United States of America (US).

This new CEO has transformed the business by divesting poor performing, or non-core, subsidiaries or business units and focusing on volume growth in the remaining units. Some of this growth has been internally generated and some has come about because of financially sound acquisitions. A particular area of strength is in non-drug pharmaceutical materials such as packaging. PM now controls the largest share of this market in the UK and Europe.

Financial objectives

PM's current financial objectives are:

- To increase EPS by 5% per annum;
- To maintain a gearing ratio (market values of long-term debt to equity) below 30%;
- To maintain a P/E ratio above the industry average.

Proposed merger

The senior management of PM is currently negotiating a merger with NQ Inc (NQ), a US-based entity with shares trading on a US Stock Exchange. NQ is an entity of similar size to PM, in terms of revenue and assets, with a similar spread of commercial and industrial interests, especially pharmaceutical materials, which is why PM originally became attracted to NQ.

NQ has had a less impressive track record of growth than PM over the last two years because of some poor performing business units. As a result, PM's market capitalisation is substantially higher than NQ's. Although this will, in reality, be an acquisition, PM's CEO refers to it as a "merger" in negotiations to avoid irritating the NQ Board, which is very sensitive to the issue.

NQ holds some software licences to products that the CEO of PM thinks are not being marketed as well as they could be. He believes he could sell these licences to a large software entity in the UK for around £100 m. He does not see the commercial logic in retaining them, as information technology is not a core business. The value of these licences is included in NQ's balance sheet at $US125 m.

Both entities believe a merger between them makes commercial and financial sense, as long as terms can be agreed. The CEO of PM thinks his entity will have the upper hand in negotiations because of the share price performance of PM over the last 12 months and his own reputation in the City. He also believes he can boost the entity's share value if he can convince the market his entity's growth rating can be applied to NQ's earnings.

Summary of relevant financial data

Extracts from the Income Statements for the year ended 31 March 2006

	PM (£m)	*NQ* ($m)
Revenue	1,560	2,500
Operating profit	546	750
Earnings available for ordinary shareholders	273	300

Extracts from the Balance Sheets as at 31 March 2006

	PM (£m)	*NQ* ($m)
Total net assets	2,000	2,100
Total equity	850	1,550
Total long term debt	1,150	550

Other data

Number of shares in issue		
Ordinary shares of 10 pence	950,000,000	
Common stock of $1		850,000,000
Share price as at today (24 May 2006)	456 pence	450 cents
High/low share price over last 12 months	475/326 pence	520/280 cents
Industry average P/E	14	13
Debt traded within last week at	£105	Par

Five-year revenue and earnings record

	PM (£m)		*NQ* (US$m)	
Year ended 31 March	*Revenue*	*Earnings*	*Revenue*	*Earnings*
2002	1,050	225	1,850	250
2003	1,125	231	1,950	265
2004	1,250	245	2,150	280
2005	1,400	258	2,336	290
2006	1,560	273	2,500	300

The two entities' revenue and operating profits are generated in the following five geographical areas, with average figures over the past five years as follows:

	PM		NQ	
Percentage of total	*Revenue*	*Profits*	*Revenue*	*Profits*
UK	30	28	20	17
US	22	23	75	76
Mainland Europe	20	17	5	7
Asia (mainly Japan)	18	20	0	0
Rest of World	10	12	0	0

Economic data

PM's bankers have provided forecast interest and inflation rates in the two main areas of operation for the next 12 months as follows:

	Interest rate Current forecast	*Inflation rate Current forecast*
UK	4.5%	2.0%
US	2.5%	1.5%

Terms of the merger

PM intends to open the negotiations by suggesting terms of 1 PM share for 2 NQ stock units. The Finance Director of PM, plus the entity's professional advisors, have forecast the following data, post-merger, for PM. They believe this is a 'conservative' estimate as it excludes their estimate of value of the software licences. The current spot exchange rate is $US1.85 = £1.

Market capitalization	£6,905 m
EPS	31.65 pence

A cash offer as an alternative to a share exchange is unlikely, although the CEO of PM has not ruled it out should the bid turn hostile. However, this would require substantial borrowing by PM, even if only 50% of NQ's shareholders opt for cash.

Except for the potential profit on the sale of the licences, no savings or synergies from the merger have as yet been identified.

Requirements

Assume you are one of the financial advisors working for PM.

(a)

(i) Explain, with supporting calculations, how the Finance Director and advisors of PM have arrived at their estimates of post-merger values.

(10 marks)

(ii) Calculate and comment briefly on the likely impact on the share price and market capitalisation for each of PM and NQ when the bid terms are announced. Make appropriate assumptions based on the information given in the scenario.

(4 marks)

(iii) If NQ rejects the terms offered, calculate

- the maximum total amount and price per share to be paid for the entity; and
- the resulting share exchange terms PM should be prepared to agree without reducing PM's shareholder wealth.

(6 marks)

(Total for part (a) = 20 marks)

(b)

Write a report to the Board of PM that evaluates and discusses the following issues:

(i) How the merger might contribute to the achievement of PM's financial objectives, assuming the merger goes ahead on the terms you have calculated in (a) (iii). If you have not managed to calculate terms, make sensible assumptions.

(12 marks)

(ii) External economic forces that might help and/or hinder the achievement of the merger's financial objectives. Comment also on the policies the merged entity could consider to help reduce adverse effects of such economic forces.

(8 marks)

(iii) Potential post-merger value enhancing strategies that could increase shareholder wealth.

(10 marks)

(Total for part (b) = 30 marks)

Up to 4 marks are available for structure and presentation.

(Total = 50 marks)

Question 8 – SHINE

Business background

SHINE is a publicly owned multinational group based in Germany with its main business centred on the production and distribution of gas and electricity to industrial and domestic consumers. It has recently begun investing in research and development in relation to renewable energy, exploiting solar, wave or wind energy to generate electricity.

Corporate objectives

Developing renewable energy sources is an important non-financial objective for the SHINE Group in order to protect and enhance the group's reputation. Renewable energy projects have been given a high profile in recent investor communications and television advertising campaigns.

Wind farm investment project

The latest renewable energy project under consideration is the development of a wind farm in the USA. This would involve the construction of 65 wind powered electricity generators which would be owned and operated by a new, local subsidiary entity and electricity that is generated by the farm would be sold to the local electricity grid. A suitable site, subject to planning permission, has been located.

Forecast operating cash flows for the project are as follows:

	Year(s)	*US$ million*
Initial investment (including working capital)	0	200
Residual value	4	50
Pre-tax operating net cash inflows	1 to 4	70

Other relevant data and assumptions:

- The initial investment is expected to be made on 30 November 2006 and cash flows will arise at any point in the year.
- However, in any net present value (NPV) exercise, all cash flows should be assumed to arise on 31 December of each year.
- The local tax rate in the USA for this industry is set at a preferential rate of 10% to encourage environmentally-friendly projects rather than the normal rate of 25%.
- Tax is payable in the year in which it arises.
- No tax depreciation allowances are available.
- No additional tax is payable in Germany under the terms of the double tax treaties with the USA.
- Net cash flows are to be paid to the German parent entity as dividends at the end of each year.

Uncertainties affecting the outcome of the project

There is some uncertainty over the US tax rate over the period of the project, with extensive discussion at local government level about raising the tax rate to 25% with immediate effect. A vote will be taken in the next six months to decide whether to retain the preferential 10% tax rate, or to increase it to 25%. Once the vote has been taken and a decision made, the tax rate will not be open for debate again for at least four years.

Economic forecasters expect the value of the euro to either stay constant against the value of the US dollar for the next four years or to strengthen by 7% per annum. Assume that there is an equal probability of each of these two different exchange rate forecasts.

There is also significant risk to the project from strong objections to the wind farm scheme from local farmers in the USA who are concerned about the impact of acid water run-off from boring holes for the 65 windmills. In addition, there are a number of executive holiday homes nearby whose owners are objecting to the visual impact of the windmills.

Investment criteria

The SHINE Group evaluates foreign projects of this nature based on a euro cost of capital of 12% which reflects the risk profile of the proposed investment.

Extracts from the forecast financial statements for the SHINE Group at 31 December 2006, the end of the current financial year:

	€ million	*€ million*
ASSETS		
Total assets		28,000
EQUITY AND LIABILITIES		
Equity		
Share capital (3,000 m €1 ords)	3,000	
Retained earnings	8,300	
		11,300

Non-current liabilities	
Floating rate borrowings	4,000
Current liabilities	12,700
	28,000

Alternative financing methods

The SHINE Group aims to maintain the group gearing ratio (debt as a proportion of debt plus equity) below 40% based on book values.

The following alternative methods are being considered by the SHINE parent entity for financing the new investment:

- Long-term borrowings denominated in euro;
- Long-term borrowings denominated in US dollars.

Requirements

(a) Calculate the NPV of the cash flows for the proposed investment for **each** of the following four possible scenarios:

- Constant exchange rate and a tax rate of 10%
- Constant exchange rate and a tax rate of 25%
- The euro to strengthen against the US dollar by 7% a year and a tax rate of 10%
- The euro to strengthen against the US dollar by 7% a year and a tax rate of 25%

In each case, assume that the exchange rate at year 0 is US$1.10 = €1.00.

(12 marks)

(b) Prepare the forecast balance sheet of the SHINE Group on 31 December 2006, incorporating the project under each of the two alternative financing structures and each of the following two exchange rate scenarios A and B:

Date	*Exchange rates under scenario A*	*Exchange rates under scenario B*
30 November 2006 (date of the initial investment and arrangement of financing)	US$1.10 = €1.00	US$1.10 = €1.00
31 December 2006 (financial reporting/balance sheet date)	US$1.10 = €1.00 (no change)	US$1.40 = €1.00

Assume that no other project cash flows occur until 2007.

(8 marks)

(c) Write a report addressed to the Directors of the SHINE Group in which you, as Finance Director, address the following issues relating to the evaluation and implementation of the proposed wind farm project:

(i) Discuss the internal and external constraints affecting the investment decision and advise the SHINE Group how to proceed. In your answer, include reference to your calculations in part (a) above.

(9 marks)

(ii) Discuss the comparative advantages of each of the two proposed alternative financing structures and advise the SHINE group which one to adopt. In your answer include reference to your results in part (b) above, and further analysis and discussion of the impact of each proposed financial structure on the group's balance sheet.

(9 marks)

(iii) Discuss the differing roles and responsibilities of the treasury department and finance department in evaluating and implementing the US project and the interaction of the two departments throughout the process.

(8 marks)

Upto 4 marks are available for structure and presentation.

(Total = 50 marks)

Answers

Question 1 – KL Group

(a) **Net present values**

Alternative 1

In £'000	t_0	t_1	t_2	t_3	$t_4 - t_8$
Equipment (note)	(4,138)	(4,082)			
Revenue		1,800	9,900	12,550	12,550
Variable costs		(540)	(2,970)	(3,765)	(3,765)
Fixed costs		(1,500)	(1,500)	(1,500)	(1,500)
Redundancy	(1,200)				
Conversion		(1,300)			
Tax					(1,457)
Lost earnings		(1,500)	(1,500)	(1,500)	(1,500)
	(5,388)	(7,122)	3,930	5,785	4,328
	1	0.877	0.769	0.675	3.433 × 0.675
	(5,388)	(6,246)	3,022	3,905	10,029

Net present value = £5,322,000 over 8 years

Note: Exchange rate in 1 year estimated as 1.45 × 1.04/1.025 = 1.47

Alternative 2

In £'000	t_0	t_1	t_2	t_3	$t_4 - t_6$
Equipment	(2,500)				
Revenue		4,500	6,300	9,700	9,700
Variable costs		(675)	(945)	(1,455)	(1,455)
Fixed costs		(1,200)	(1,200)	(1,200)	(1,200)
Redundancy	(240)				
Conversion		(1,300)			
Tax				(1,409)	
Lost earnings		(1,500)	(1,500)	(1,500)	(1,500)
	(2,740)	(175)	2,655	5,545	4,136
	1	0.877	0.769	0.675	3.433 × 0.675
	(2,740)	(153)	2,042	3,743	6,483

Net present value = £9,375,000 over 6 years

These calculations assume:

- The WACC is the appropriate discount rate, but this may not be the case if the business or financial risk changes.
- In alternative 1, we have assumed that we accept the supplier's offer to pay a 50% deposit to secure the price.
- The two alternatives have been assessed over the lives of the machines. They therefore have not considered the loss in earnings from KL3, or any other cash flows, beyond this.
- Cash flows beyond year 3 have been assumed to remain constant but this may not be realistic. The objectives say that KL intend to increase operating cash flows by 5% per

annum but this may be achieved by undertaking new projects or increasing revenues on certain projects, rather than increasing cash flows of all projects across the board. Any increase in cash flows beyond year 3 would clearly increase the net present values.

(b)

REPORT

To: Board of KL Group plc
From: Financial Manager
Date: xx of x 20xx

New subsidiary in KL15

This report will discuss how the new subsidiary might help the group achieve its objectives, look at the risks and limitations involved and make recommendations on the way forward.

(i) *Achievement of objectives*

The two alternatives give different net present values; although both give positive values which would suggest the investment is viable, the greater net present value is achieved under alternative 2 with £9.375 m. In terms of shareholders' wealth, in theory both alternatives should help it to increase, with alternative 2 making the greater contribution. However, the current value of the company is over £800 m so the NPV of approximately £9.4 m will not make a significant impact.

The establishment of KL15 might help the employees and other stakeholders as it will produce employment and demand instead of the subsidiary KL3 which is only operating at 50%.

The company also wants to improve cash flows and dividends by 5% per annum. The cash flows in alternative 1 are greater than those in alternative 2, both inflows and outflows. As the first two years have cash outflows, the group will see a drop in cash flows in the first two years (and a greater drop under alternative 1). The investment will therefore be detrimental to the achievement of this objective, although, as with the first objective, the impact is insignificant in the group context.

(ii) *Risks and limitations*

The risks can be analysed under the areas of commercial, political, operational and financial:

The main commercial risk in alternative 1 is that there are fewer customers, on whom we will be more dependent, while alternative 2 has customers in developing countries, which might cause credit risk problems.

Although there are political uncertainties in the UK relating to safety issues, as mentioned in the scenario, there are further political risks in alternative 2 which include many customers in developing countries.

The main operational risk is that a change in the regulations means that the equipment specified in alternative 2 cannot be used, as it only allows for a modest change in regulations. One possibility is to go for the least-risk option of alternative 1, despite the lower NPV; this could be used in PR and corporate image projection to show the high environmental standards achieved by the group.

The financial risks refer to the calculation of the NPV. The WACC was used as a discount rate but it may not be appropriate to the investment under consideration; we would ideally find a proxy quoted company in the same business and use its beta but this might be difficult in practice.

We have assumed that we will take up the supplier's offer for the equipment purchase; this will protect us against the price rising but means that we pay the cash 6 months earlier than we would otherwise. We therefore need to look at the opportunity cost of this finance.

The revenue estimates have different possible ranges and those in alternative 2 are more likely to be in the mid-range while those under alternative 1 are more likely to be at the lower end. We need to use sensitivity analysis and simulation to establish the likelihood of these outcomes more accurately.

Currency risk is introduced in alternative 2 with diverse overseas customers; it would be sensible to look at the possibilities of hedging these revenues.

The equipment in alternative 2 will need replacing before that in alternative 1 but this is based on current estimates; in a field such as this in which technology is evolving, it is possible that lives may be shorter or alternatively could be extended through adaptive technology.

(iii) *Recommendations*

Maximising shareholders' wealth would suggest alternative 2, as would the employment prospects for the workforce. Alternative 1, however, is environmentally better and therefore may have other, less easily quantifiable, advantages for the group image. The risks discussed above are fairly balanced.

Neither contribute significantly to either objective and as such it is worth seeing if there are any larger scale investments that could be undertaken in preference to this.

(c) **Real options**

KL Group have three possible options relating to this investment – the abandonment option, the delay option and the follow-on option:

Abandonment option

An abandonment option is when a company can decide not to continue with an investment as circumstances change; this can increase the value of a project as there is less risk of being stuck with an unviable investment. Usually this is difficult when expenditure on capital equipment is involved as the main costs have been incurred and abandoning the project will only sacrifice revenues. In this situation alternative 1 could be abandoned if it did not take up the supplier's offer and risked the 5% increase in price; this, along with the redundancies and loss of KL3, seems a high price to pay for this option. In alternative 2 the project could be abandoned up until the factory is fully converted in 6 months' time.

Delay option

There may be scope for delaying the investment until the government decisions and regulations relating to these environmental issues are clearer. This may then allow a much better estimate of revenues and costs and consequently a more reliable decision on the investment. The current NPV has been calculated by using expected values based on subjective probabilities of the different courses of action by the government. We could therefore calculate different NPVs and estimate the probability of us undertaking the investment, based on expected values, but achieving a negative NPV; this would give us an idea of the value of the delay option.

Follow-on option

Sometimes investment decisions give other opportunities even if the original investment was not particularly beneficial in its own right (and possibly even had a negative NPV). In this situation, the knowledge gained in the operation or the reputation of a good environmental record in this area may lead to substantial other work. By its nature this will be difficult to quantify but could be valuable in an industry where safety and environmental concerns are important.

Question 2 – Dobbs

(a)

(i) *Present value of cash flows*

In millions	t_1	t_2	t_3	t_4
US$ cash flows	35.5	43.5	46.5	52.5
Inflated at 2.5%	36.4	45.7	50.1	58.0
Exchange rate (decrease by 1.035/1.045)	1.436	1.422	1.409	1.395
£ cash flows	25.3	32.1	35.5	41.6
Discount factors (13%)	0.885	0.783	0.693	0.613
Present values	22.4	25.1	24.6	25.5

Net present value = £97.6 m

Using a discount rate of 11% gives an NPV of £102.3 m

The present value of future cash flows over the next 4 years is a reasonable method of estimating the value of the company; asset valuations would not take account of the intellectual capital in the company in the form of the authors' contracts and without any kind of market price other methods could be difficult to apply.

The cash flows could have been discounted at a local cost of capital and then the present value translated at the spot rate, or as here translated at the different exchange rates likely to be ruling and discounting the home currency cash flows at the home country cost of capital.

The discount rate should be appropriate to the risk of the investment and therefore may need to be adjusted for additional currency risks and difference in operations. However, overseas diversification may help to decrease the risk to shareholders. The 11% usually used may not fully incorporate the difference in risk in the American investment; the 13% from a similar business to Alice Jain is more appropriate, although this is assuming the Finance Director has already adjusted it for the lower gearing in Alice Jain than Dobbs.

(ii) *Shares and debt*

In the worst case scenario the two majority shareholders take 50% in cash and the other shareholders all take cash.

Proportion taking shares = 0.50 × 60% = 30%

Proportion taking cash = 70%

Shares needed in Dobbs = (30% × £97.6 m/£8.85 = 3.31 m) shares at Dobbs' current share price.

Debt needed = (70% × £97.6 m) − £30 m = £38.3 m

This assumes that the full £30 m is still available from the sale of the other company and that there are no other demands on the money.

(b)

REPORT

To: Board of Dobbs plc
From: Financial Manager
Date:XXofX20XX

Potential acquisition of Alice Jain

This report will look at the viability of the purchase, strategies for enhancing the value, other recommendations for use of the funds and the directors' responsibilities in respect of fair treatment of all shareholders.

(i) *Viability of purchase*

The present value of the first 4 years' cash flows is approximately £97.6 m; the asset values at today's spot rate are worth approximately £40 m but this does not recognise the intellectual capital in the company in the form of the authors' contracts. Another possibility is to use an earnings multiple approach and use Dobbs' P/E ratio, giving (11.9 m × 10.3)/1.45 = £84.5 m. However, this again reflects the risk of Dobbs' operations in the UK and the expected growth prospects; the 13% cost of capital calculated by the Finance Director would suggest that the American company has a higher P/E ratio reflecting the higher growth potential often associated with a smaller company. This would therefore lead to the higher value mentioned above.

(ii) *Strategies for enhancing the value after acquisition*

There are a number of actions that could be taken to enhance the value after acquisition, including:

- Review the individual business units for costs that could be cut or assets that could be sold.
- Consider what economies of scale could be enjoyed across the group to reduce costs or improve revenues.
- Ensure that any reorganisation does not demotivate the staff, particularly in the acquired company, by improving and maintaining communication with the workforce.

- To safeguard the revenue stream we should review the contracts with authors and start looking at terms to renew them on expiry.
- Look at marketing the US magazines and books in the UK and vice versa to enhance revenue streams, and generally look at a more aggressive marketing strategy.
- Re-evaluate the group cost of capital which may have changed to reflect the investors' new perception of risk in the shares.

(iii) *Other recommendations for the funds*

The other possibility for the funds was to repay some debt and buy a smaller UK company. Whether it is worthwhile repaying debt depends on the opportunity cost of capital. If the cost of debt is less than 11% (which seems likely) and the group has investment opportunities which give an IRR in excess of 11%, the company should continue to use debt finance to maximise shareholders' wealth, in theory. If the debt is at a floating rate and the group expects an increase in the rate so that the cost rises above 11%, it might be appropriate to repay some debt.

We do not have information on industry averages, but the gearing of 46% by book values in the last balance sheet does not seem excessive and the interest cover was comfortable. Based on market values, the gearing is only 125/(125 + 398) = 24%

The £30m cash has not been included in this balance sheet and would be used to reduce the debt in the calculation, while the assets sold would reduce the equity. As the sale price would have exceeded the net asset value, this would reduce the gearing calculated.

The smaller UK company identified may or may not be a better acquisition for the group; no information is given about the target or about any potential synergies that might arise. It may reduce the risk associated with an overseas investment, but it may not provide as much in the way of strategic potential.

(iv) *Directors' responsibilities*

The UK Takeover code does not have the force of law but the Takeover Panel can reprimand a listed company, suspend the listing or effectively ensure that no regulated professionals want to work with the company. The objectives are to ensure fair and equal treatment between all shareholders; specifically they forbid:

- Action contrary to shareholders' best interests, such as agreeing or rejecting a bid to suit the managers' interests rather than those of the shareholders.
- Shareholders being treated differently in terms of the price offered.
- Information being restricted in its release and associated manipulation of the share prices.
- Insider dealing (this is also illegal).

Dobbs will also have to obey the US rules on competition.

Question 3 – C&C Airlines

(a) **Discount rate**

Using the competitor's beta we can degear it and calculate the asset beta:

1.3 (4/4.7) + 0.15 (0.7/4.7) = 1.13

Using CAPM, discount rate = 5 + (12 − 5) 1.13 = 12.9 or approximately 13%

(Note that assuming a debt beta of zero gives an asset beta of 1.106 and a discount rate of 12.75% or still approximately 13%.)

Limitations of CAPM are:

- It assumes that all the investors are diversified and that all unsystematic risk has been eliminated in the shareholders' portfolios.
- We have used another company as an approximation, but the listed company is likely to have rather different activities and the shareholders will view an unquoted company as far more risky than a listed company because of the marketability of the shares.
- CAPM gives a return which is valid for the next year (a single period model) but we intend to use it to discount a 3-year project.

(b) **Net present value**

Expected number of passengers:

Year 1 = 220 × (1 × 0.1 + 0.8 × 0.5 + 0.5 × 0.3 + 0.4 × 0.1) = 151.8

Year 2 = 220 × (1 × 0.15 + 0.8 × 0.6 + 0.5 × 0.2 + 0.4 × 0.05) = 165

The revenues generated will be the above 48 × 6 × £300 and inflated at 2%

Predicted exchange rates:

t_0	1.530	
t_1	1.530 × 1.04/1.03	1.545
t_2	1.545 × 1.04/1.03	1.560
t_3	1.560 × 1.04/1.03	1.575

In £'000	t_0	t_1	t_2	t_3
Income		13,378	14,832	15,129
Sterling costs (inflated at 3%)		(2,987)	(3,077)	(3,169)
Overheads		(600)	(600)	(600)
Fuel costs (translated and 5% inflation)		(2,855)	(2,969)	(3,087)
		6,936	8,186	8,273
Tax on operating cash flows		(2,081)	(2,456)	(2,482)
Capital costs	(19,608)			10,159
Tax on capital allowances		1,471	1,103	261
	(19,608)	6,326	6,833	16,211
Discount factor at 13%	1	0.885	0.783	0.693
	(19,608)	5,598	5,351	11,234

(i) Net present value = £2.575 m

(ii)

Net cash flows	(19,608)	6,326	6,833	16,211
Certainty equivalents	1	0.90	0.85	0.80
	(19,608)	5,693	5,809	12,969
Discount factor at 9%	1	0.917	0.842	0.772
	(19,608)	5,220	4,891	10,012

Net present value = £0.515 m

Based on these calculations, the investment should go ahead. Both methods do depend heavily on the resale value of the plane, however.

(c)

REPORT

To: Board of C&C Airlines plc
From: Assistant to Financial Manager
Date: xx of x 20xx

Investment appraisal of new plane

This report will look at the major economic factors that will impact on the investment decision, the commercial areas of greatest uncertainty and the strategies for dealing with these risks.

1. *Major economic forces*

   The major economic forces that might impact on the success of the investment, include:

   - The changes in interest rates, both in absolute terms and relatively between those in the Caribbean and the UK. This will affect the borrowing costs, the fuelling costs and the demand.
   - Increased interest rate might increase prices in the Caribbean and impact on the tourist business.
   - The airline industry is affected by political and safety concerns which can impact on the access to airports and the number of flights, and their timing allowed.

2. *Commercial aspects involving uncertainty*

   Those commercial aspects which carry the greatest uncertainty and hence risk to the project are:

   - The future state of the tourist trade and estimates of the expansion in demand; are there sufficient numbers of tourists wanting flights only rather than a pack age holiday?
   - Whether there is a realistic demand for a low-cost no-frills airline to fly to an up-market destination.
   - The level of competition in the industry and particularly rivals flying to similar destinations.
   - The high passenger loading required to be viable.
   - The resale value of the plane which will be dependent upon the availability of second-hand planes in 3 years' time.
   - The insurance and security costs may increase as airlines come under attack more.

3. *Strategies for dealing with risks*

   Dealing with these might include:

   - Hedging exchange rates and possibly buying fuel forward to mitigate the effect of rising prices.

- Aim for a mixed demand of tourist and business visitors; in the long term, consider whether an alliance could be made with larger airlines that do not fly to the destination.
- Assess the impact on the viability of the investment of a lower resale value and consider the possibility of agreeing a deal now to take place in 3 years' time.
- Take out insurance and employ security guards to combat the security risks, although this can only mitigate them to a limited extent and can be very expensive.

4. *Recommendations*

- There are large number of estimates and probabilities involved in the calculations. The probabilities attached to the loadings should be reviewed carefully, and all estimates assessed to determine the decision's sensitivity to changes in each. The certainty equivalents are not justified at all and there is an argument for applying different certainties to the operating cash flows and the resale of the plane. The 9% also seems high if the cash flows have been converted into certainty equivalents and there is no justification given for this rate.
- Overall, all the estimates need looking at carefully and sensitivity analysis should be carried out, but based on these calculations the investment should go ahead and the various methods for mitigating the risks identified above implemented.

Question 4 – Hi-Clean

(a) **2005 forecasts**

	Public Sector £m	*Hotels/Restaurants* £m	*Total* £m
Sales revenue	104.90	131.00	235.90
Direct costs	57.69	65.50	123.19
Gross profit (45%, 50%)	47.21	65.50	112.71
Fixed overheads (apport'd)	31.93	39.87	71.80
Operating profit	15.28	25.63	40.91
Interest (25 m × 0.06)			1.50
			39.41
Taxation (18%)			7.09
Profit after tax			32.32
Dividends (30%)			9.69
Retained earnings			22.63
EPS			
107.7pence			

Sales revenue

Public sector $= [(102 \times 0.55) + (112 \times 0.45)] \times 0.6 + [(95 \times 0.5) + (110 \times 0.5)] \times 0.4$
$= 104.9$

Hotels $= (123 \times 0.6) + (143 \times 0.4) = 131$

Gross profit is forecast to grow at a faster rate than the fixed costs. As this will lead to an increased operating profit and as interest costs are falling, the constant payout ratio will lead to an increase in dividends of 15%.

(b)

REPORT

To: Board of Hi-clean plc
From: Financial Manager
Date: xx of x 20xx

Company valuation and venture capitalist

This report will look at possible valuations for the company and the stake held by the venture capitalist.

1. *Asset valuation*

   We could value the company by adding up the value of all the assets less liabilities of the company. This would give £147 m at the end of 2004 and a further £22.63 m of retained earnings in 2005 giving £169.6 m at the end of 2005. However this does not take account of the value of the future revenue streams, as it makes no allowance for the goodwill that has been generated by the business. In addition, the asset values of buildings, land and other fixed assets may not be up to date in the balance sheet.

2. *Dividend valuation model*

   We could value the future projected dividends by discounting the forecasts. The industry cost of capital is 9% and to estimate growth we could look at past growth. As earnings have grown by 20% each year and dividend payout ratio has remained constant at 30%, dividends have also grown by 20% per annum. Even between 2004 and 2005, dividends are forecast to increase by 15%. As both of these are in excess of the return required, it cannot continue at this level indefinitely. To give a base position we could assume a zero growth:

   $$\frac{D_1}{(k_e - g)} = \frac{9.69}{0.09} = £107.7\text{ m}$$

   As this is less than the asset valuation, it is not very reliable. With 5% growth, it would give:

   $$\frac{(9.69 \times 1.05)}{(0.09 - 0.05)} = £254.4\text{ m}$$

3. *Earnings capitalisation*

   We could assume steady earnings which are all paid out rather than only 30%, giving:

   $$\frac{32.32}{0.09} = £359\text{ m}$$

4. *Earnings multiple*

   The industry P/E ratio is forecast to be somewhere between 12 and 15; applying these to post-tax profits gives a variety of estimates:

P/E ratio	12	13	14	15
Value (£32.32 × multiple)	£388 m	£420 m	£452 m	£485 m

5. *Summary of valuations*

The venture capitalist owns 20% of the company so the range of values gives:

	Group total £m	*VC share (20%)* £m
Assets	170	34
Dividends	108	22
Capitalised earnings	359	72
Earnings multiple	388–485	78–97

The highest values are given by the earnings multiple calculated from the industry P/E ratios, even at the lower end of the forecasts.

6. *Venture capitalist's share*

Although the venture capitalist has a seat on the Board, the seat may not be transferable to a new holder, particularly if the shareholding is split up. It therefore does not give control and a 20% stake may be worth substantially less than suggested above; as there is not a stock market listing there is no liquid market in the shares which will also reduce the value of the holding. However, if the venture capitalist exercised the warrants, it would give control of over 26% which could increase its value substantially, as it gives the power to block special resolutions.

(c) **Venture capital return**

The return achieved by the venture capitalist will depend on the price obtained on the sale. If we use the earnings multiple approach based on a P/E ratio of 12 and capitalised earnings:

	P/E ratio	*Earnings capitalisation*
20% of value	78	72
Investment	25	25
	53	47
Dividends (Working)	7	7
Total return	60	54
Percentage of investment	240%	216%
Annual return (Working)	27.7%	25.9%

Working

Working backwards at 20% growth per annum, dividend = 0.20 × (9.69 + 8.43 + 7.02 + 5.85 + 4.88)

Annual return given by $(1 + r)^5 = 3.40$ or 3.16

It can be seen from this that the venture capitalist will not make the required return of 50% per annum. If a simple interest approach had been used instead of compound capital growth, the results would have been 48% and 43% respectively, which are closer. A sale value near the top end of the multiple range would have to be achieved to satisfy this objective.

These calculations also do not take into account the possible downgrading of the value of the stake on sale from a straight 20% of the total value of the company, as discussed above. This would reduce the return further.

Typical exit routes would be to sell them on the open market or privately to a third party. In this case the company is unquoted so the venture capitalist will have to find another private investor; this may be another venture capitalist or the current owners, managers or employees. It is possible that the second group would have difficulty raising the finance required and would try to negotiate an earn-out which would delay payment even longer. The venture capitalist may therefore want the company to float on the stock market as it would give a much easier exit route, probably at a better price and would enable them to exercise their warrants, giving them a greater return.

(d) **Risks and opportunities**

The main risks and opportunities facing the company are:

- The outcome of the election. This will directly affect the sales to the public sector; if party B wins, the company will need to try to increase the sales to the private sector. This may not be easy as all the industry competitors will have the same objective.
- Exchange rate fluctuations. As the company imports equipment a change in the exchange rate could have a dramatic impact on the profitability of the company. The company should consider hedging the risk.
- Interest rate fluctuations. As the loan is a floating rate, an increase in rates could cause a problem. The current rates seem to be lower so it may be an opportunity to refinance the loan (which has to be repaid in 2006) and possibly increase the gearing of the company, which is currently low.
- The change in ownership of the venture capitalist stake. The new owner may want to be more actively involved in the management of the company. This could be an opportunity if they bring additional skills or bring a risk of unwanted interference.
- A listing on the stock market. Flotation would bring greater marketability of shares and the ability to raise finance more easily but also brings greater public scrutiny. The sale of a large stake held by the venture capitalist might also depress the share price.

Question 5 – JHC Group

(a) (i) **Net present values**

Alternative 1

In €'000

	t_0	t_1	t_2	t_3	t_{4-8}
Equipment	(3,200)	(4,800)			
Revenue		4,480	11,800	17,600	17,600
Variable costs		(1,568)	(4,130)	(6,160)	(6,160)
Fixed costs		(2,500)	(2,500)	(2,500)	(2,500)
Redundancy	(2,100)				
Conversion		(2,800)			
Tax					(1,788)
Lost earnings		(2,200)	(2,200)	(2,200)	(2,200)
	(5,300)	(9,388)	2,970	6,740	4,952
Discount factor	1	0.917	0.842	0.772	3.890 × 0.772
	(5,300)	(8,609)	2,501	5,203	14,871

Net present value × €8,666,000 over 8 years

Alternative 2

In €'000

	t_0	t_1	t_2	t_3	t_{4-6}
Equipment	(4,500)				
Revenue		7,800	9,680	13,130	13,130
Variable costs		(1,560)	(1,936)	(2,626)	(2,626)
Fixed costs		(1,500)	(1,500)	(1,500)	(1,500)
Redundancy	(420)				
Conversion		(2,800)			
Tax					(1,801)
Lost earnings		(2,200)	(2,200)	(2,200)	(2,200)
	(4,920)	(260)	4,044	6,804	5,003
Discount factor	1	0.917	0.842	0.772	2.531 × 0.772
	(4,920)	(238)	(3,405)	(5,253)	(9,776)

Net present value = €13,276,000 over 6 years

On the basis of these calculations, it would appear that alternative 2 is the better option.

These calculations assume:

- The WACC is the appropriate discount rate, but this may not be the case if the business or financial risk changes.
- In alternative 1, we have assumed that we accept the supplier's offer to pay a 50% deposit to secure the price.
- The two alternatives have been assessed over the lives of the machines. They, therefore, have not considered the loss in earnings from CC, or any other cash flows, beyond this.
- Cash flows beyond year 3 have been assumed to remain constant but this may not be realistic. The objectives say that JHC intend to increase operating cash flows by 4% pa but this may be achieved by undertaking new projects or increasing revenues on certain projects, rather than increasing cash flows on all projects across the board. Any increase in cash flows beyond year 3 would clearly increase the net present values.

(ii) **MIRR**

The MIRR calculates the Internal Rate of Return, having first converted all cash flows into two single cash flows – the initial investment and a final terminal cash flow. This second cash flow is produced by compounding forward all cash flows, except the initial investment, at the normal cost of capital to the end of the project life. The advantages and disadvantages include.

- Having only two cash flows makes the calculation of the IRR straightforward and avoids the possibility of multiple IRRs.
- The MIRR will usually give the same ranking as the NPV.
- However, compounding cash flows at the cost of capital rather than the true IRR (implicit in a 'normal' IRR) will understate the value of good projects and overstate poor ones.
- In addition, because of the use of the cost of capital to take cash flows to their terminal value, the longer the project the more approximate it becomes.

In this case, the alternatives have different lives, which makes the MIRR less appropriate.

(b)

REPORT

To: Board of JHC Group
From: Financial Manager
Date: xx of x 20xx

New subsidiary, SP

This report will discuss how the new subsidiary might help the group achieve its objectives, consider other relevant factors and make recommendations on the way forward.

(i) *Achievement of objectives*

The two alternatives give different net present values; although both give positive values which would suggest the investment is viable, the greater net present value is achieved under alternative 2 with €13.276 m. In terms of shareholders' wealth, in theory both alternatives should help it to increase, with alternative 2 making the greater contribution. However, the current value of the company is over €2,900 m so the NPV of approximately €13 m will not make a significant impact. In theory this would add about 4 cents to the current share price of €8.31. In this respect there is little to choose between them.

The establishment of SP might help the employees and other stakeholders as it will produce employment and demand instead of the subsidiary CC which is only operating at 60%.

The company also wants to improve cash flows and dividends by 4% per annum. Under both alternatives, the first two years have cash outflows, so the group will see a drop in cash flows in the first two years (and a greater drop under alternative 1). The investment will, therefore, be detrimental to the achievement of this objective, although, as with the first objective, the impact is insignificant in the group context. There will be little significant impact on dividends.

(ii) *Other factors to consider*

The main commercial risk in alternative 1 is that there are fewer customers, on whom we will be more dependent, while alternative 2 has customers in developing countries, which might cause credit risk problems.

Although there are political uncertainties in the UK relating to safety issues, as mentioned in the scenario, there are further political risks in alternative 2 which includes overseas customers.

The main operational risk is that a change in the regulations means that the equipment specified in alternative 2 cannot be used, as it only allows for a modest change in regulations. One possibility is to go for the least-risk option of alternative 1, despite the lower NPV; this could be used in PR and corporate image projection to show the high environmental standards achieved by the group.

In the calculation of the NPV, the WACC was used as a discount rate but it may not be appropriate to the investment under consideration; we would ideally find a proxy quoted company in the same business and use its beta but this might be difficult in practice.

We have assumed that we will take up the supplier's offer for the equipment purchase; this will protect us against the price rising but means that we pay the cash 6 months earlier than we would otherwise. We, therefore, need to look at the opportunity cost of this finance.

The revenue estimates have different possible ranges; we need to use sensitivity analysis and simulation to establish the likelihood of these outcomes more accurately. Currency risk is introduced in alternative 2 and it would be sensible to look at the possibility of hedging these revenues.

The equipment in alternative 2 will need replacing before that in alternative 1 but this is based on current estimates; in a field such as this in which technology is evolving, it is possible that lives may be shorter or alternatively could be extended through adaptive technology.

(iii) *Recommendations*

Maximising shareholders' wealth would suggest alternative 2, as would the employment prospects for the workforce. Alternative 1, however, is environmentally better and therefore may have other, less easily quantifiable, advantages for the group image. The risks discussed above are fairly evenly balanced.

Neither contribute significantly to either objective and as such it is worth seeing if there are any larger-scale investments that could be undertaken in preference to this.

(c) **Real options**

JHC Group have three possible options relating to this investment – the abandonment option, the delay option and the follow-on option.

Abandonment option

An abandonment option is when a company can decide not to continue with an investment as circumstances change; this can increase the value of a project as there is less risk of being stuck with an unviable investment. Usually this is difficult when expenditure on capital equipment is involved as the main costs have been incurred and abandoning the project will only sacrifice revenues. In this situation, alternative 1 could be abandoned if it did not take up the supplier's offer and risked the 5% increase in price; this, along with the redundancies and loss of CC, seems a high price to pay for this option. In alternative 2 the project could be abandoned up until the factory is fully converted in 6 months' time.

Delay option

There may be scope for delaying the investment until the government decisions and regulations relating to these environmental issues are clearer. This may then allow a much better estimate of revenues and costs and consequently a more reliable decision on the investment. The current NPV has been calculated by using expected values based on subjective probabilities of the different courses of action by the government. We could, therefore, calculate different NPVs and estimate the probability of us undertaking the investment, based on expected values, but achieving a negative NPV; this would give us an idea of the value of the delay option.

Follow-on option

Sometimes investment decisions give other opportunities even if the original investment was not particularly beneficial in its own right (and possibly even had a negative NPV). In this situation, the knowledge gained in the operation or the reputation of a good environmental record in this area may lead to substantial other work. By its nature this will be difficult to quantify but could be valuable in the health food industry.

Question 6 – GAS plc

(a) *Investment criterion 1*

Year	*1*	*2*	*3*	*4–9*	*10*
	B$ million	*B$ million*	*B$ million*	*B$ million*	*B$ million*
Operating cash flows	20	150	150	300	300
Loss on realisation of working capital					−10
Net profit before depreciation	20	150	250	300	290
Deduct depreciation	−35	−35	−35	−35	−35
Annual accounting profit	−15	115	215	265	255
Tax at 20% (see note 1)	0	−20	−43	−53	−51
Net cash flow repatriated to the UK = (operating cash flows − tax)	20	130	207	247	249

Average annual profit $216 = \dfrac{(-15 + 115 + 215 + (6 \times 265) + 255)}{10}$

Average investment $570 = \dfrac{(700 + 50 + 350 + 40)}{2}$ (see note 2)

Accounting rate of return $37.9\% = \dfrac{216}{570}$

Note 1: Alternative assumptions regarding the offset of losses for tax purposes were also acceptable.

Note 2: Average investment of (700 + 50 + 350 + 40)/2 was also acceptable.

Workings: Loss on realisation of working capital: BS$10m = 20% × B$50m Cash flow repatriated Year 10: 249 = 300 − 51 (ignoring loss on realisation of working capital and depreciation)

Conclusion: The project gives a pre-tax accounting rate of return of 37.9%, well in excess of the minimum requirement of 25%.

Investment criterion 2

Year	*0* B$ *million*	*1* B$ *million*	*2* B$ *million*	*3* B$ *million*	*4* B$ *million*	*5–9* B$ *million*	*10* B$ *million*	*11* B$ *million*
Net cash flow repatriated to the UK		20	130	207	247	247	249	
UK tax paid at 30% paid one year in arrears			−6	−39	−62.1	−74.1	−74.1	−74.7
less tax relief on Bustan tax			0	20	43	53	53	51
Net UK taxes			−6	−19	−19.1	−21.1	−21.1	−23.7
Post-tax repatriated funds		20	124	188	227.9	225.9	227.9	−23.7
Initial investment & working capital	−750						390	
Net cash flow in $million	−750	20	124	188	227.9	225.9	617.9	−23.7
Converted to £million at 0.7778	−964.3	25.7	159.4	241.7	293.0	290.4	794.4	−30.5
Discount factor at 16% *(W1)*	1	0.862	0.743	0.641	0.552	1.807 *(W2)*	0.227 *(W3)*	0.195
NPV	−964.3	22.2	118.5	154.9	161.7	524.8	180.3	−5.9
Cumulative NPV	192.2							

Workings:

W1 (1 + 10.5%)(1 + 10%)/(1 + 4.8%) − 1 = 15.983% so use 16% as an approximation

W2 Either: AF5yrs@16% × DF4yrs@16% = 3.274 × 0.552 = 1.807
Or: AF9yrs@16% × AF4yrs@16% = 4.607 − 2.798 = 1.809

W3 DF10yrs@16% = 0.227

Alternative approach using a discount factor of 10.5%

Year	*0*	*1*	2	3	4	5	6	7	8	9	10	11
	B$ *million*	B$ *million*	B$ *million*	B$ *million*	B$ *million*	B$ *million*	B$ *million*	B$ *million*	B$ *million*	B$ *million*	B$ *million*	B$ *million*
Net cash flow repatriated to the UK		20	130	207	247	247	247	247	247	247	249	
UK tax paid at 30% paid one			−6	−39	−62.1	−74.1	−74.1	−74.1	−74.1	−74.1	−74.1	−74.7
year in arrears less tax relief on Bustan tax			0	20	43	53	53	53	53	53	53	51
Net UK taxes			−6	−19	−19.1	−21.1	−21.1	−21.1	−21.1	−21.1	−21.1	−23.7
Post tax repatriated profit		20	124	188	227.9	225.9	225.9	225.9	225.9	225.9	227.9	−23.7
Initial investment & working capital	−750										390	
Net cash flow in $million	−750	20	124	188	227.9	225.9	225.9	225.9	225.9	225.9	617.9	−23.7
Exchange rate (*W1*)	0.7778	0.8164	0.8569	0.8994	0.9440	0.9909	1.0401	1.0917	1.1458	1.2027	1.2624	1.3250
£ Sterling equivalent	−964.3	24.5	144.7	209.0	241.4	228.0	217.2	206.9	197.1	187.8	489.5	−17.9
Discount factor at 10.5% (*W2*)	1	0.9050	0.8190	0.7412	0.6707	0.6070	0.5493	0.4971	0.4499	0.4071	0.3684	0.3334
NPV	−964.3	22.2	118.5	154.9	161.9	138.4	119.3	102.8	88.7	76.5	180.3	−6.0
Cumulative NPV	193.2											

Wl: Exchange rate: 0.8164 = 0.7778 × 1.10/1.048 and so on

W2: Discount factor: 0.9050 = 1/1.105 0.8190 = $1/1.105^2$ and so on

[*Examiner's Note:* The slight difference in the NPV's on pages 297 and 298 is due to roundings.]

Note: An alternative approach, using a discount factor of 10.5% is shown on the next page.

Conclusion: The project has a positive NPV of £192m at a risk-adjusted cost of capital of 10.5% and therefore meets investment criterion 2.

(b) The key risks that should be discussed include:

- Costs and revenue estimates
  - Realisation of the plant and equipment – How reliable is this estimate? It may be totally unrealistic to assume that the investment in plant and equipment could be not realised at all, let alone as early as the last day of the project.
  - Operating cash flows – How reliable are the forecasts here, for example, could capital expenditure on plant and equipment exceed budget?
- Timings of cash flows – What is the risk that construction takes longer than planned and hence receipt of positive cash flows being delayed?
- Regulator/political interference
  - Taxes – Could these change either in the UK or in Bustan?
  - Repatriation of profits – Might this be blocked?
  - What is the risk that the regulator might restrict the operation of the networks and generators in favour of local operators in future?
- Exchange risk – Will exchange rates mirror interest rate differentials?
- Discount rate – Does this adequately reflect the risk profile of the project?

(c)

REPORT

To: Board of GAS plc
From: External Management Consultant
Date: 23 November 2005
Subject: Share price volatility

Introduction/terms of reference

The purpose of this report is to address the following three issues relating to the entity's share price:

(i) Possible reasons for the unusually volatile movements in the entity's share price.
(ii) Fair market price for the entity's shares.
(iii) How and to what extent the share price can be influenced by the Board.

(i) ***Possible reasons for the unusually volatile movements in the entity's share price in the twelve months up to and including 1 January 2005***

Introduction: the semi-strong efficient market
In a semi-strong efficient market, the share price will reflect all publicly available information, including anticipated results or actions.

Beginning of 2004: proposal invitation
It is likely that the invitation to submit a proposal would be widely known and in the public domain. Any impact on the share price of GAS plc would depend on.

- Expectations that the entity would submit a proposal (for example, has the entity been interested in similar projects in the past and does this fit its business strategy);
- Expectations that the entity would be successful in having its proposal accepted (for example, the number of projects available and the number of entities invited and/or intending to submit proposals);
- Expectations of the profitability of the project.

June 2004: submit proposal
Any impact on the share price in June 2004 will largely depend on the extent to which the project announcement has already been factored into the entity's share price ahead of the formal announcement of the acceptance of the proposal.

January 2005: proposal accepted
The share price of GAS plc would be expected to rise on announcement of the acceptance of the proposal unless GAS plc had been singled out as the most likely contractor at an earlier stage and the market had already factored the effects of the proposal being accepted into the share price.

The extent of a rise in share price in January 2005 will depend on market perceptions of

- the profitability of the project
- the risk profile of the cash flows
- the likelihood of obtaining further similar contracts in the future as a direct result of this proposal being accepted.

General economic and business conditions
The share price of GAS plc will also be affected by changes in general economic and business conditions such as.

- energy prices
- national disasters and other disruptions to supplies
- world demand for energy.

(ii) Fair market price for the entity's shares in January 2005

Theoretical ex-rights price (TERP) before project cash flows
Ignoring the new project and looking at the impact of the rights issue in isolation, the entity's share price can be forecast as 328pence after the rights issue.

Workings:

$$\text{Amount to be raised} = \frac{\$700\,\text{m}}{0.7778} = £900\,\text{m}$$

Number of shares to be issued at 1 for 4 = 300

So price rights at £3 each in order to raise £900m (300 × £3)

$$\text{TERP} = \frac{1,200 \times 335\text{ pence} + 300 \times 300\text{ pence}}{(1,200 + 300)} = 328\text{ pence}$$

If the market is optimistic about the outcome of the proposed new investment and a semi-strong efficient market applies, the share price would be expected to respond positively to the announcement of the acceptance of the proposal and rise above the TERP.

TERP after adjusting for project cash flows
A valuation based on the NPV of the project gives a predicted share price of 341 pence after the rights issue as follows:

NPV of project cash flows	192.00
Current value of shares	4,02000 (1,200 shares × 335 pence)
Proceeds of rights issues	900.00 (300 shares × £3)
	5,11200
New number of shares	1,500
New share price	341 pence $\left(\frac{5,11200}{1,500}\right)$

However, this assumes that:

- The market has sufficient information to produce an accurate estimate of the NPV of the proposed project, which is unlikely to be the case.
- The whole of the added value is reflected in the share price before commencement of the project.

Workings: $\frac{(£5,11200) - (30\% \times 192)}{1,500} = 337$

Dividend growth model valuation
The dividend growth model valuation gives a much higher share price valuation of 512 pence as follows:

	Pence	*Workings*
2005	12.80	$= 14/1.094$
2006	11.70	$= 14/1.094^2$
2007	10.69	$= 14/1.094^3$
2008 on	476.70	$\frac{14(1.07)}{(0.094) - 0.07)(1.094^3)}$
	511.89 pence	

This would suggest that the intended dividends are unsustainable from the projected profits of the project.

On the evidence of the earnings of this project alone, it is unreasonable to assume that the entity will be able to afford to increase dividend growth per share from 5% to 7% per annum and pay these dividends on a larger share base.

The dividend forecast is also based on the unrealistic premise that the 7% dividend growth rate will continue indefinitely, even beyond the 10-year time horizon of the project before taking into account any growth in earnings in other parts of the business.

Conclusion

In practice, the share price is likely to be quite close to the TERP of 328 pence plus some small premium to reflect the likely increase in shareholder value as a result of the new project.

Examiner's note:

The following calculations are included for tuition purposes and are beyond what would be expected from a good 'pass' in the examination:

Note that 'freezing' dividends at 14 pence per share represents an increase in dividend per amount invested in shares of 2% due to the effect of the rights issue discount.

Workings:

14 pence dividend post rights issue = 13.71 pence dividend pre-rights issue where 13.71 = 14 pence × 328/335.

The share price can be shown to be highly sensitive to the underlying dividend growth rate. At a growth rate of 6% from 2008, the current share price would be 369 pence:

	Pence	*Working*
2005	12.80	$= 14/1.094$
2006	11.70	$= 14/1.094^2$
2007	10.69	$= 14/1.094^3$
2008 on	333.35	$\frac{14(1.06)}{(0.094 - 0.06 \times 1.094^3)}$
	368.54 pence	

At a growth rate of 5% from 2008, the current share price would be 290 pence

	Pence	*Working*
2005	12.80	$= 14/1.094$
2006	11.70	$= 14/1.094^2$
2007	10.69	$= 14/1.094^3$
2008 on	255.16	$\frac{14(1.05)}{(0.094 - 0.06 \times 1.064^3)}$
	290.35 pence	

The project cash flows would therefore only appear to support a rise in dividends of between 5% and 6% rather than the 7% growth that was announced.

(iii) *How and to what extent the share price can be influenced by the Board*

Informing the market

It is important that the directors keep the market informed promptly of any changes affecting the performance or future business developments. The market will then factor this information into the share price of the entity and ensure that the share price is a fair reflection of the value of the entity and its future prospects.

Releasing price sensitive information on a regular basis should reduce the volatility of the share price. This can be achieved by regular release of information to the market on current performance and business developments.

Dividend predictions
Dividend plans need to be achievable and sustainable out of forecast future earnings to give a fair indication to the market of the future prospects of the entity. A smooth dividend stream enables individual shareholders and institutions to plan their portfolio and income stream and should reduce share price volatility. Announcing a 7% increase in dividends that the market views as unsustainable would not lead to the large increase in share price that would be expected based on the dividend growth model.

Regulatory issues
Consider potential conflicts of interest arising. For example, an over-optimistic projection of project returns could improve director bonuses if these are linked to the share price.

Summary and conclusion

The volatility of the share price in the last 12 months can largely be explained by the speculation surrounding the Bustan project.

Note also that the dividend forecasts appear to be unrealistic in relation to the profits to be generated by the proposed project and may need to be revised. However, this could have a serious impact on the credibility of the management and on the entity's rating and share price if the market has already factored the increased dividends into the share price.

Assuming that the market has largely ignored the new dividend forecasts, the share price on 1 January 2005 is likely to be based on the TERP of 328.08 pence. There may also be a small premium of no more than 10 pence a share to take into account the additional wealth generated by the new project.

Examiner's note:
The answer to this question is fuller than was expected from a well-prepared candidate.

Question 7 – PM Industries

(a) (i) *Preliminary calculations*

It is useful to convert some of NQ's figures from US$ to £ at spot of 1.85:

Earnings	\$300 m/1.85	=	£162.2 m
Share price	450 cents/1.85	=	243 pence
Market capitalisation	243 pence × 850 m shares	=	£2,065 m

The Finance Director and advisors of PM have assumed that PM's own pre-merger P/E ratio will be applied by the market to the combined earnings of the merged entity, as follows:

Pre-merger	*PM*	*NQ*	*PM + NQ*	
Earnings (£m)	273	162.2	435.2	
Number of shares (million)	950	850	1,375	(950 + 850/2)
EPS (pence)	28.74	19.08	31.65	
P/E ratio	15.87	12.73	15.87	
Share price (pence)	456	243	502	
Market value (£m)	4,332	2,065	6,903	(502 pence × 1,375 m shares)

Post-merger

Proportion of merged entity owned by the present shareholders of:

PM (950/1,375 × 100)	69.1%		
NQ (425/1,375 × 100)		30.9%	
Market value (proportion × 6,903)	4,770	2,133	6,903
Number of shares pre-merger (m)	950	850	
Post-merger share price per existing share (pence)	502	251	

PM has assumed its own P/E ratio of 15.87 will be applied to the combined earnings of the merged entity. The combined total of the current market capitalisation of PM and NQ in sterling is £6,397 m (£4,332 m + £2,065 m). The difference between the estimated post-merger value and the current value is £506 m. This is the 'bootstrapping' effect – the difference between the P/E ratios is 3.14 (15.87 – 12.73) × NQ's earnings of £162.2 m.

Note: Precise reconciliation is difficult because of roundings.

(ii) In the absence of any synergy, and assuming the market is unaware of PM's estimate of the value of the software licences, there is no reason why the stock market value of the merged entity should be any different from £6,397 m. This would suggest post-merger prices per existing share of:

PM – £6,397 × 69.1% = £4,420 or 465 pence per share compared with 456 pence now

NQ – £6,397 × 30.9% = £1,977 or 233 pence per share compared with 243 pence now

This implies a transfer of wealth from NQ's shareholders to PM's as the share exchange offered is more generous to PM than the ratio of old share prices. Pre-merger share prices would suggest 456:243 or 1 for 1.88 not 1 for 2.

(iii) If PM genuinely believes it can bootstrap NQ's earnings and also believes the software licences are worth £100 m, it could offer the following:

	£m
Value of merged entity	6,903
Plus: Sale of licences	100
Less: Current value of PM	4,332
	2,671

Maximum price £2,671 m, or 314 pence per share

If a share exchange, this suggests a maximum offer in the region of 1 PM for 1.5 NQ.

(b)

REPORT

To: Board of PM
From: Financial Advisor
Date: 24 May 2006
Subject: Evaluation of merger with NQ

Introduction

The purpose of this report is to evaluate the proposed merger between PM and NQ. In accordance with the terms of reference, the following issues are discussed:

- The contribution of the merger to the achievement of PM's financial objectives.
- The external economic forces that might help or hinder the achievement of the merger's financial objectives. Some comments are also provided on the policies that the merged entity could consider to help reduce the adverse effects of such economic forces.
- Potential post-merger value enhancing strategies that could increase our share holders' wealth.

The report proceeds as follows:

In sections (i), (ii) and (iii) each of the above issues is discussed followed by a short conclusion.

An appendix is provided that shows figures to support the discussion in section (i).

Section (i) – How the merger might contribute to the achievement of PM's financial objectives

Increase EPS by 5% per annum

- PM has demonstrated steady growth in both revenue and earnings since 2002 (this could be supported by growth percentages as shown in appendix 1), although earnings as a percentage of revenue is declining – which might suggest the entity is aggressively reducing prices to obtain market share, but is also managing to control costs to allow earnings growth.
- If PM acquires NQ immediately, the effect would be to increase revenue in the first full year of operations. Earnings per share have been projected as 31.65 pence per share. Assuming around 567 m new shares are issued (850 m old NQ shares in issue/1.5) this would mean 1,517 billion in total. This implies earnings of £480 m. Clearly, as a percentage increase on only PM's 2005 earnings this is an increase well above 5%. On the combined earnings it is an increase of 10%.
- If the more realistic projections are taken, it is unlikely PM will 'grow' earnings at the rate expected, at least in the first full year of operations. Assuming both entities' earnings grow at the same rate as 2005/06, this would imply earnings of £457 m [PM's 2005/06 earnings of £273 m × 1.058 plus NQ's 2005/06 earnings of £162.2 m × 1.034]. This is an increase of just 5% (£457 m compared with combined earnings of £435.2 m in 2005/06].
- On the positive side, no real savings or synergies have yet been identified and these might help boost earnings. It is, therefore, quite possible PM's management will be

able to increase NQ's earnings sufficiently more than 3.4% to more easily clear the 5% hurdle, so the merger could make a greater contribution to the achievement of this objective.
- There will, of course, be an impact on future earnings of the sale of the licences. There is insufficient information in the scenario to quantify this.

Maintain a gearing ratio below 30%

- Current gearing is 28% [market value of debt is £1,207 m [£1,150 m × £105/100 as percentage of market capitalisation of £4,332 m].
- If the merger is on the basis of a share exchange, and assuming a market capitalisation of the merged entity of £6,903 m, the ratio falls to 21.8% [PM's debt of £1,207 m as calculated above plus NQ's debt of £297 m ($550 m/1.85) as percentage of £6,903].
- If a cash alternative is offered and 50% or 100% of NQ's shareholders accept, the gearing would clearly rise well in excess of 30% (*Note:* calculations could be provided here, but are not expected.).
- All these calculations ignore movements in the market prices of debt and equity and the exchange rate, but they are unlikely to be substantially different unless there is a major market crash.

Maintain a P/E ratio above the industry average

- Future growth rating by the market depends on how the merger is received by the market. Typically, bidders overpay for their acquisitions and as a result are downgraded by the market. However, PM does appear to have a better track record than NQ and if it is an agreed merger there is less likelihood of PM overpaying.
- Unlikely PM's P/E ratio will maintain for the merged entity, at least in the immediate future. The P/E is more likely to be a weighted average as follows:

PM 15.87 × 69.1% = 11
NQ 12.73 × 30.9% = 3.9
Say, 15.

This is still above the industry average of 14, but ignores potential downside risks, such as problems with integration and exchange rate volatility affecting the increased percentage of the business now conducted overseas.

Section (ii) – External economic forces that might affect the achievement of the entity's objectives

The success of the merger depends on a number of factors:

- The NQ shareholders' willingness to accept sterling denominated shares (and dividends).
- The movement of the exchange rate between sterling and the US$. A merger such as this may take between 6 and 12 months to complete. Well over 40% of the merged entity's profits will be generated in the US and exchange rates in countries in the rest of the world may be pegged to the US$. However, interest rate parity suggests the £ will depreciate against the US$ by around 2% a year, which implies a net exchange rate benefit. Nevertheless, parity theories have not held recently in the US$–£ relationship so there is still a risk.
- External factors such as unforeseen changes in interest and/or inflation rates in any of the two entity's major areas of operation.

- PM could use the capital and money markets to hedge $ and other currency denominated transactions, but it is difficult to do this on all operations long term. Internal or informal methods may be preferable here, and may already exist.
- Competition controls – unlikely here, but it is possible certain areas of the entity's operations might attract the attention of the competition authorities, for example the pharmaceutical materials sector referred to. PM is already market leader in UK and Europe, acquiring NQ would increase this even further.
- A general crash in the stock market – this would affect the second and third objective, but probably not the first. Little can be done about the P/E ratio, but if the second objective were to be restated so that gearing is measured in book value terms not market value terms, the volatility of stock markets can be overcome.
- While not strictly an 'economic' force, the integration of the two entities could be a challenge. It is already stated that the NQ board is 'sensitive' to whether this is termed a merger or an acquisition, so there is clearly scope for disagreements. How these issues are managed is mentioned in the next part of this report.

Section (iii) – Post-merger value enhancing strategies

- Position audit – need to understand NQ's entity culture, its staff, products and other stakeholders.
- The integration strategy must be in place before the merger is finalised.
- Improve efficiency – Synergies have not yet been identified, but there are bound to be some administrative savings. If these involve redundancies – and they surely must – the effect on the workforce in both the UK and the US must be considered together with the need to recognise local employment laws and sensitivities.
- Improve profitability/earnings – undertake a comprehensive, but realistic and time-bound action plan.
- Review and improve marketing strategy, especially for key areas such as pharmaceutical materials.
- Asset sales – already considered in respect of the software licences, but there may be other assets that will be surplus to requirements.
- The entity's cost of capital should be re-evaluated: the level of diversification obtained by merging two different income streams might reduce this and therefore increase the value of the entity.

Conclusion and summary

This report has shown that the merger will meet at least two of the entity's three objectives. Earnings will increase by 5% per annum, at least in the first full year of operations. On the positive side no real savings or synergies have as yet been identified, which would help boost earnings. On the negative side, the effect on earnings of the disposal of the licenses has not yet been quantified. PM's P/E ratio is likely to be maintained above the industry average, but there are potential downside risks.

The effect on gearing is difficult to predict with accuracy as the proportion of NQ's shareholders who will opt for cash, necessitating additional borrowings, is unknown.

A number of economic forces were identified that could help or hinder the achievement of the objectives. These include exchange rate movements, changes in interest and inflation rates, competition controls and stock market volatility.

Post-merger value enhancing strategies were identified as the need for a position audit, marketing and integration strategies, and strategies to improve efficiency and profitability. Also considered are the sale of surplus assets and the need to re-evaluate the cost of capital.

In summary, the merger has potential, but is not without its downside risks.

Examiner's note:
The answer to this question is fuller than was expected from a well-prepared candidate.

Appendix 1

Year Earnings end	*PM Revenue* £m	*%*	*PM Earnings* £M	*% Growth*	*Earnings as % of Revenue*	*NQ Revenue* $m	*% Growth*	*NQ Earnings* $m	*% Growth*	*as % of Revenue*
2002	1,050		225		21.4	1,850		250		13.5
2003	1,125	7.1	231	2.7	20.5	1,950	5.4	265	6.0	13.6
2004	1,250	11.1	245	6.1	19.6	2,150	10.3	280	5.7	13.0
2005	1,400	12.0	258	5.3	18.4	2,336	8.7	290	3.6	12.4
2006	1,560	11.4	273	5.8	17.5	2,500	7.0	300	3.4	12.0

Question 8 –SHINE

(a)

Tables showing separate workings for each year

	millions	*millions*	*millions*	*millions*	*millions*	
Years	*0*	*1*	*2*	*3*	*4*	
1. Constant exchange rate and 10% tax rate						
Net operating cash flows ($)	–	70.00	70.00	70.00	70.00	
Less tax at 10%	–	(7.00)	(7.00)	(7.00)	(7.00)	
Initial/residual investment	(200.00)				50.00	
Net $ cash flows	(200.00)	63.00	63.00	63.00	113.00	
Convert to € at rate of:	1.10	1.10	1.10	1.10	1.10	
Net $ cash flows	(181.82)	57.27	57.27	57.27	102.73	
Discount factor	1	0.893	0.797	0.712	0.636	
PV of € cash flows	(181.82)	51.14	45.65	40.78	65.34	**TOTAL 21.09**
2. Constant exchange rate and 25% tax rate						
Net operating cash flows ($)	–	70.00	70.00	70.00	70.00	
Less tax at 10%	–	(17.50)	(17.50)	(17.50)	(17.50)	
Initial/residual investment	(200.00)				50.00	
Net $ cash flows	(200.00)	52.50	52.50	52.50	102.50	
Convert to € at rate of:	1.10	1.10	1.10	1.10	1.10	
Net $ cash flows	(181.82)	47.73	47.73	47.73	93.18	
Discount factor	1	0.893	0.797	0.712	0.636	
PV of € cash flows	(181.82)	46.62	38.04	33.98	59.26	**TOTAL (7.92)**

	millions	*millions*	*millions*	*millions*	*millions*	
Years	*0*	*1*	*2*	*3*	*4*	
3. Euro strengthening and 10% tax rate						
Net operating cash flows ($)	–	70.00	70.00	70.00	70.00	
Less tax at 10%	–	(7.00)	(7.00)	(7.00)	(7.00)	
Initial/residual investment	(200.00)				50.00	
Net $ cash flows	(200.00)	63.00	63.00	63.00	113.00	
Convert to € at rate of:	1.1000	1.1770	1.2594	1.3476	1.4419	
Net $ cash flows	(181.82)	53.53	50.02	46.75	78.37	
Discount factor	1	0.893	0.797	0.712	0.636	
PV of € cash flows	(181.82)	47.80	39.87	33.29	49.84	**TOTAL (11.02)**
4. Euro strengthening and 25% tax rate						
Net operating cash flows ($)	–	70.00	70.00	70.00	70.00	
Less tax at 25%	–	(17.50)	(17.50)	(17.50)	(17.50)	
Initial/residual investment	(200.00)				50.00	
Net $ cash flows	(200.00)	52.50	52.50	52.50	102.50	
Convert to € at rate of:	1.1000	1.1770	1.2594	1.3476	1.4419	
Net $ cash flows	(181.82)	44.60	41.69	38.96	71.09	
Discount factor	1	0.893	0.797	0.712	0.636	
PV of € cash flows	(181.82)	39.83	33.23	27.74	445.21	**TOTAL (35.81)**

Workings: exchange rates

Year1	1.10 × 1.07	=	1.177
Year 2	1.177 × 1.07	=	1.2594
Year 3	1.2594 × 1.07	=	1.3476
Year 4	1.3476 × 1.07	=	1.4419

Examiner's notes:

1 These figures were based on the discount factors quoted in the tables provided. Candidates who used calculators to obtain discount factors would have obtained slightly different answers due to rounding differences.
2 Candidates who used a correctly adjusted discount rate (approximately 20%) instead of applying forward rates in the two scenarios where the Euro is strengthening against the $ would have gained full credit.

Summary of results

	NPV *€ million*
Constant exchange rate and tax rate of 10%	21.1
Constant exchange rate and tax rate of 25%	(7.9)
Euro strengthening against the dollar by 7% pa and tax rate of 10%	(11.0)
Euro strengthening against the dollar by 7% pa and tax rate of 25%	(35.8)
Expected average NPV at tax rate of 10%	5.0
Expected average NPV at tax rate of 25%	(21.9)

Alternative approach using aggregate cash flows for constant exchange rate scenarios:

Years	*0*	*1 to 4*	*4*	
1. Constant exchange rate and 10% tax				
Net operating cash flows ($)	–	70.00		
Less tax at 10%	–	(7.00)		
Initial/residual investment	(200.00)		50.00	
Net $ cash flows	(200.00)	63.00	50.00	
Convert to € at rate of:	1.10	1.10	1.10	
Net $ cash flows	(181.82)	57.27	45.45	
Discount factor	1	3.037	0.636	
PV of € cash flows	(181.82)	173.93	28.91	**TOTAL 21.02**
2. Constant exchange rate and 25% tax				
Net operating cash flows ($)	–	70.00		
Less tax at 10%	–	(17.50)		
Initial/residual investment	(200.00)		50.00	
Net $ cash flows	(200.00)	52.50	50.00	
Convert to € at rate of:	1.10	1.10	1.10	
Net $ cash flows	(181.82)	47.73	45.45	
Discount factor	1	3.037	0.636	
PV of € cash flows	(181.82)	144.96	28.91	**TOTAL (7.96)**

Examiner's note:

This alternative approach produces slightly different answers due to rounding differences.

(b)

	SCENARIO A		SCENARIO B	
	borrowings denominated in euro €millions	**borrowings denominated in US dollars €millions**	**borrowings denominated in euro €millions**	**borrowings denominated in US dollars €millions**
Assets	28,182 (W1)	28.182 (W1)	28,143 (W3)	28,143 (W3)
Non-current liabilities	4,182 (W2)	4,182 (W2)	4,182 (W2)	4,143 (W4)
Current liabilities	12,700	12,700	12,700	12,700
Equity	11,300 (balance)	11,300 (balance)	11,261 (balance)	11,300 (balance)
Total liabilities and equity	28,182	28,182	28,143	28,143

W1	28,182	=	28,000 + 200/1.1
W2	4,182	=	4,000 + 200/1.1
W3	28,143	=	28,000 + 200/1.40
W4	4,143	=	4,000 + 200/1.40

(c)

To: The Directors of the SHINE Group
From: Finance Director Date: 22
November 2006

Report on proposed wind farm project

Purpose

This report considers the financial viability of the proposed wind farm project and whether or not it would be in the best interests of the group to proceed with the project. Alternative financing structures are also evaluated. The report concludes with a review of the different roles of the treasury and finance departments in the implementation process.

(i) **Discussion of the internal and external constraints**

External constraints
Uncertainty over the tax rate

- The tax rate is highly significant to the success of the project. The 'expected' NPV is negative (€22.15 m) at a tax rate of 25%, but positive at a tax rate of 10%.
- If a tax rate of 25% is voted in by the local government, SHINE must take account of the risk of loss from the project and weigh that risk against the public relations benefits that would arise from undertaking the project.
- SHINE could also choose to wait until the tax rate is known before deciding whether or not to proceed with the project.

Uncertainty over the exchange rate

- Exchange rate movements are also key to the profitability of the project.
- Assuming that SHINE only proceeds with the project if the tax rate is fixed at 10%, exchange rate movements could make the difference between a positive NPV of €21.1 m at constant exchange rates to a negative NPV of €7.9 m if the euro were to strengthen against the US dollar by 7% per annum.
- The 'expected' NPV result at a tax rate of 10% is positive at €5.0 m.
- SHINE would be well advised to use forward contracts to fix the exchange rate on future cash flows. If forward rates reflect current exchange rate expectations, it could then 'lock into' a positive NPV result.

Objections from local holiday home owners and farmers

- The project may not be permitted at all if local holiday home owners and farmers succeed in their objections to the project.
- SHINE should take these objections seriously and employ local lawyers and a public relations organisation to assist them in defending the project.
- The main motivation of the wind farm project is to boost the reputation of the group and SHINE needs to assess the risk that negative publicity from local holiday home owners and farmers might significantly reduce the potential public relations benefit of the project.

Internal constraints

The decision on whether to proceed, even with a 25% tax rate, will largely depend on whether a suitable alternative project can be found that meets the group's public relations requirements and gives a positive NPV result.

However, the corporate objective to enhance the group's reputation by engaging in projects involving renewable energy is regarded as an important objective and may override any doubts about the potential profitability of the project.

Note that the 40% gearing ratio target is not perceived as a constraint since the project has very little impact on group gearing levels and is currently well within the 40% limit.

Conclusion

- The decision on whether or not to proceed will be largely dependent on how important the project is considered to be from a public relations viewpoint. If it is seen as regarded as very important and there are no suitable alternative projects, SHINE should proceed with the project regardless of the tax rate. If not, SHINE should hold back until the actual tax rate is known and only accept the project if a 10% tax rate is adopted.
- It is strongly recommended that exchange rates should be fixed by using forward contracts.

(ii) **Financing the project**

A large multinational group such as SHINE would be able to borrow from both domestic banks and international banks and financial markets in either euro or US dollar, who would be largely indifferent to the choice of currency.

Euro borrowings

- Euro borrowings have the disadvantage that they do not provide a natural hedge of the US$ assets. The value of equity would fall from €11,300 m to €11,261 m as a direct result of a rise in the value of the euro from US$ 1.10 = €1.00 to US$ 1.40 = €1.00.
- Gearing is likely to increase slightly with a rise in the value of the euro. However, the impact is negligible.

US dollar borrowings

- The dollar borrowings, however, provide a natural hedge against the dollar denominated investment, protecting the value of equity at €11,300 m despite a significant rise in the value of the euro.
- They may also enable US dollar net revenue streams to be netted against interest payments in US dollars.
- However, gearing levels are still slightly affected by changes in exchange rate movements. In this case, gearing improves marginally from 27.0% to 26.8% as a result of a rise in the value of the euro.

Conclusion:

- The project is so small in comparison in relation to the size of the SHINE group, that the type of financing has no major impact on either gearing levels or exposure of equity to exchange rate movements.

Workings:

Gearing:	*Scenario A*	*Scenario B*	*Workings:*
Euro borrowing	27.0%	27.1%	27.0% = 100 × 4,182/(4,182 + 11,300)
US dollar borrowings	27.0%	26.8%	

These figures compare to a pre-project gearing of 26.1%
Workings: 26.1% 5 100% × 4,000/(4,000 + 11,300)

(iii) **Differing roles and responsibilities of the treasury department and finance department**

	Treasury	**Finance**
Evaluating the project	Quantify risks and look for ways of hedging or managing risks such as exchange rate and interest risk. Advise on an appropriate discount factor to be used in the investment appraisal evaluation.	Assess costs and revenues. Analyse risk factors. Evaluate the project.
Evaluating financing options	Treasury department to investigate alternative sources of finance.	Liaise with treasury on wider implications of financing options.
Arranging finance	Treasury to liaise with the banks and other intermediaries to arrange finance.	

Implementation of the project	Provide liquidity, and so on, as required. Prepare cash forecasts. Arrange interest rate and exchange rate hedging.	Set the budget and timetable. Monitor and control costs and revenues against the budget. Oversee the implementation.

Conclusion

The financial viability of the project is highly dependent on the final tax rate. At 10%, the project is highly attractive, but at 25% it is no longer financially viable, and we have to consider whether the public relations benefits outweigh the financial cost. We could also choose to delay the project until the final tax rate is known.

In terms of financing the project, the currency of any loan is insignificant from the group's perspective as the project is so small. The choice of currency would only affect overall cost of the project after taking the type of financing into account.

Both the treasury and finance departments would play an important and distinctive role in the implementation of the project and it is important that the departments work closely together throughout the process.

Examiner's note:

The answer to this question is fuller than would be expected from a well-prepared candidate.

Exam Q & As

At the time of publication there are no exam Q & As available for the 2010 syllabus. However, the latest specimen exam papers are available on the CIMA website. Actual exam Q & As will be available free of charge to CIMA students on the CIMA website from summer 2010 onwards.